Cambridge Philosophical Te

This innovative series offers a fresh way of understanding and teaching the canonical texts in the history of philosophy. Its purpose is to allow students to appreciate the contexts in which the philosophical classics emerged by providing the primary materials that constitute their immediate intellectual background. These contextual materials are often neglected because they are hard to find, or unavailable in English translation, or both. Now this background source material will be available in convenient editions with helpful explanatory introductions and annotations. The series thus aims to provide an important new resource, enabling both teachers and students to achieve an enriched understanding of the great texts in the Western philosophical tradition.

Descartes' *Meditations*

No single text has more importance for the history of philosophy than Descartes' *Meditations*. This unique collection of background material has been translated from the original French and Latin. The texts gathered here illustrate the kinds of principles, assumptions, and philosophical methods that were commonplace when Descartes was developing his ideas. The selections are from Petrus Ramus, Francisco Sanches, Christopher Clavius, Francisco Suàrez, Pierre Charron, Eustachius a Sancto Paulo, Scipion Dupleix, Marin Mersenne, Pierre Gassendi, Jean de Silhon, François de la Mothe le Vayer, Charles Sorel, and Jean-Baptiste Morin.

Roger Ariew is Professor of Philosophy at Virginia Polytechnic Institute and State University, Blacksburg, Virginia. John Cottingham is Professor of Philosophy at the University of Reading. Tom Sorell is Professor of Philosophy at the University of Essex.

CAMBRIDGE PHILOSOPHICAL TEXTS
IN CONTEXT

General Editors

John Cottingham, *University of Reading*
Daniel Garber, *University of Chicago*

Descartes' *Meditations*, edited by Roger Ariew, John Cottingham, and Tom Sorell.

Forthcoming
Berkeley's *Principles and Dialogues*, edited by Ian Tipton and Charles McCracken.
Kant's *Groundwork of the Metaphysics of Morals*, edited by J. B. Schneewind.

Contents

Preface

The planning and execution of this volume has been very much a joint venture. The hard decisions about which texts to include, and how much of them, were made at a series of virtual and actual meetings, and the work of translation was divided up between the three of us (the initials of the relevant translator appear in square brackets at the end of the introduction to each text). All the work was then checked by at least one other member of the team before the final version was prepared. In the case of the extracts from Dupleix and de Silhon, Roger Ariew was joined as translator by Marjorie Grene, and her invaluable work on this material is gratefully acknowledged here. We have tried in the introductions to each text to provide the reader with essential historical information about the authors and the provenance of the materials, and also to give a brief indication of some of the main points of philosophical importance, and the principal ways in which the materials shed light on the intellectual context of Descartes' philosophy. The explanatory footnotes appended to the texts have all been added by the present editors, unless otherwise stated. Constraints of space, as well as considerations of philosophical relevance, have made it necessary to abridge much of the material, and deletions are indicated throughout by ellipses. The great bulk of the material included in this volume is here translated into English for the first time, but our understanding of the texts has greatly benefited from the work of previous editors of the relevant Latin or French writings, as well as from the contributions of many scholars and commentators who have written on the philosophers in question; further details may be found in the footnotes and the bibliography.

RA
JGC
TS

Abbreviations

AT   C. Adam and P. Tannery, eds. *Œuvres de Descartes.* 12
            vols., revised edition. Paris: Vrin/CNRS, 1964–76.
CSM   J. Cottingham, R. Stoothoff, and D. Murdoch, eds. *The
            Philosophical Writings of Descartes.* Vols. 1 and 2. Cam-
            bridge: Cambridge University Press, 1985.
CSMK   J. Cottingham, R. Stoothoff, D. Murdoch, and A.
            Kenny, eds. *The Philosophical Writings of Descartes.*
            Vol. 3, *The Correspondence.* Cambridge: Cambridge
            University Press, 1991.

For other works, referred to in the notes by author or editor and brief
title, full details are given in the Bibliography.

General Introduction

Philosophy, more perhaps than any other discipline, has always been preoccupied with itself – with what kind of activity it is, or should be. In dissections of the current state of the subject, a distinction is often deployed between approaches to philosophy that take pride in meticulous attention to its history, and those that disdain the close study of past ideas as irrelevant to the cutting edge of modern philosophical research. Though each of these polar stereotypes has its instantiations, the sharp contrast can mislead, since many, if not most, practitioners of the subject fall somewhere between the extremes – and so much the better for that. For the truth is that the history of philosophy can easily turn sterile if it lacks a sense of how the great issues of the past are related to the continuing philosophical debates of our own time; and conversely, the practice of "up-to date" analytic philosophy risks becoming obsessive and shortsighted unless it is informed by a lively awareness of the philosophical tradition that delivered us where we are today. Fruitful philosophical analysis, like individual self-discovery, operates at a point of interplay between the struggle toward a future not yet achieved, and the effort to recover and understand the past we have (partly) left behind.

Yet to acknowledge the vital role of inherited tradition for productive philosophical inquiry is immediately to confront the problem of how that tradition is itself generated. Again, more than perhaps any other subject, philosophy has a tendency to canonize, or to demonize, the great figures of its past. Of these two opposite tendencies, over-reverential hagiography is a lesser danger (at least in the anglophone philosophical world) than the kind of polemicism that wildly caricatures famous dead philosophers in order to dismember their supposed doctrines. The fate of Descartes in the twentieth century is a spectacular example of this latter process, so much so that the label "Cartesian" has become in many quarters almost a term of abuse, designating all the confusions and errors from which today's philosophical champions claim to protect us: an obscurantist immaterialism in the philosophy of mind; a suspect foundationalism in epistemology; an incoherent subjectivism in the theory of meaning; a blinkered apriorism in the philosophy of science.

This is not the place to attempt to "rescue" the progenitor of modern philosophy from the charge of having fathered these monumental errors;[1] and, in any case, the modern detractors of "Cartesianism" are often less interested in what Descartes actually wrote than they are in furthering their own particular philosophical agenda. But for those who have any interest in studying Descartes' own writings – and for anyone remotely concerned with the Western philosophical tradition, such a study is in the end unavoidable – a problem of perspective immediately arises: how are we to discern the significance of the arguments Descartes advances, and the force of the claims he puts forward, when so much of our vision is clouded by the heavy accretion of subsequent interpretation and criticism?

We cannot, of course, go back in time, nor can we escape the influence of the contemporary philosophical atmosphere that surrounds us. But as the great Cartesian scholar Geneviève Rodis-Lewis once observed, we "can at least glimpse the originality of the Cartesian outlook if we consider it in relation to the views of Descartes' own contemporaries."[2] The rationale for this volume, and indeed the Cambridge series of "Texts in Context" as a whole, is the belief that our understanding of the great canonical philosophers can be greatly enriched if their ideas are set against the work of their immediate predecessors and contemporaries; by displaying the intellectual soil out of which the theories of the great philosophers grew, one may hope to reveal some of the philosophical concerns that motivated and conditioned their arguments – concerns that are all too easily obscured if we look at their writings only from the standpoint of later developments.

Mention of the "originality" of Descartes' ideas is especially in point here. The contextualizing of a great writer may, on first inspection, seem

---

1. For such a defense, see J. Cottingham, "The Cartesian Legacy."
2. "On peut du moins cerner l'originalité de la position cartésienne en la situant parmi ses contemporains." See "Le paradox cartésien," in G. Rodis-Lewis, L'anthropologie cartésienne, chap. 3, p. 86.

to diminish that sense of uniqueness which we associate with true genius. The lover of Shakespearean sonnets may be taken aback to find that the Bard was but one of a score of Elizabethan poets who had mastered the form; the devotee of Schubert's string quartets, shocked to discover the plethora of chamber music composed in the early nineteenth century. In the same way, those brought up (as most undergraduates are) to think of Descartes as the inaugurator of the modern age may be surprised at the extent to which the seeds of "modernity" had already been widely sown by the time he published the *Discourse*. Disenchantment with Aristotelianism, as some of the texts included in this volume make abundantly clear, had set in many decades before Descartes wrote, and the Cartesian search for new standards of knowledge followed closely in the wake of a protracted earlier critique of traditional methods of inquiry. Yet for all that, a reading of the texts included here in the end enhances rather than diminishes one's appreciation of the special genius of the "French cavalier who set out with so sprightly a step."[3] In style, as well as content, the writings of Descartes have a clarity and power that the work of his predecessors and contemporaries often lacks; the new worldview toward which many early seventeenth-century thinkers were groping, or against which they were starting to dig in, comes alive in Descartes' writings with unprecedented vigor and confidence. But one needs to see the precedents to appreciate just what is special in the work of the master.

A theme that emerges repeatedly in the texts collected here is the status of Aristotle – a figure who, by a curious quirk of history, was subject in the early modern period to exactly the same kind of *peripeteia* as has beset Descartes himself in our own time: the transition from a revered source of true philosophizing to a bête noire from whose shadow every aspiring philosopher must escape. There is, moreover, much food for thought in the realization that just as nowadays certain Cartesian modes of thinking often still seem surreptitiously to influence those who claim to have cast off Descartes' doctrines, so Descartes himself, for all his insistence on a "new start," often lapses into the language and presuppositions of the Scholasticism that it was his mission to overthrow.

This last fact should come as no surprise. The Jesuits who educated Descartes were steeped in Scholasticism, but wherever he had learned his metaphysics, it would have been likely to have been powerfully in-

---

3. "Descartes, dans l'histoire de la pensée, ce sera toujours ce cavalier français qui partit d'un si bon pas." C. Péguy, *Oeuvres*, p. 1303.

fluenced by the long Peripatetic tradition that had dominated European thought for so many centuries. Descartes' own account of his early life reveals something of his struggles against Aristotelian orthodoxy, but often provides only the most schematic indication of what precisely the traditional doctrines actually were. A good many of the materials gathered in this volume illustrate the kinds of principles, assumptions, and philosophical methods that were commonplace when Descartes was growing up, together with the special terminology that, so far from being a mere instrument, often plays such a crucial role in structuring a conceptual scheme. Being able to read the texts themselves will, we hope, do more to enhance appreciation of the climate in which Descartes operated than a host of textbook summaries.

Alongside the general purposes of the volume just indicated, a complementary aim has been to bring to the reader source materials that are often difficult to find and not readily available in English. Almost all of the texts included are here translated into English for the first time. Two of the authors who appear in the following pages will be familiar from Descartes' own writings: Pierre Gassendi, Descartes' trenchant critic in the Fifth Objections, and Marin Mersenne, Descartes' faithful correspondent and editor. Here, both of them figure as philosophers in their own right: Gassendi as a fierce opponent of Aristotelian orthodoxy, Mersenne as an exponent of the kind of philosophical theology that strongly influenced Descartes' outlook in the *Meditations*. The volume (which is arranged chronologically) opens with four much earlier figures who published in the second half of the previous century. Two of these are from the Iberian peninsula, a fertile seedbed for philosophical research during this period: Francisco Sanches, one of the spokesmen for the widespread disillusionment with existing systems of "knowledge" in the late sixteenth century, and Francisco Suárez, a leading scholastic of brilliant intellect whom Descartes studied, and whose brand of Aristotelianism influenced him as much if not more than that of Aquinas. The other two are from Italy and France respectively: Christopher Clavius, senior professor of mathematics at the Collegio Romano, whose enthusiasm for a subject then often held in low esteem heralds the crucial importance it was to attain in the Cartesian revolution, and Pierre de la Ramée (Petrus Ramus), whose work illustrates how the reformation of philosophical methodology was very much on the agenda well before Descartes. Moving on to the early seventeenth century, we next have extracts from Pierre Charron, whose arguments on the need to void the mind of false beliefs as a preliminary to the attainment of wisdom clearly

anticipate Descartes' approach in the *Meditations*; then come two substantial sets of extracts from important textbooks of the period, the *Compendium of Philosophy in Four Parts* (1609) by Eustachius a Sancto Paulo,
and (published a decade or so later) the *Corpus of Philosophy* by Scipion
Dupleix. Descartes is known to have studied the former text as a schoolboy, and both works illustrate the aspirations of Scholasticism to provide
a complete philosophical system embracing logic, physics, metaphysics,
and ethics – an aspiration, albeit pursued in a very different way, that
was to remain one of Descartes' central goals. Proceeding chronologically, we come (after Mersenne and Gassendi) to the religious apologist
(and friend of Descartes) Jean de Silhon and the controversialist and
freethinker François de la Mothe le Vayer: the arguments of both concerning the status of religious truth, the demonstrability of God's existence, the relation of reason to faith, and the nature of the soul do much
to set the scene for Descartes' preoccupations in the *Meditations*. Our
selection ends with two exact contemporaries of Descartes, Charles Sorel, whose proposals for a new "universal science" (begun in 1635 and
completed the same year as the *Meditations*) bear many interesting sim-
ilarities and contrast with the Cartesian project, and Jean-Baptiste
Morin, whose "geometrical" proof of God's existence was read by Descartes shortly before he published the *Meditations*. Finally, a brief appendix, recording the condemnations of Cartesianism later in the century, indicates something of the robust resistance that Scholasticism
continued to put up to the "new" philosophy many years after Descartes'
death.[4]

Apart from their intrinsic interest, the writings included here throw
light on many issues that are still subjects of debate among scholars of
the early modern period. How far, for example, did Descartes really
succeed in making the break from Scholasticism that he claimed to have
achieved?[5] What was the significance for "modern" philosophy of the
great revival of skepticism in the sixteenth and early seventeenth centuries?[6] What role was played in Descartes' intellectual development by

4. This appendix is included for the reader's interest as a kind of "sampler." The
reception of Cartesianism is a vast and fascinating topic that would require a
separate volume in its own right.
5. See especially the texts by Clavius, Suárez, Eustachius, and Dupleix; and compare E. Gilson, *Etudes sur le rôle de la pensée médiévale dans la formation du système
cartésien*.
6. See the texts by Sanchez, Ramus, Charron, Mersenne, Gassendi, de Silhon,
and le Vayer; and compare R. Popkin, *History of Scepticism from Erasmus to
Descartes*.

the circle of philosophers, theologians, and scientists who knew or corresponded with Mersenne?[7] How does Descartes' approach to the need
for a "new start" in philosophy compare with that of other reformers
of the period?[8] The list could no doubt continue, but since part of the
purpose of this volume is to help the reader to escape from the fixed
agenda of topics so often associated with the great philosophers, we hope
that reading these relatively little studied texts will generate fresh per-
spectives, new lines of inquiry, and a richer sense of the many complex-
ities and contrasts that marked one of the most fascinating periods in
Western philosophy.

We have learned much from working on the materials provided here,
and we hope that readers will find them as enjoyable to examine as we
have found them to translate. Philosophical understanding is like a jig-
saw: the picture often changes from what was first expected as the missing pieces are filled in. To achieve a final and definitive picture of the
intellectual context of Descartes' philosophy is, of course, beyond the
scope of this or any volume; what we have tried to do here is to present
at least some of the important missing pieces.

[JC]

7. See the texts by Mersenne, Gassendi, de Silhon, le Vayer, Sorel, and Morin.
8. Any comprehensive study of Descartes' intellectual context would of course
need to set his philosophy against the work of the giants among his contemporaries such as Bacon, Galileo, and Hobbes. Writings of such major figures
(each of whom would require a "Texts in Context" volume in his own right)
are not included here; much of their work is, in any case, widely available in
English editions.

ONE

Petrus Ramus, *Dialectic*

[*La dialectique*, 1555]

Introduction

A teacher in various colleges in Paris for most of his adult life, Petrus Ramus (or Pierre de la Ramée, 1515-1572) was known as a strong critic of Aristotle and the Aristotelian tradition in the university curriculum, and as a constructive philosopher interested in "logic" and "method" as well as rhetoric. His writings were distinctive for, among other things, their emphasis on the practice or exercise of arts and doctrines. *La dialectique* was one of many versions of a theory of the use of discourse in general that Ramus published from the 1540s to the 1560s. Although this theory was intended to challenge a number of Aristotle's logical writings, Ramus' critics pointed out that he remained heavily indebted to his ancient opponent.

This excerpt from *La dialectique* is to do with "method," which was the subject of a large literature in the sixteenth century, long before Descartes took it up.[1] In the pre-Cartesian period, "method" often meant a technique for the effective presentation of different subjects in the university curriculum, and sometimes effectiveness was tied to abbreviation, or the identification of a key idea. Method was not primarily a series of steps for making discoveries. In Ramus, effective presentation is linked with the passage – perhaps deductive – from the general to the specific, especially in the natural sciences. Observations about particular things are methodically understood when they are seen as the consequences of the genera and species

1. For a comprehensive survey of the context, see W. J. Ong, *Ramus: Method and the Decay of Dialogue*. For the main types of pre-Cartesian literature on method, see Ong, chap. 9.

to which the things observed belong. But methodical understanding in this sense is possible not only in the natural sciences of the university curriculum, according to Ramus, but quite generally. There is a method of prudence, for example, which aims not at illuminating observed fact, but at presenting things to an audience in a way that will lead it to act in a desired way. This method differs systematically from the method of tracing the specific and less clear to the general and more evident. For it sometimes depends on obscuring or distracting attention away from the important thing and presenting other things in a deceptive or confusing order.

In describing preferred starting points according to a method of nature, Ramus refers to what is clear or manifest or evident, identifying it with what is prior or comes first in the natural order. The Cartesian language of clarity was not entirely new, then, though Descartes would have denied that species and genera met his own standards of clarity and distinctness. Not only was Ramus one of many pre-Cartesian methodologists of science; he was also a pre-Cartesian reformer of some of the established sciences, as his implied criticism of Euclid's method in geometry shows.

[TS]

DIALECTIC

Method

Method is the disposition by which, when several things are considered, the first of note is put first, the second second, the third third, and so on. The term covers any discipline or dispute, yet method is commonly taken to show and shorten the way of proceeding. Method is practiced in the schools by the Greek and Latin writers under that figure of speech. When speaking of it in rhetoric they also call it "disposition." In rhetoric, no doctrine of proposition or syllogism is taught under that name and by that genus; only method is mentioned.

Method of Nature

There is a method of nature and a method of prudence. Cicero and Quintilian divide disposition in this way. Aristotle's teaching about the parts of method is similar.

The method of nature takes what is completely and absolutely the most evident and manifest and places that first. This is what Aristotle, at the beginning of *Posterior Analytics*, calls both the most manifest in nature, and what is prior in nature. That which is naturally more evident must take precedence in the order and exposition of doctrine, just as causes must come before effects and, in symbols, the general and universal must come before the specific and particular.

This method is also called the method of art because it is observed in the transmission of arts and theories and has as much authority over them as the necessary proposition and a valid syllogism have over judgment. Besides, in all real disciplines the rules are general and universal, albeit to different degrees. And the more general each is, the more precedence it has. And the most general will come first in rank and order because it is first in clarity and knowledge. The others will fall into line according as they approximate in clarity. And of these the most manifest will precede, and the less manifest will follow. And finally the most specific examples will be placed last. This method is singular and unique to well-founded doctrines, as it alone proceeds by placing first of all what is absolutely most clear and manifest so as to illuminate and make clearer the unknown and obscure things which come next. Thus all the ancients, such as Hippocrates, Plato, and Aristotle, have endorsed this method. Hippocrates, saying that it is necessary to begin with the greatest and easiest things, greatest in the sense of greatest use and power, easiest in the sense of easiest to understand. Galen correctly interprets Plato in the *Philebus* when he says that even though all arts are hit upon by an induction from particular to general, nevertheless they must be deduced the opposite way, descending from the chief genus to the multitude of lowest species.[2] Or again, in the *Phaedo*, he teaches that in the disposition of the art we must consider two ideas: the definition of the genus and the distribution of it in the species. He teaches something similar in the *Charmides* by the example of the doctors who do not begin to cure the part that is diseased before they treat the whole body. This is how Aristotle carefully proceeds at the beginning of *Posterior Analytics* when he teaches that every genuine theory and science must start off with general things and descend little by little to the specific. And it is not possible to set up an art in any other way, as we showed at length in the ninth book of the *Animadversions* against Galen and the interpreters of Aristotle. In short, this method of art seems to

2. Reading "espèces infimes" for "espèces infinies."

me to be a long golden chain, such as Homer imagined, and whose links
are so interdependent and intertwined, that none can be taken away
without breaking the order and integrity of the whole. But in order that
something of such great moment should be better understood, we must
make use of a familiar example.

Let us suppose that all the definitions, distributions, and rules of
grammar are discovered and each correctly judged, and that all of these
teachings are written on different tablets, which are thrown together
and jumbled up out of order and put in a jug, as in the game of *blanque*.
What branch of dialectic could teach me to deal with such confused
precepts and restore them to order? No method of discovery is necessary, for everything is already discovered. Every particular proposition
is judged and proved. We will need neither the first judgments of propositions nor the consequences of syllogisms. Method alone is left as a
reliable way of putting things together. Therefore, going by the light of
the method of nature, the dialectician chooses from this jug the definition of grammar, for this is the most general and puts in the first place,
"Grammar is the doctrine of speaking properly." Afterward he will look
in this same jug for the divisions of grammar and will put them in the
second place: "Grammar has two parts: etymology and syntax." Later
he will take out of the jug the definition of the first part and add that
in the third place. Thus, in defining and distributing, he will descend to
specific examples and put them last. And he will do the same with the
other part, taking the same pains we have taken up to now in placing
the most general precepts of dialectic first, the less general second, and
the specific last.

This method is not only applicable to arts and theories but to anything that we can set about teaching easily and clearly. For example, it
is common to orators, poets, and all writers. Orators, in their preambles
and narrations, confirmations and perorations, like to follow this order,
and so call it the order of art and of nature. . . .

This then is the method of nature and doctrine, easy to teach, but
very difficult to exercise and practice, as Socrates says, and not without
reason, in the *Philebus* of Plato. . . . But furthermore it is an infinitely
greater and more difficult task to arrange and combine by this method
of art than to discover and judge well by proposition and syllogism. And
no doubt the art in this case is far more excellent than it is in the first
of proposition and the second of syllogism. What might be considered
a very good example of a science and discipline where many things are
perfectly judged by the first and second judgment (namely, the elements

of Euclid, the method of which is considered very perfect) is not judged carefully enough and put together by the standards of the artificial method, as will be shown very amply one day when these elements are arranged in the preferred way.

And consequently, as Socrates said in the same place, "the light of this method is a gift of the gods conferred on men by a Prometheus with a bright and resplendent torch. Thus have the ancients, more perfect than ourselves, and better acquainted with the gods, taught us this oracle." We understand by this passage of Socrates the antiquity and excellence of such an order. . . .

Method of Prudence

Next comes the method of prudence, in which the prior things are not necessarily the most manifest, but are nevertheless more suitable to the one that has to be taught, and more likely to guide him and lead him where one would like. The orators call it the disposition of prudence, because it has more to do with the prudence of man than with an art or precepts of theory. If the method of nature was a judgment based on knowledge, the method of prudence is a judgment based on opinion. All the same, this method has been noted by philosophers, poets, and orators and we can bring in here what Aristotle calls *crypse*, that's to say, a hidden and false insinuation of which he spoke in the second chapter of the Syllogism, the eighth book of the *Topics*, and the first of the *Sophistical Refutations*, identifying it in a number of ways, which can be summarized as follows: begin in the middle and never state at the beginning what your aim is, or deduce its parts, but look hard for ways and means of achieving it and pursue them forthwith by simile and parabole if the audience is imprudent, for such minds let themselves be overcome forthwith. If one's audience is defiant and subtle, it is better not to play one's cards one after the other but to change and mix them, pretend to do otherwise, resume, never show any sign of thinking about it, say that is a common and usual thing, make haste, wager, debate, proceed with great boldness, and in the end spring the trap so that the adversary, astonished, says: "What is this all about?" Aristotle learned these things from his teacher, Plato, in whose dialogues Socrates often employs these ruses against the Sophists, who do not want to be taught by him. And consequently, when their foolish opinions are refuted in this way, they get angry with Socrates and call him a stingray or Dedalus, now wizard, now sophist, as if it was by this method that he numbed them, as if they were roughed up by a ghost, charmed and deceived by some mark or semblance of reason. The poet, who is often excellent in the various areas of logic, is in this part even more admirable. He sets about teaching the people, that is to say the many-headed beast, and, consequently, deceives by a number of means. He begins in the middle and there the beginning is often contained; and he comes to the last part with a few uncertain and tentative verses. . . .

The wisdom of this method is apparently noted by orators when they advise that in the exordium, before having proposed or talked about the thing in question, it is necessary to engage the intelligence, or even better the attention and favor, of the hearer, and retain it in the course of the speech by some change of subject and some repetition, and in the peroration to move him to favor us. These exordia and perorations are unnecessary for teaching the good hearer, who loves and seeks truth in his own right, as Aristotle says in the third chapter of the *Rhetoric*. And in short, although anything taken from outside the method of doctrine is often criticized by Aristotle in the *Organon*, it is nevertheless often prudently recommended given the circumstances of the hearer, and by Aristotle himself as well as by the orators, who further advise that in a dishonest and spirited cause it is better not to take the direct route but always to make one's approach oblique, and never express in advance any proposition or division of a thing into parts. In just the same way, to borrow from Quintilian, a surgeon would be ill advised to show the knife to the timid patient before he has made the incision. And Cicero has spoken similarly about the disposition in saying that nothing weighs more with a man, once he has seen what is good and bad in a given cause, than to embrace the good, fortify it, increase it, take it to heart, and flee the contrary. Indeed, sometimes this can mean not running away and giving up one's arms, when faced by aggravating and difficult circumstances, but putting up a show of bravado, not from fear, but in order to occupy a better position from which to fight. And this the orator wisely practiced himself. There is a long insinuation in book 2 of *De lege agraria* under the guise of giving thanks when he pretends to be of the people and devoted to the people but which is expressly designed to subvert the cause of the people. . . .

Conclusion

Now it is in the judgments of the method of doctrine as well as prudence that men differ not only from the animals, . . . but also from one another.

For although all enjoy a capacity to reason syllogistically, only a few who study it are able to make good use of it and, of these, an even smaller number knows how to proceed by a good method and judge (accordingly). To the same degree that man surpasses the beasts in respect of syllogism, so among men he excels who has method. In no part of reason does the divinity of man stand out so prominently as in the sun of this universal judgment. . . .

And finally, as Aristotle says in the ninth book of the [*Nicomachean*] *Ethics*, it is not enough to know what virtue is: it is necessary to take the trouble of acquiring and making use of it. In the same way, no one is considered a logician who has learned the laws and rules of logic: rather, things stand as in the arts in general, for example, the mechanical ones: the apprentice spends some time receiving and considering the instructions of his master, but is much more profitably engaged when he observes the master's products and samples, and gradually follows him in producing the same so that by the end of his apprenticeship, by this combination of thought and imitation, he makes some masterwork of his own to prove his diligence and attain the status of master himself. And then, continuing the practice of his profession over many years, making each person aware of the excellence of his work, he gradually acquires the stature and reputation that make him a grand master of his profession. In the same way, it is not enough in logic to parrot its laws in the schools: one has to practice them in the manner of poets, orators, and philosophers, that is, in all of the minds in which they might be applied, considering their strengths and weaknesses, imitating in writing and speech their good invention and disposition, and then by trying to equal them, that is, to prevail in treating and disputing all things by oneself, without having any more regard to particular disputes. And when this apprentice-logician has by such diligence and assiduousness acquired the knowledge of logic, then he can present himself confidently for the tests associated with mastership in this art. . . . And it is worth far more to have applied oneself in practice without an art than to have an art that one has never applied. For there are men to be seen throughout the republic who have made themselves wise and able through the use of reason without art, that is to say who are great logicians and dialecticians. But we can point to countless Mercures de Passon [who do not know whether the science is within them or withheld from them on the outside] who have art without having applied it.

TWO

Francisco Sanches, *That Nothing Is Known*
[*Quod nihil scitur*, 1581]

Introduction

Francisco Sanches, the Portuguese philosopher and medical writer, published his *Quod nihil scitur* at Lyons in 1581 – one year after Montaigne's *Essays*. To those brought up to believe in the seventeenth-century revolution in philosophy, the opening of the *Nihil scitur* comes as a salutary shock. Sanches "withdraws into himself" (*ad memetipsum retuli*) and "calls all into doubt" (*omnia in dubium revocans*); this is the "true way of knowing" (*verus sciendi modus*). The parallels, both in phrasing and in content, with what Descartes was to write sixty years later in the *Meditations* are remarkable. Traditional appeals to authority are swept away: Aristotle, for all his wisdom, was just wrong on many points; at the end of the day *homo ut nos* – he was an ordinary human being like us. To say "thus spake the Master" is unworthy of a philosopher; better, in our reasonings "to trust nature alone."

   Part of the fascination in reading Sanches is the sense it gives to the present-day reader of the arbitrariness and artificiality of standard historiographical boundaries; we are made to realize just how protracted and gradual was the parturition of the "modern age." The Cartesian attacks on conventional philosophical jargon, on the barrenness of conventional uses of the syllogism, on the emptiness of elaborate definitions *per genus et differentiam* – all these are anticipated in Sanches; and if this diminishes the originality of the seventeenth-century moderns, it also enriches our understanding of the task they faced – the task of dispatching that exasperatingly resilient animal, late Scholasticism, which was able to retain its dominance for so long after its shortcomings had first been exposed.

Though Sanches, unlike Descartes, proposes no new method for the acquisition of knowledge, he does produce some interesting anticipations of the Cartesian approach, particularly when he distinguishes between "external" objects of cognition and the "inner" objects of the mind (e.g., its own inner awareness of its willing and thinking). The verdict that emerges bears interesting comparisons with that of Descartes: the "external" deliverances of the senses, argues Sanches, are in some respects superior to the mind's inner reflections on itself (since they provide a precise image for the intellect to grasp), but the internal objects have a greater certainty (since "I am more certain that I am now thinking this than that I see a temple").

Despite the modernity of so many of Sanches' utterances, reading the *Quod nihil scitur* also brings an awareness of the extent to which he was trapped in the inescapable ignorance of the pre-Enlightenment world. Whenever he reviews conventional claims to knowledge, he can only glumly rehearse the unsatisfactory explanatory apparatus of qualities and forms, sympathies and antipathies, with no clear notion of what might be used to replace it: "Coldness can come about from motion, as in the agitation of the heart, thorax, and arteries, or of hot water, but also from rest, as when someone stops after moving but is still hot. Heat can come from motion, as when running, but also from rest, like the heart when it is still, or when some boiling water is kept motionless. Blackness can come from heat, as in the Ethiopians, or from cold, as in a rotting limb. ... Decay may occur from any combination of qualities, apart from dryness. This is not all: one quality may be produced by its opposite, such as heat from cold, as when cold lime is soaked ... or in the Ethiopians who are cold inside, as are we, even in summer." So it goes on, a catalog of obscurities illuminated only by the honest realization that no materials are to hand that could merit the title of genuine understanding. Sanches' achievement was to grasp the nettle and admit the speciousness of most sixteenth-century claims to knowledge: "wretched is our condition; in the midst of light we are blind."[1]

Richard Popkin's groundbreaking *History of Scepticism* (1960) highlighted Sanches as "more interesting than any other sceptic of the sixteenth century except Montaigne," but devoted only four or

---

1. "Misera est conditio nostra: in media luce coecutimus."

five pages to discussing his ideas. There is now an excellent full
critical edition of the Latin text of *Quod nihil scitur*, edited by Doug-
las Thomson, containing an English version by the editor, and a
historical introduction and notes by Elaine Limbrick. The extracts
that follow, freshly translated for the present volume, are chosen for
their relevance to themes appearing in the *Meditations*, or for the
comparative light they throw on various general features of Descartes' methodology and epistemology. References in square brackets are to page numbers of the first (Latin) edition (which are reproduced in the margins of the Limbrick and Thomson edition).

[JC]

THAT NOTHING IS KNOWN

[Preface] The desire to know is innate in humankind;[2] but to few is it
granted to know how to pursue this desire, and to fewer still to succeed
in it. I have had no better luck than others. From my early youth I made
it my sworn task to contemplate nature and I began to investigate everything in minute detail. In my avid zeal for knowledge I was at first
content with any fare that was offered; but after a short time I suffered
from indigestion and began to vomit everything up. I began to seek
something to give my mind that it might embrace fully and enjoy entirely, but there was nothing to satisfy me. I turned over the sayings of
the ancients, and examined the views of my own time; but the answers
I got were all the same and gave me no satisfaction whatever. I admit
that some shadows of truth were produced by some people, but I found
no one who could provide the basis for a candid and absolute judgment
on things.

So I then withdrew into myself, and called everything into doubt.
Ignoring anything that anyone had previously said, I set about examining
the things themselves, which is the true way of knowing. I began to
resolve everything back to ultimate principles. And then, as I start to
contemplate, the more I think, the more I doubt: I cannot seize hold of
anything perfectly. I am in despair, but I carry on. I go to the learned
doctors, looking eagerly to them for the truth. What do they offer? Each
of them constructs knowledge for himself from imaginings either borrowed from others or of his own making; from these they draw conclu-

2. The first sentence of Aristotle's *Metaphysics*.

sions, and from the conclusions yet more conclusions. They give no attention to the things themselves, but carry on until they produce a labyrinth of words far removed from any foundation of truth. From all this you could never get any understanding of the things in nature, but merely learn a tapestry of new invented things, unintelligible to any mind. . . .

I call on you then, you who find yourself in the same situation and with the same outlook as myself. You who have so often entertained your own doubts about the natures of things, now join your doubts to mine: let us together exercise our native intelligence. Let my judgment range freely, but within the bounds of rationality, and I will allow and encourage the same freedom in you.

You may say: "But after so many great men, what can you contribute that is new? Was the truth waiting to reveal herself to you?" Certainly not; but then she was not waiting on the great men of the past either. Is there then nothing new that men can discover? If so, why did Aristotle write? Or why should we now keep silent? Did Aristotle mark out the whole power of nature? Did he grasp the universal span of things? I can hardly accept this, though there are very learned men of recent times who are so in awe of him that they actually call him the "Dictator of Truth," the "Tribunal of Truth," and so on. . . . I certainly would judge Aristotle to rank very highly among the most acute investigators of nature, and to be preeminent among the outstanding intellects that our weak human frame has produced. But I would not assert that he never went astray. I would say that he was ignorant of very many things, and I can see plainly that he wavered on many matters, that he made confused pronouncements on several points, that he dealt with some things overbriefly, and passed over others in silence or refused to deal with them at all. He was a human being, like us. . . .

As one era gives way to the next, so do the various opinions of men, and though everyone thinks he has found the truth, of the thousand various views only one can have hit the mark. So allow me, along with the others, or even without them, to follow the same inquiries; I may even be successful. . . . I do not at all promise you the truth; for I am ignorant of the truth, as of all other matters. But I will pursue the inquiry as best I can, and you alongside me will chase after the truth, out in the open, like a quarry driven out of the thickets. You should not hope ever to track her down, or grasp hold of her in full knowledge that you have succeeded; being engaged on the hunt will be enough for us both. This is my goal and object, and you should seek the same end.

With this in mind, we shall take as our starting point the first principles of things, examining the major headings of philosophy from which
all the rest may be more easily inferred. . . . You should not ask me to
cite numerous authorities, or expect a reverential attitude to the established authors, since this is the mark of a servile and undisciplined mind,
rather than a free inquirer into the truth. I use my reason, and follow
nature alone. Authority orders us to believe, but reason provides demonstrations; the former is more suited to faith, but the latter to the
sciences. . . .

[1] This one fact, that I know nothing – even this I do not know. But I
conjecture that neither I nor anyone else knows anything. Let this proposition be the banner under which I march; this is the flag I must follow.
Nothing is known. If I eventually know how to prove it, I shall rightly
conclude that nothing is known; but if I fail, so much the better, for
such was my claim in the first place. You may say: "if you discover how
to prove it, this will contradict your thesis, since you will now know
something." But I have got there ahead of you, and now will begin to
turn it around: from this very conclusion it follows that nothing is
known. Perhaps you did not understand what I meant, or are calling me
ignorant or a quibbler. You are right, and I can say the same of you,
since you did not understand me. So we are both ignorant. And hence
in your ignorance you have reached the conclusion I was after. . . .
    Come then, sharpen your mind and I will follow you. Are we to set
about drawing conclusions about things from the meanings of words?
In my view every definition is about words, not things, and so is almost
every question. Let me explain. We cannot know the natures of things,
or at least I cannot. You may say you can, and I will not argue, but you
are wrong, for why should you be able to do so any more than I? . . .
You may say that there is a definition that demonstrates the nature of
the thing. Give me one: you cannot, so my conclusion stands. Moreover,
how are we to apply words to something we do not know? . . .
    [2] You may say that you can define the thing which is a man by
means of the definition "man is a mortal, rational animal"; and that this
is a real, not merely verbal, definition. I deny as much; for I will now
raise doubts about the terms "animal," "rational," and so on. You may
define these by means of higher genera and differentiae, as you call
them, until you reach Being; but I will raise the same questions about
each of these terms, right up to the ultimate "Being," for you do not
know what it means. You may say you cannot define it since it has no

higher genus; but I do not understand what this means, nor do you. You do not know what "Being" is, and much less do I. You may say that all inquiry must eventually have a halt, but this does not dissolve the doubt or satisfy the mind. You must admit your ignorance; fine, so do I.

Let us proceed. Man is one thing, which you deck out with a host of names – being, substance, body, living, animal, man, and finally Socrates. Are not all these words? To be sure. If they signify the same thing, they are superfluous, but if they signify different things, then man is not one and the same thing. You may say you consider many aspects in the same man, to each of which you give their appropriate names. But this makes the thing more doubtful still. Moreover, you have still not reached an understanding of the whole man, since man is something large, solid, and perceptible by the senses, and yet you divide him into categories, traced out by weak and obscure reason, which are so minute that they escape the perception of the senses – the surest judge of all. . . .

[4] Let us see, then, what is to be understood by the word "knowledge." For if there is no such thing, no one will be entitled to lay claim to it. What is Aristotle's view? It will suffice to examine him as a representative of all the others; for he was the most acute investigator of nature, and is generally followed by the great majority of philosophers. . . . On his account, knowledge is a disposition acquired by demonstration. I do not understand this, and, worst of all, it is explaining something obscure by what is even more obscure – this is how they fool people. What is a disposition? I know even less of what it is than I do of what knowledge is. You say it is a "settled quality" – I am even less clear. The more you go on, the less you achieve, and the more verbiage you produce, the greater the confusion. . . . And what is a demonstration? You will provide a new definition: "a syllogism producing knowledge." This is circular, and you have fooled yourself along with me. But what is a syllogism? How wonderful! Strain your ears and stretch your imagination, for it may not be capable of taking in such a barrage of words. How subtle, long, and difficult is the science of syllogisms! . . . Listen: prove that man is an entity. You proceed as follows: "man is a substance, a substance is an entity, therefore man is an entity." I doubt both premises. Suppose you give the following proof: "man is a body, body is a substance, therefore man is a substance"; again, I doubt both. You may say "man is a living thing; a living thing is a body, therefore man is a body"; I have the same doubts here. Or again, "man is an animal, an animal is a living thing, therefore man is a living thing." Almighty God, what a

long series of moves, what a mess, just to prove that man is an entity! The proof is more obscure than the original question. . . .

[11] So what use have all these syllogisms been? Why did Aristotle spend so much effort on teaching them? And why do all his successors still expend their labor on them? When it comes to writing, we do not make any use of syllogisms, nor did Aristotle. No science has ever emerged from them; indeed, they have led many sciences into error and confusion. As for discussions and disputes, we make even less use of syllogisms; we are content with a simple inference from one point to the next. Otherwise, our disputes would never end, but we would have to struggle at every stage to reduce a syllogism to its correct mood and figure, or to convert it, and endless other games of this sort. In fact there are foolish people who do this, even today: they reject any argument not couched in the proper mood and figure. Such is their stupidity, such is the wonderful subtlety and benefit of this syllogistical science, that they turn wholly to shadows, and real things are entirely forgotten. . . . [12] Their "science" is nothing else than constructing a syllogism out of nothing, that is, from A, B, and C. If they had to construct out of something, they would fall silent, since they do not understand the simplest proposition.

So, returning to our inquiry, if someone is teaching us to build a house, but has never built one himself, and does not know how to, nor has any pupils who do, why should we believe his account of how to build? Because "there can be no knowledge where there is no demonstration"? But it is false that demonstration produces the disposition for knowledge. Knowledge arises in someone who is ignorant but has an aptitude for knowledge; demonstration merely points to the thing to be known, as the very term "demonstration" implies. . . . [13] True knowledge, by contrast, if it existed, would be free, and would come from a free mind. If such a mind does not, by itself, perceive the thing in question, it will never be compelled by any demonstrations to perceive it. . . .

[14] If they had said "knowledge is amassing many things in the mind," they might have been nearer the mark, though still not entirely correct. For there can be knowledge of just one single thing; indeed, knowledge relates to each individual thing taken on its own, [15] not to a plurality of objects taken together, just as vision is of each individual single object taken on its own. We cannot perfectly view two objects at the same time, just as we cannot perfectly understand two objects at the same time, but only one after the other. Hence, the saying "bent on too

many things, you lose clear sight of each." Now as all men, in virtue of their species or, better, in virtue of the name applied to them, are re- garded as a single item, "mankind," so vision is said to be one thing, even though it is of many things, and though there is a plurality of acts of vision. Similarly, philosophy is said to be one science, even though it is contemplation of many things; but the contemplation relating to each thing, and the knowledge of each thing arising from that contemplation, is something single. The saying "knowledge is an accumulation of many things in the mind" is not even true, notwithstanding the silly view of people who regard as "learned" those who have the ability to recite the many things they have seen and heard, whether in one science or in many different ones. Rather, he who wishes to embrace all things loses all. A single science suffices for the entire world, though the whole world is not enough for it. As for me, even the smallest thing in the world is more than enough for the contemplation of an entire lifetime, but even so I do not hope to achieve knowledge. On the contrary, believe me, many are called but very few chosen. . . .

[16] Some think that it suffices for knowledge that the things known are within us. This position is mistaken. . . . For there are many things within us, body, soul, intellect, faculties, images, and so on, of which we in no way have perfect knowledge. . . . It is not existing items within us, things, or images of things, that produce knowledge or are knowledge; they are rather the contents filling the memory, which are then contem- plated by the mind. I conclude that it is quite wrong for knowledge to be called a disposition. For a disposition is a quality that is relatively stable; but knowledge is not a quality, unless you are prepared to call vision a quality. It is rather a simple action of the mind that can be perfect even at the first moment of intuition; and it lasts no longer than the mental activity that brings it about, just like vision. Such contem- plation and awareness, which is produced by the mind, gives rise to an image that is transmitted to the memory [17] and retained there; if it is firmly imprinted there it is called a permanent disposition and, if less so, a temporary one. But the images will now be the proper objects of memory, not knowledge. If we recall them afterward, we will be said to remember what was known, but not to know – unless we contemplate them afresh (just as someone who recites what he has seen is not now seeing). But someone who holds in his memory many things once known is said to know them, since he did indeed know all these things before, and can know them whenever he wishes; for even with a very small effort he can understand these things by looking back, since he did understand

them previously. Hence it is clear that the permanent disposition
whereby many things are held in the memory is not to be called knowledge, unless those things were known previously by the intellect. . . .

[22] Aristotle [in the *Physics*] remarked that "knowledge of the things of
which there are principles, causes, and elements depends on our awareness of these principles." . . . Earlier he said that there was knowledge
of these first principles, but that it could not be demonstrated. Elsewhere, he calls awareness of first principles "intellection," not knowledge; but this is not well put, since if we did have access to these principles, then, as in other cases, it would amount to perfect knowledge.
But in fact we have no such grasp either of the first principles or of what depends on them, from which it follows that nothing is known. . . .

[23] What has hitherto been accepted by the majority seems to me
false, as I have already shown, but what I shall now say seems true. You
may take the opposite view, and you may well be right, which will confirm the proposition that nothing is known. So let us now see what
knowledge is, to try to make it clearer whether anything is known.
KNOWLEDGE IS THE PERFECT AWARENESS OF A THING. Here is a simple
but true explication of the term "knowledge." If you are looking for the
genus and differentia, I will not provide them, for such words are more
obscure than what I have just defined. What is "awareness" [*cognitio*]? I
really would not know how to explain it any other way, and if I were to
define it, you could raise exactly the same questions about the definition
and its parts, so that we would never reach an end, but would be em-
broiled in perpetual doubt about terms. . . .

[40] Yesterday, with your perfect knowledge, established for many centuries, you said that the whole Earth was surrounded by the ocean, and
was divided into three general parts, Asia, Africa, and Europe. Now what
will you say? A new world has been discovered, new things, in Nova
Hispania, or the West and East Indies. You used to say that the land
south of the equator was uninhabitable because of heat, and the polar
zones too cold to live in; but now experience has proved both false.
Construct another science, then, for the first one is now revealed to be
false. How can you claim your propositions are eternal, incorruptible,
infallible, and incapable of being otherwise, you miserable worm, who
scarcely even knows who you are, where you come from, or where you
are heading? . . .

[41] As for what occurred long before us, or what may come after-

ward, who can assert anything for certain? This is the source of all the debates among philosophers about the beginning, or eternity, of the world, and the controversy over its duration and end; no one we know of has been able to settle the argument, and no one perhaps will ever do so from scientific knowledge. For how can a corruptible being establish anything about what is incorruptible, or a finite being about what is infinite? How can one who lives for a single instant, and who, were he to cease to live, is as if he has no being at all – how could he have the power to establish anything about what is eternal and certain? The question of whether there is anything eternal and certain, and the rest, is the most fundamental of all other questions, but it is one of which we neither have, nor can have, any knowledge whatsoever. . . .

[44] A further cause of our ignorance is the perpetual duration of some things, while other things are subject to perpetual generation and corruption and change; so you cannot ever give an account of the former, since you do not live forever, nor of the latter, since they are never entirely the same and appear and disappear from moment to moment. . . . [48] The same effect produced by contrary causes gives rise to the greatest uncertainty as far as we are concerned. Coldness can come about from motion, as in the agitation of the heart, thorax, and arteries, or of hot water, but also from rest, as when someone stops after moving but is still hot. Heat can come from motion, as when running, but also from rest, like the heart when it is still, or when some boiling water is kept motionless. Blackness can come from heat, as in the Ethiopians, or from cold, as in a rotting limb, or one that has had a tourniquet applied for some time, especially when the passage of spirits through the arteries is prevented. Decay may occur from any combination of qualities, apart from dryness. This is not all: one quality may be produced by its opposite, such as heat from cold, as when cold lime is soaked, or in winter time, in our own bodies, or in fountains, or the earth (hence the saying "the belly is hottest in winter and spring"), or in the Ethiopians who are cold inside, as are we, even in summer. How all this can happen, I wholly fail to understand. . . .

[52] All awareness comes from the senses. Beyond this, everything is confusion, doubt, perplexity, and guesswork: nothing is certain. But the senses see only what is on the outside, and do not have true awareness (by "the senses" in this context, I mean the eye). The mind then considers what is taken in by the senses. If the senses are deceived, so too will the mind be; but if not, what follows? The mind views only the images of

things, let in by the eye; it then inspects them on every side, turns them around, asking "What is this?" "How does it come to be such and such?" "Why?" This is all it can do, for it sees nothing certain. . . .

[53] Being, however, is the object, subject, and principle of all awareness, and of all acts and motions. And you see how great is our opportunity for ignorance in respect of things. . . . Yet the problems in things are minute when they are compared with the obstacles to knowledge which arise in the subject who seeks awareness. Someone endowed with a perfect, razor-sharp mind and faultless sense perception could perhaps overcome all these obstacles (I concede this for the sake of argument, but in fact the task would be impossible, even were one to have access to the most perfect objects); but in our actual situation, things are far worse.

Now in our definition of knowledge, namely "perfect awareness of things," the other element was "awareness." There are three aspects to this: the thing of which we have awareness (just mentioned), the subject who is aware (to be dealt with later), and the awareness itself, which is the act of the subject directed toward the thing. I shall say a word about this now, but as briefly as possible, for it belongs in a treatise on the soul. It is indeed a most difficult matter, full of perplexity, for the soul to contemplate its faculties and actions; nothing is harder. And this is especially true in respect of the awareness we are now inquiring about. Just as there is nothing that has higher worth than the soul, so there is nothing more excellent than this awareness; it is quite unparalleled. If one had this faculty in a perfect form, one would be like God – indeed, God himself. For none can have perfect awareness of [54] what he has not created; nor could God have created anything, or be able to rule over his creation, had he not had perfect prior awareness of it. He alone, then, who is wisdom, awareness, and perfect understanding, goes deep within all things, knows all, is aware of all, and understands all; for he is all things and in all, and all things are him and in him. But poor man, imperfect and wretched – how should he be aware of other things, since he cannot even know his own self, in whom and with whom he exists? How is he to know the most abstruse mysteries of nature, including spiritual things, and our own soul, when he does not fully understand even the clearest and most obvious things – what he is eating and drinking, what he is touching, seeing, and hearing. Even what I am now thinking and writing I do not understand; nor will you understand what you read. You may perhaps think it is all fine and true, as I do. But neither of us knows anything. . . .

[55] What is awareness [*cognitio*]? The apprehension of the thing.

What is apprehension? You must apprehend this by yourself; I cannot implant everything in your mind for you. But if you persist in asking me, I will say that it is understanding, perspicuous vision, intuition. If you go on to ask about these, I have nothing to say: I cannot, since I do not know. But you must distinguish apprehension from mere reception. A dog receives the image of a man, a stone, or of some quantity, but does not have awareness. Our own eye receives, but does not have awareness. Often, the soul merely receives, without having awareness, as when what it takes in is false, or when what is presented to the dull intellect is obscure. You must also distinguish awareness in the strict sense, which we have just described, though without full awareness of what it is, from another kind which is inaccurately so called. In this latter sense, a person is said to have awareness of what he saw on a previous occasion, and retains in his memory, flagged by the appropriate signs. This is the sort of awareness by which a child is said to recognize his father or brother, or a dog his master or the path it follows. Finally, you must divide all awareness into two kinds. The first is perfect, and enables the thing to be scrutinized and understood on all sides, from inside and outside. This is the knowledge [*scientia*] that it is our present purpose to secure for mankind, despite her reluctance to be captured. But the second kind is imperfect – a haphazard apprehension of the thing in any fashion whatever. We are all familiar with this; but it can differ in scope, be more or less clear or obscure, and finally be enjoyed in varying degrees as the native mental endowments of people vary.

There are two sorts of such imperfect awareness: the one external, which comes about via the senses, and is hence called "sensory awareness," and the other internal, which arises in the mind alone, but is no less important. There are different ways of thinking about all this. The person who has awareness is a single entity, and the awareness in all these cases is one and the same. For it is the same mind that has awareness of what is external and what is internal. The senses do not have awareness of anything or make any judgment, but merely receive items that they pass on to the mind, which subsequently exercises its awareness (just as the air does not see colors or light, but is merely the medium for their being presented to our vision).

[56] There are, however, three classes of object of which the mind has different kinds of awareness. Some are entirely external, and separated from any action of the mind. Others are entirely internal, of which some do not involve any contribution from the mind, while others do. Others are partly external and partly internal. Furthermore, the first

kind manifest themselves via the senses, the second never via the senses
but immediately through themselves, and the third partly via the senses
and partly through themselves. Let me explain. Color, sound, and heat
cannot present themselves to the mind to be objects of awareness
through themselves, but only by imprinting a form on the sense organ
that is apt for receiving them (let us take it for now that sensation comes
about by the reception of such sensible forms); such a form, or something like it, is offered to the mind, enabling the mind to be aware either
of it or, by its means, of the thing of which it is a form. But the items
that arise entirely through the action of the intellect, which is their
begetter, and which are within us, offer themselves and are displayed to
the intellect not through forms but through themselves. Such are the
countless objects that the mind fashions for itself, as when, after protracted reflection, it thinks up something new, and makes an inference,
or when it understands its own acts of understanding, or when it constructs within itself conjunctions and divisions and comparisons and
predications and notions, and then applies its attention to them and
achieves awareness of such items through themselves. The second class
includes everything internal that arises along with the understanding,
but without its direct operation, such as will, memory, the appetites,
anger, fear, and the other passions, together with all other internal items
of which, through themselves, the intellect itself is immediately aware.
Finally, there are the many items that reach the mind partly through
the senses and partly from the understanding itself. The nature of a dog,
or of a magnet, cannot in any way be grasped by the senses; they are
clothed with color, size, and shape, and conveyed to the mind, which
strips them of these accidents [57] and considers, turns over, and compares what remains, and finally fashions some common nature for itself,
as far as it is able.

The learned philosophers propose that there are intelligences in the
heavens. I hear what they say, but I do not understand. Yet I can construct something that gives me some representation of intelligence. The
air is something I continuously perceive by the sense of touch; but it
certainly does not provide any image in my mind, other than a kind of
image I invent for myself of a kind of quasi-incorporeal body – I do not
know what. I think of a vacuum in the same way. The infinite is something I comprehend in virtue of never comprehending a limit; but even
in the midst of this act of awareness I am forced to stop, thinking that
the infinite is something whose limits I shall never reach in my apprehension, though I continue to add forever, reaching on infinitely in my

imagination. Thus I fashion a form of something bounded, but with neither of its extremities bounded and perfect, but somehow defective; my notion is of something not bound or capable of being bounded, since an infinite number of parts can be added on to it, on either end, forever. What are we to do? Our condition is indeed wretched: in the midst of light, we are blind.

I have often thought about light, but have had to abandon it, as something of which I have no awareness, which is unknown and uncomprehended. It is the same if you contemplate the will, or the intellect, or anything else that is not perceived by the senses. I am certain, admittedly, that I am now thinking what I am writing down, that I want to write it down, and that I desire what I am writing to be true, and to meet with your approval. But even this is something I cannot regard too highly; for when I try to consider what this thought, or wanting, or desiring, or not regarding, amounts to, my thought gives out, my will is thwarted, my longing increases, my anxiety grows. I see nothing that I can grasp or apprehend. Indeed, the awareness of internal objects, which arises without the senses, is in this respect outclassed by that which I have of external objects via the senses. For the latter enables the [58] intellect to grasp something, namely the shape of a man, a stone, or a tree, derived from the senses; it at least seems to the intellect that it grasps the man by means of his image. But in the kind of awareness that occurs with regard to internal objects, it finds nothing it can grasp; it runs here and there, and can do no more than grope around like a blind man in the attempt to hold something fast. Yet the awareness of external things attained via the senses is inferior in certainty to that which is derived from the internal objects that are in us or arise in us. For I am more certain that I have appetite and will, and that I am now thinking this, or shunning and detesting that, than that I am seeing a temple, or Socrates.

I have just said that we are certain of the reality of those items that are, or arise, within us. As for the opinions we reach in our judgments of things by argument and reasoning, when we infer that they really are as we judge them to be, here there is the greatest uncertainty. It is much more certain to me that this paper I am writing on exists and is white than that it is composed of four elements, or that these elements are actually in it, or that it has a form derived from them. Moreover, if you exclude what is in us, or produced by us, the awareness arising from the senses is the most certain of all, while that arising from formal discourse is the most uncertain. For the latter is not truly awareness, but feeling our way, doubt, mere opinion, guesswork. And once again it emerges from this that what is arrived at through syllogisms, distinctions, predications, and other mental actions of this sort is not knowledge [scientia]. Were it possible to grasp the internal essence of each thing just as we perceive the external qualities of things by various kinds of sensation, then we could truly be said to know. But no one, so far as we know, has ever been able to achieve this. And hence, we know nothing. . . .

[59] Let it suffice to say something of one or more of the senses – for example, vision. Even though this comes about by means of the most perfect organ, and is the most certain and noblest of the senses, it still is deceived on very many occasions. . . . [60] If you put a coin in a small wide vessel, place the vessel on the ground, move away from it until you cannot see the coin, then have the vessel filled with water, you will immediately see the coin, larger then it was before. Why could you not see it before through the air, when this is supposed to be the best medium? And why does the coin now appear [61] larger? We do not know. . . . [62] Someone at a distance, even if he is running very fast, may seem to move slowly, especially if you are looking down from above, or looking up from below. What happens very slowly escapes the senses, like the movement of the hand in a clock. How can you judge for certain? You do not know, and still less do I. That we should have knowledge in such cases is of great importance, since all the perpetual doubts about the size of the stars (not to mention their distance, speed, and location) all seem to hinge on this. As for objects close at hand, we may simultaneously investigate them with various senses, if they are perceivable by more than one, and arrive at a more certain awareness from nearby. But how is this possible with distant objects? And it is not only distant objects that present problems. If from a distance you see a stick half submerged in water, it will appear bent or broken. You will still say that it is straight, because of previous experience. But if it is really broken, it will still appear broken – no reasoning based on opposite cases is valid here. You may assert that it is straight, relying on the previous reasoning, but you are wrong. What are you going to do if you cannot remove it from the water? You will stay in doubt. . . .

[69] From so many thousands of men, how few are suited to the sciences – even such sciences as we have? Scarcely more than one or two; and if we are talking of perfect science, then the answer will be none at all. I will show you why: to know something perfectly, one would have to be a perfect human being. But is there any such creature? You must see

that he would have to be perfect. You may say that the soul is equally perfect in all men . . . but the body is the cause of one person's being more learned than another, or of the fact that some lack learning altogether. Very well. But is our soul perfect enough to enable a human being to know anything perfectly? No. So the degree of perfection of knowledge will depend on the degree of perfection of the body (this seems the most reasonable inference from the line of argument you are pursuing). But who has been given a perfect body? No one. . . .

[75] What follows? The human soul, most perfect of all God's creatures, needs the most perfect body in order to achieve the most perfect of all its possible actions, namely perfect awareness. You may say that understanding does not depend on the body, and is not in any way assisted by it, but is accomplished by the mind alone. This is false. . . . It is as silly to say that the soul understands as to say that it hears. It is the human being who does both, using both body and mind; here, as in all its other actions, the two assist each other, cooperate and act together. . . . Since a perfect body is nowhere to be found, there will be no such thing as perfect awareness, and hence no such thing as knowledge. . . .

[90] Wretched human beings have two ways of finding the truth. They cannot know things through the things themselves; if they could understand them in this way, as they ought, they would not need any other means. But since they do not have this power, they have lighted upon two props for their ignorance: these do not enable them to increase their knowledge, at least in a perfect way, but do help them to perceive and learn something. I am referring to experience and judgment. Neither of these can rightly stand without the other . . . but see how it again follows that nothing is known. Experience is everywhere deceptive and difficult; and even if we could have it in a perfect form, it shows us only what happens from an extrinsic point of view, never anything of the natures of things. Judgment is exercised on the items that are discovered by experience, and hence it too can only relate to externals, and that badly. It can approach the natures of things only by conjecture; since it did not acquire them previously by experience, it cannot reach them by itself, and its guesses are often opposed to the truth. So where is knowledge to come from? Certainly not from experience or judgment. But these are all we have. . . .

THREE

Christopher Clavius, *The Promotion of Mathematics*

[*Modus promovendi mathematicas disciplinas*, 1586]

Introduction

Christopher Clavius (1537–1612) was a Jesuit astronomer and mathematician who taught in the order's Collegio Romano (from 1565 to his death). His importance was due in part to the influential textbooks he published and to his training of numerous professors of mathematics who went on to teach in other Jesuit colleges (such as La Flèche, where Descartes was educated). John Pell, writing to Charles Cavendish about a meeting with Descartes in 1646, relates that "He [Descartes] says he had no other instructor for Algrebra [*sic*] than ye reading of Clavy Algebra above 30 yeares agoe," that is, his reading of Clavius' *Algebra* before 1616, when he was a student at La Flèche.[1] In 1586, the Jesuits, having decided to reorganize and standardize their collegiate curriculum, carried on significant debates about teaching, the importance of various disciplines to learning, and their relations with each other. These position papers (or *Monumenta paedagogica*) resulted in the order's set curriculum (*Ratio studiorum*). The following pedagogical paper was written by Clavius for this occasion. It is significant as part of Descartes' context because of the picture it imparts of the relation between mathematics and philosophy at the start of the century: the implied low status of professors of mathematics in contrast with the one accorded to professors of philosophy; the emphasis on mixed as opposed to pure mathematics: "the division of continuous quantities into infinity, of the tides, the winds, comets, the rainbow, the halo,

1. AT IV, 730–731.

and other meteorological matters, the proportions of motions, qualities, actions, passions, reactions, and so on concerning which the *calculatores*[2] wrote much"; and the disavowal of the claim that mathematics should be thought of as subordinate to philosophy – one should not teach that "the mathematical sciences are not sciences, do not have demonstrations, abstract from being and the good, etc."[3]

[RA]

THE PROMOTION OF MATHEMATICS

First a teacher must be chosen with uncommon knowledge and authority; for if either of these is absent, as experience shows, students seem unable to be attracted to the mathematical disciplines. In order that the teacher may have greater influence over his students, the mathematical disciplines themselves be more highly valued, and the students come to understand their utility and necessity, the teacher must be invited to the ceremonial proceedings in which doctorates are granted and public disputations held, so that, if he is capable, he may also at times put forward arguments and help those arguing. For, by this means, it will easily happen that the students, seeing the professor of mathematics taking part in such proceedings and also disputing at times with other instructors, will be convinced that philosophy and the mathematical sciences are connected, as they truly are – especially because up to now students seem almost to have despised these sciences, for the sole reason that they think these sciences are considered not valuable, even useless, since the person who teaches them is never called to public proceedings with the other professors.

2. *Calculatores* refers to a group of fourteenth-century Oxford natural philosophers linked by a common interest in and approach to logic, mathematics, and physics; they are also referred to as "Mertonians," since some of them were fellows at Merton College, Oxford. See E. D. Sylla, "The Oxford Calculators," in N. Kretzman, A. Kenny, and J. Pinborg, eds., *The Cambridge History of Later Medieval Philosophy*, pp. 540–564.
3. For more on Clavius as a mathematician and astronomer, see J. M. Lattis, *Between Copernicus and Galileo*, and P. Dear, "Mersenne's Suggestion: Cartesian Meditation and the Mathematical Model of Knowledge in the Seventeenth Century," in R. Ariew and M. Grene, eds., *Descartes and His Contemporaries*, pp. 49–62.

It also seems necessary that the instructor should have a certain inclination and desire for lecturing on these sciences, and should not be
taken up with many other concerns; otherwise he will scarcely be able
to help his students. Now, in order that the society may always have
capable professors of these sciences, some people should be selected who
are fit and capable for carrying out this task, so that they may be in-
structed in various mathematical subjects in a private school. Otherwise
it does not seem possible that these studies would last long in the society,
let alone be promoted, even though they might bring honor to the society and are very frequently the subject of discussion in colloquia and
meetings of leading men, where Jesuits are seen as lacking knowledge
in mathematical matters. This is the reason why the Jesuits become
speechless in such meetings, with great shame and disgrace, as has often
been reported by those to whom this has happened. I omit the fact that
natural philosophy without the mathematical disciplines is lame and incomplete, as we shall show a little later. So much for the teacher of
mathematical disciplines; now let us add a few words about his pupils.

Second, then, it is necessary that the students should understand that
these sciences are useful and necessary for rightly understanding the rest
of philosophy, and that they are at the same time an embellishment to
all other arts, so that perfect knowledge might be acquired; indeed, these
sciences and natural philosophy have so close an affinity with one another that unless they give each other mutual aid they can in no way
preserve their own status. For this to happen, it will be necessary first
that physics students should study mathematical disciplines at the same
time – a habit that has always been retained in the society's schools thus
far. For if these sciences were taught at a different time, philosophy
students would think, and understandably so, that they were in no way
necessary to physics. And so very few would want to understand them,
even though it is agreed among experts that physics cannot be correctly
grasped without them, especially what pertains to that part concerning
the number and motion of the celestial orbs; the multitude of intelligences; the effects of the stars, which depend on the various conjunctions, oppositions, and other distances between them; the division of
continuous quantities into infinity; of the tides, the winds, comets, the
rainbow, the halo, and other meteorological matters; the proportions of
motions, qualities, actions, passions, reactions, and so on concerning
which the *calculatores* wrote much. I omit countless examples in Aristotle,
Plato, and their more illustrious commentators, which can by no means
be understood without some knowledge of the mathematical sciences.

Indeed, because of their ignorance of these, some professors of philosophy have very often committed many errors, and those most grave; and what is worse they have even published them; it would not be difficult to produce examples.

By the same token, instructors of philosophy should be skilled in mathematical disciplines, at least moderately, lest they run into similar shoals with great disgrace and loss of the reputation the society has in letters.

It goes without saying that the professors would hereby gain great influence over their pupils, if they understood that they treated the passages in Aristotle and other philosophers concerning the mathematical disciplines as they deserved. As a result, it will also come about that the students understand better the necessity for these sciences. It will also contribute much to this if the instructors of philosophy abstain from those questions that do not help in the understanding of natural things and very much detract from the authority of the mathematical disciplines in the eyes of the students, such as those in which they teach that the mathematical sciences are not sciences, do not have demonstrations, abstract from being and the good, etc.; for experience teaches that these questions are a great hindrance to students and of no service to them; especially since instructors can hardly teach them without bringing these sciences into ridicule (as has been reported to me on more than one occasion).

It would also help if, in individual conversations, teachers would encourage students to learn mathematics, impressing on them its usefulness, and not doing the opposite, as many have done in the past. In this way all the disagreement that outsiders observe among us, when such opinions are heard in our schools, will be removed.

Moreover, Schoolmen will be greatly encouraged to study mathematics, if once a month all the philosophers are assembled in one place, where a student would read a short appreciation of the mathematical disciplines, and then with one or two others would explain a problem from geometry or astronomy, as would be pleasant to hear and be of use for the humanities; such problems can be found in abundance. Or let him explain a mathematical text from Aristotle or Plato, in whose works such texts are numerous. Or even let him propose new and original demonstrations of some of the propositions of Euclid. Let praise be given there to those who best solve the proposed problem, or are guilty of the fewest fallacies (which are common enough) in the invention of new demonstrations. The result of this would be that they would become eager for such studies, when they see such honors before them, and at the same time they would come to understand their importance, and would make greater progress in them.

Furthermore, toward the end of the course in philosophy, those who wish to take the honors of master or doctor should be examined in mathematical matters, as is usual in some other schools. At this examination, let the mathematics professor be present with the other professors of philosophy.

FOUR

Francisco Suárez, *Metaphysical Disputations*
[*Disputationes metaphysicae*, 1597]

Introduction

Born in Granada, Suárez was a member of the Jesuit order, and taught at Salamanca and Coimbra. His lengthy *Metaphysical Disputations* (the work is divided into fifty-four major sections, "disputation 1," "disputation 2," etc.) was a comprehensive treatise on metaphysics and one of the first to be developed in its own right, rather than as a commentary on Aristotle. Descartes, who was educated by the Jesuits, certainly studied Suárez's work, and a considerable amount of the framework for the *Meditations* (particularly the reasoning in the Third Meditation) bears the clear imprint of Suárez's ideas. We also know that Descartes had access to a copy of the *Disputationes metaphysicae* about the time he wrote the *Meditations*: he makes an explicit reference to disputation 9, section 2, §4 (the relevant extract is included here) as a source for his use of the term "material falsity."[1]

A facsimile reprint of the complete Latin text of the *Disputationes* was published in two volumes in 1965. The complete works of Suárez in the original Latin are available in the standard edition in twenty-six volumes (1861). There is a translation by F. Freddoso of a portion of the *Disputationes*, entitled *On Efficient Causality: Metaphysical Disputations 17–19*.

The *Disputationes* is of great interest to the student of Descartes both because it gives a vivid and detailed picture of the style and method of philosophical argument that Descartes would have imbibed as a schoolboy, and because it deploys a framework of theo-

---

1. Fourth Set of Replies, AT VII 235: CSM II 164.

logical and metaphysical assumptions that continued, sometimes almost subliminally, to influence Descartes, despite his official program for casting aside all preconceived opinions. The work, however, is an enormous one, and constraints of space have meant that it has been possible to include only a small selection of extracts here; these have been chosen for their particular relevance to the argument of the *Meditations*. The extracts are arranged not in the sequence in which they come in Suárez's own text, but following the order in which the various corresponding topics arise in the development of the *Meditations* (thus, extracts that throw light on the argument of the Third Meditation come before those relevant to the Fifth). In selecting material from Suárez to translate for the present volume, I have been very greatly influenced by the choice of texts made by Etienne Gilson in his invaluable *Index scolastico-cartésien.*

[JC]

METAPHYSICAL DISPUTATIONS

Metaphysics

Divine and supernatural theology relies on the divine light and on principles revealed by God; yet since it is carried out through human discourse and reasoning, it is also assisted by truths known by the light of nature, and employs such truths as ministers and, as it were, instruments in order to carry forward its theological inquiries and to shed light on divine truths. Among all the natural sciences, that which comes first of all, and has taken the name "first philosophy," does special service to sacred and supernatural theology. For it comes closest of all to the knowledge of divine things, and also explicates and confirms those natural principles that include universal things and in a certain way support and sustain all learning. . . .

The science of metaphysics is not only valuable in its own right, but also most useful for the perfect acquisition of the other sciences. This proposition is taken from Aristotle, *Metaphysics*, book I, chapter 2, and book 3, chapter 2, where among the other characteristics of wisdom he includes the fact that the other sciences minister to it, and that it has priority over the others. According to Aristotle its superior position is not in respect of practical expertise, which has to do rather with prudence or the moral sciences, but in respect of speculative guidance; he adds that metaphysics has this status above the other sciences because it deals with the most important things and the first causes of things, and the ultimate end and the supreme good. He adds in the *Posterior Analytics*, book I, chapter 7, that metaphysics alone deals with the first principles of the other sciences. The principles of the sciences are twofold (as he explains in the same book, chapter 8): some are proper to each individual science that unfolds them; others are common to many or rather all the sciences, since all the sciences use them, as the subject matter demands, and insofar as the other particular principles depend on them. . . . Now since all the sciences depend to a very great extent on these principles, it must necessarily be through metaphysical science that they are to a great extent developed; for as previously noted, the knowledge and contemplation of these principles cannot belong to any special science, since it consists of the most abstract and universal terms. Therefore this science is of great utility for the development and perfection of the others. Again, Saint Thomas in various places says that metaphysics is more basic than the other sciences, since it considers the definition of absolute being, while the others consider a determinate notion of being; and he also says that metaphysics directs the other sciences. Finally, from these points we have made concerning the object and subject matter of metaphysics, it can easily be proved that this science considers the supreme definitions of entities, and the most universal properties and the proper notions of essence and being, and all the manners of distinction that there are in things; without distinct knowledge of all these, it is not possible to achieve perfect knowledge of particular things. This conclusion can be known by experience, since all the other sciences often use metaphysical principles, or presuppose them in order to move forward in their demonstrations or arguments; and hence it often happens that errors in the other sciences come about through ignorance of metaphysics.[2]

Is a Substance Known Prior to Its Accidents?

Some say that with respect to us, and originally, a substance falls within our knowledge before its accidents, at least if we are talking of confused and imperfect knowledge, even though in respect of distinct and proper

2. Preface, and disputation 1, section 4, §5; cf. First Meditation, AT VII 17; CSM II 12.

knowledge a substance is known through its accidents. . . . The latter part of this view is clear from experience itself, and the authorities do not disagree on this point. For we arrive at knowledge of substances, and of their proper genera or differentiae, only via their accidents or properties, by means of some intermediate effects or sensible signs. The first part is proved from the sayings of the authorities: the intellect cannot conceive of an accident except by conceiving of a substance, since the whole nature of an accident is to belong to a substance; hence Aristotle said that an accident cannot be defined except through a substance, and therefore the concept of an accident necessarily presupposes the concept of a substance. Other authorities, however, think that we can conceive of accidents before a substance. . . . The proof of this is that though a substance may be in itself more perfect and intelligible, yet as far as we are concerned, an accident has a greater power to impinge on the intellect, since our intellect is affected only by means of the impressions of sensible kinds; now the senses are not impressed with the forms of a substance, but only with its accidents; and therefore accidents are what first of all impinge on the intellect, and hence are conceived of by the intellect before the substance. In my view the latter opinion seems absolutely true, but should be understood in such a way that the substance should not be taken to be excluded entirely from the first conception of the intellect.[3]

The Natural Light

The natural light of any created intellect, as it intrinsically flows from a created essence, is commensurate with it in its power and manner of acting, and looks on it as its first and appropriate object. It is as it were an instrument joined to such an essence for the purposes of eliciting all the acts of understanding of which the essence itself, which is the basis of that light, is the proper and principal cause, acting through its own proper influence. But the light of glory, which the theologians say pours upon the blessed, cannot be naturally joined to any created things, and hence in a peculiar manner or relation it flows from the divine essence, being as it were a singular participation in its uncreated light. And hence it looks to such divine essence as its proper and appropriate object, and shares its modes of operation, and is its proper instrument for producing

3. Disputation 38, section 2, §§8, 9; cf. Second Meditation, AT VII 27; CSM II 18; Third Replies, AT VII 176; CSM II 124.

a vision of the divine essence. No created essence is the principal and, as it were, radical cause of such vision, but rather the divine essence itself. For just as the intellect is the instrument of the soul, so the light is the instrument of God. . . . As heat is said to be the instrument of fire with respect to its power of heating, and the intellect the instrument of the soul with respect to its power of understanding, in this manner the light of glory is the instrument of no created thing but of God; and in this sense God is said to be the principal cause of this vision.[4]

Formal and Objective Existence

We must first of all assume the common distinction between a formal and an objective concept. A formal concept is said to be the act itself, or (which is the same) the word whereby the intellect conceives some thing or common definition [*ratio*], which is called a concept because it is, as it were, the offspring of the mind. It is called "formal" either because it is the ultimate form of the mind, or because it represents formally to the mind the thing that is known, or because it really is the intrinsic and formal term of the mental conception, thus differing from an objective concept, as I shall now explain. An *objective* concept is said to be the thing, or notion [*ratio*] which is strictly and immediately known or represented by means of the formal concept. For example, when we conceive of a man, that act which we perform in the mind in order to conceive of man is called a formal concept; but the man thus known and represented by that act is called the objective concept. As a concept, it is so called through a denomination that is extrinsic to the formal concept through which its object is said to be conceived; and hence it is rightly called "objective." For it is not a concept in the sense of a form intrinsically determining a conception, but in the sense of the object and subject matter round which the formal concept is deployed, and to which the mind's eye directly moves; in view of which it is called by some, following Averroes, the *intention formed by the intellect*, and by others the *objective relation*. From this we may gather the difference between the formal and objective concept, namely that the formal concept is always a true and positive thing, and a quality in created things inhering in the mind; but an objective concept is not always a true positive thing. For we conceive from time to time of privations and other items which are

4. Disputation 30, section 11, §46; cf. Third Meditation, AT VII 40, 52; CSM II 28, 36.

called "entities of reason," which have being only objectively in the intellect. Again, the formal concept is always a singular and individual thing, since it is a thing produced through the intellect and inhering in it; but an objective concept can indeed sometimes be a singular and individual thing, insofar as it can be presented to the mind and conceived by a formal act, but often it is a something universal, or confused and common, such as "man," "substance," and so on.[5]

Containing Perfections Eminently

It belongs to the perfection of this being [i.e., God] that he contains all these perfections [life, knowledge, etc.] *eminently*. To contain them in this way is the manner appropriate to the excellence of such a being, which has a more eminent grade and mode of being than every entity in which these perfections are found formally; hence, it must contain these perfections in a more eminent manner than that found in created beings.

But what is it for one thing to contain another thing, or its perfection, *eminently*? This is matter on which various theologians dispute with Saint Thomas in [*Summa theologiae*] part I, question 4. To put it briefly, we may say that to contain something eminently is to possess such a perfection in a superior manner, which contains in virtual form whatever is to be found in the lower perfection. The best way for us to explain this is with respect to causality or effect. All the perfections of created things, insofar as they are eminently in God, are nothing else than the creative essence of God itself. . . . Now creative essence is said to be all things *eminently*, insofar as by itself alone, and by its eminent virtue, it has the power to communicate its perfections to all things. Not that formally speaking, and in strictness of definition, the power to bring things about is to be identified with containing them eminently: we can make a distinction of reason between these two notions, and we believe that the following causal locution is a true way of putting the matter: since it contains the perfections eminently, it follows that it can bring them about. But we explain this "containing" by reference to the bringing about of an effect, since this is the clearest and most convenient way we can find to put the matter.

Some people say that to contain the perfections of creatures eminently is to contain whatever perfection they have, with all their imper-

5. Disputation 2, section 1, §1; cf. Third Meditation, AT VII 40ff.; CSM II 28ff.

fections removed. This is not so clear. For when God is said to contain whatever perfection a creature has, with the imperfections removed, either we are tacitly understanding "eminently" with "contains," in which case nothing is explained, or else we are supposing he contains the perfections formally, which would involve a contradiction. For if every imperfection is removed from a created thing, we are not left with formal perfection, since imperfection is included in the intrinsic formal definition and concept of a created thing.

You may say it follows from what has been said that no created perfection is present formally in God, since there is no created perfection that, taken formally, does not include some imperfection. I reply that it is true that no created perfection is present in God formally in a way corresponding to the precise definition appropriate to a created thing, but it is present in God only eminently. For God does not have created wisdom, since this as such is an accident and a finite perfection; and the same holds for other perfections. Hence God is said to contain some of these perfections formally, since in respect of them he has some formal similarity with a created thing, by virtue of which the perfection is attributed to God and to a created thing in the same terms, and according to the same definition or formal concept, notwithstanding the fact that any relation between God and a created thing will always involve an element of analogy. But when there is no such similarity or formal connection of terms, but it is merely a question of the efficacy of the divine power, then we say that what is involved is a relation of [eminent] containment.[6]

Material Falsity

Composition and division can be found either in the apprehension of a concept alone, abstracting from any judgment, or in a conception that involves a judgment at the same time. In the former case we have said that complex truth is properly found in the composition of our judgments; and the same must therefore be said of falsity, for contraries are of the same kind. Hence, no one thinks he is deceived or goes astray until he judges how many false compositions he apprehends. But since the apprehension that happens without judgment regularly comes about by concepts of words, rather than things . . . (for in the composition of

6. Disputation 30, section 1, §§9–12; cf. Third Meditation, AT VII 41; CSM II 28.

words there is falsity just as in the composition of signs), it can be admitted that in such apprehension, although there is something as it were materially false, it is not something false in the judgment that affirms or puts something forward, but merely in the sign, which signifies something false in its own right. Thus there is falsity in the proposition "There is no God," either written down or materially put forward by him who reports "The fool hath said in his heart 'There is no God'"; and, hence, the account of this kind of falsity is the same as that which applies to the falsity which occurs in some verbal composition, as in a sign. But if the apprehension comes about by means of concepts of things, it is scarcely intelligible how there could be a composition of the apprehending mind without some judgment. . . . [7]

Causality and Perfection

It is certain that an effect cannot exceed in perfection all its causes taken together. The proof of this is that there is nothing of perfection in the effect that it does not have from its causes; therefore, an effect can have nothing of perfection that did not previously exist in one of its causes, either formally or eminently. For causes cannot bestow what they do not in any way contain in themselves. . . .

It must be said that an effect can never exceed in perfection all the efficient causes that, taken together, go to produce it; nor indeed can it exceed in perfection any given single cause that goes to produce it as the principal and total cause in some kind. Conversely, what is truly a principal efficient cause always exceeds its effect in perfection. . . . The proof of the first point is that the whole perfection of an effect flows from its efficient causes; hence, it is impossible that there should be some perfection in the effect that is not present in an equal or more noble manner in one of the efficient causes. Therefore it is impossible for effects to exceed in perfection all their efficient causes taken together. . . . The second point, which involves comparing effects with single efficient causes, is easily established by distinguishing a principal and an instrumental cause. For an instrumental cause can be less noble than its effect, . . . since the effect does not proceed principally from its power. But a principal cause can never be less noble, especially if it is the complete and total cause in its kind (in the case of a partial cause, the matter

7. Disputation 9, section 2, §4; cf. Third Meditation, AT VII 43–44; CSM II 30.

is more doubtful). . . . When it is the total principal cause, it cannot be inferior in perfection to its effect, since it cannot give to the effect a perfection that it does not have in itself.[8]

The Divine Attributes

The predicates as attributed to God by us do not express precise knowledge of his nature, since they are either used analogically, as expressing some features common to God and other things, or if they are properties of God they are very confused and are scarcely properties at all, except in a negative sense. This is clear from the fact that all the following – being, good, perfect, substance, wise, just, and so on, which are properly asserted of God – are common to created things; and if we wish to conceive of them as properties of God, we cannot do so except with a certain confusion, as when we say that God is supremely wise, or a being embracing all perfection, or something similar. Most often we do so by adding a denial of some imperfection that is normally predicated of created things, in order to attempt to explain in some way what we apprehend confusedly of such a perfection as it is in God. . . .

But although we do not conceive of God distinctly and in accordance with a proper representation of him, we nonetheless conceive of him truly, by a concept that directly and immediately represents him or some perfection that is proper to him. Such a concept, if it is positive and absolute, is indeed very confused . . . as it is opposed to a conception that properly and clearly represents the thing as it is in itself. But if a negation is included in this conception, although it does not pertain to the essence[9] of God, it nevertheless enables us to understand a foundation or root which is an essential property of God, and not some common notion or analogy. Thus when we conceive of God as an infinite being, we do not understand the substrate of this negation to be being as such, but we understand it as a certain singular being that has such great perfection that it is not limited by any boundaries. This is universal in us whenever we use negative differentiae in order to mark out positive genera, as when we say "irrational animal": we do not conceive of the genus animal as such, as the foundation of this negation,

8. Disputation 26, section 1, §§2, 5–6; cf. Third Meditation, AT 40–50; CSM II 28–35.
9. Latin *quidditas*, literally "whatness."

but we conceive of a certain restricted differentia of an animal, which, since we cannot conceive of it in a positive way, except very confusedly, we explicate through this negation.[10]

Knowledge of God's Existence through Our Own Imperfection

Although the existence of God is not known to us as something entirely evident, this truth is nonetheless so in accord with the natural light and the assent of all men that it can scarcely be unknown by anyone. As Augustine says in his *Treatise on the Epistle of John*, 106: "I have manifested thy name to men – not that name of thine whereby thou art called God, but that whereby thou art called my Father. For as for being called God, this name could not in any way have been unknown to the whole of creation and to all nations, before they believed in Christ."

This knowledge of God, however, can be understood in two ways. The first is under a confused and common notion [*ratio*], as under the notion of some superior power, which can help us or make us blessed, or something similar; such a concept may be appropriate to the true God, but can also apply to false deities, and this may have been Cicero's meaning when he said in *De natura deorum*, book I, "There is no people that does not have some primitive notion of what God is." The second way to understand "knowledge of God" is as referring to knowledge of the true God through the concept of a supreme being – that than which there can be nothing greater, and that which is the origin of all other things. This is the way Augustine appears to talk in the passage cited, and he adds: "For this is the power of the true Deity, that he cannot be entirely or completely hidden to a rational creature who actually employs his reason; for with the exception of a few in whom nature is extremely depraved, the entire human race confesses that God is the author of this world." ... And the other authorities I have mentioned have similarly asserted that knowledge of the true God is naturally implanted in mankind.

But this knowledge does not come about in all people by means of a demonstration, since not everyone is capable of grasping such a proof, nor is it established merely by the self-evidence of the terms involved.

10. Disputation 30, section 12, §§8, 11; cf. Third Meditation, AT VII 45; CSM II 31.

For although we take the name of God to signify a being that is necessary through itself, and than which nothing greater can be thought (as Anselm proposes, and Augustine takes it in his *De doctrina Christiana*, chapter 7), it is still not immediately evident whether the meaning of this term is a true thing, or merely something invented or thought up by us. Hence the knowledge in question can arise under a twofold heading. First, it can arise from the very great correspondence that this truth has with the nature of man; for when this truth is put forward, and the terms explained, although it may not immediately appear entirely evident, it still immediately appears in itself to be in accord with reason, and very easily carries conviction for a person who is not altogether corrupt. For nothing appears in this truth that is inconsistent or that makes it difficult to believe; on the contrary there are many things that at once incline us to assent to it – many things, I say, not only of a metaphysical or physical nature, but also of a moral nature; and not external things alone, but internal ones also. For if a man turns his reflection toward himself, he becomes aware that he does not exist from himself, and is not self-sufficient with respect to his perfection; and that none of the other created things of which he has experience are self-sufficient; but he still recognizes in himself a nature that, though imperfect in its own degree, is more excellent than these other created things, since both in knowing the truth and in loving the good he recognizes himself to be weak and infirm. Hence, by a very easy train of thought, a man will persuade himself that he lacks something, and requires a superior nature from which he derives his origin, and by which he is ruled and governed.

Second, this general notion is based on the tradition of the majority and is passed on from parents to children and from the learned to the ignorant. As a result, the general belief that God exists has grown and become accepted among all nations. Hence this knowledge seems in large part to be due to faith, especially among the mass of people, rather than to the self-evidence of the matter; but it still seems to have been attended with a certain practical and moral self-evidence that was sufficient to oblige people both to assent to the truth of God's existence and also to propagate it. And accordingly we may easily understand everything that the doctors of the church say about knowledge of God being naturally implanted.[11]

11. Disputation 29, section 3, §§35–37; cf. Third Meditation, AT VII 47ff.; CSM II 32ff.

The Total Perfection of God

It is of the essence of God that he is a being that is perfect in every respect, and this can be evidently demonstrated by the natural light. To prove it, we have to suppose that "perfect" applies to something which has no defects. . . . This can be understood either in a privative or a negative sense. In the former sense, something is called perfect if there is nothing missing that is owed to it by its nature to make up its integrity or fullness; in this sense many entities are perfect in their species or genera, but are not quite simply perfect – perfect in the whole breadth of their being. In the latter sense, something is called perfect when absolutely no element of perfection is missing, and in this sense a being is said to be absolutely perfect when every perfection is owed to it, and is necessarily in it, in such a way that it is wholly impossible for any perfection to be missing, either in a privative or a negative sense. In both these senses it is said to be of the essence of God that he is quite simply perfect.[12]

Being from Itself and Being from Another

Beings may be divided into those which have being from themselves and those which have being from another. Augustine touched on this division in chapter seven of *De cognitione verae vitae*,[13] and made it central to the proof of God's existence. In these terms it is a very well known and evident distinction, which is quite manifest, namely that there are many entities that have being communicated from another, and would not exist unless they received being from another; experience indeed establishes this point quite adequately. Again, it is evident that not all entities can have this mode of being, for if all individuals of a species have being from another, it is necessary that the whole species has being from another, since a species does not exist except in the individuals that make it up, nor do individuals have any common natural mode of receiving being apart from that required by the nature of the species; hence, if all individuals are such as not to have being from themselves, but need the efficient power of another to receive being, the whole species has the same lack and imperfection. Accordingly, it is not pos-

12. Disputation 30, section 1, §1; Third Meditation, AT VII 47; CSM II 32.
13. *De cognitione verae vitae* (Knowledge of the true life) is of doubtful authorship; it was also attributed to Honorius of Autun. The work was published circa 1470–1475.

sible that the whole species should have being from some individual of that species, since no such individual is capable of bringing itself about; and therefore it must receive being from a superior entity. And we should have to further investigate whether this entity had being from itself, or from another; for if it has being from itself, then we have reached our desired distinction; but if it has it from another, it would similarly be necessary for the whole species of such an entity to derive its origin from another higher being. There cannot be an infinite regress here. . . . And hence we must necessarily stop with some entity that has being from itself, and which is the origin of all things that merely received being from another. . . .

When something is said to have being out of itself or from itself, though this may seem something positive, it merely adds a negation to the entity itself; for an entity cannot have being from itself by a positive origin and emanation, and is said to have being from itself insofar as it has being without emanation from another. By this negation we declare the positive and simple perfection of this being, because it holds fast within itself its own existence and its essence, in such a way as to receive it from nothing else. . . . Some of the church fathers use this way of explaining the matter, when they say God is, for himself, the cause of his own being, or substance. Thus Hieronymus says (in his commentary on Ephesians, 3), "God is the origin of himself and the cause of his own substance." And Augustine in *De diversis quaestionibus LXXXIII*, questions 15 and 16, says that "God is the cause of his own wisdom"; and in *De trinitate*, chapter 1, speaking of the Father, he says that "to him belongs the cause that there is even a cause that he is wise." These locutions are all to be interpreted in a negative way.[14]

The Distinction of Reason

A distinction of reason is a distinction that does not formally and actually obtain in the things that are called distinct in this way; it does not obtain in the things as they exist in themselves, but only as they subsist in our conceptions, and have some label applied to them from our conceptions – as we distinguish one attribute of God from another, or a relation of identity from its term (as when we say "Peter is identical with himself"). This distinction is often itself broken down into two kinds: the former,

14. Disputation 28, section 1, §§6–7; cf. Third Meditation, AT VII 49–50; CSM II 34.

which does not have any foundation in the thing, is called a distinction of "reasoning reason"; . . . the latter, which has some foundation in the thing, is called by many a distinction of "reasoned reason."[15]

The Ineffability of God

Can it be demonstrated that God is ineffable? The sense of this attribute is not that God is a being such that he cannot in any way be named or described in speech. For it is a matter of common agreement that there are many things we say of God and his properties; and similarly it is agreed that God has many names, even in Holy Scripture. The sense of the proposition, then, is that God cannot be described in speech in accordance with his entire perfection, and no name can be given him by us or any created being that expresses his nature as it is in itself. In this sense the attribute of ineffability does not refer to another perfection in God alongside the previous ones we have discussed [namely his invisibility and his incomprehensibility]; it is based simply on the principle that names are signs of concepts, and hence, just as we cannot conceive of God sufficiently, or as he is in himself, so we can neither name him nor declare his perfection in speech. . . . [16]

The Nature of Perfection

How are the good and the perfect to be compared? Aristotle says in his *Metaphysics*, book 5, chapter 16, that "we call perfect that which does not require any part to be added to it, or which lacks nothing." In this sense, not every good thing is perfect, as is clear in itself, nor is every entity perfect, even though it may be good. A boy is an entity, like a man, but is not yet perfect; and a man may have a perfect quantity but not the qualities or dispositions that accord with his nature; and hence, though he may be good in a way, he is not perfect. In this sense we call perfect not whatever is good, but that which is complete in every part, and which is quite simply good. But in another way of speaking, we may call perfect anything that under some category of being possesses a perfection that is simply necessary and essential. . . . In this second sense, "good" and "perfect" are convertible terms; indeed they are entirely the same, since "good" signifies what is good in itself, or has goodness, that is, the perfection that is owed to it; and this is nothing else than pos-

15. Disputation 7, section 1, §4; cf. Third Meditation, AT VII 49; CSM II 33.
16. Disputation 30, section 13, §1; cf. Third Meditation, AT VII 52; CSM II 35.

sessing the essence or entity owed to it. Hence "good" under this definition signifies nothing else, essentially and formally, than being; for charity to be a good in the said fashion is in reality nothing else than its being charity, and so in other cases. But to be perfect in the first sense described, that is, to be quite simply good, is nothing else than to be an entity possessing the whole being required to make up its perfection.[17]

The Nature of Evil

It was an ancient error to regard evil as a positive nature of certain things which were thought to be entirely bad, and having their origin in a supremely bad principle. This was the Manichaean heresy. . . . But since Holy Scripture clearly teaches that there is only one first principle of things, which is supremely good, and that all things brought about by it are good, . . . among Christian philosophers it is certain that evil cannot be some positive thing, which of its nature and in its entirety is evil. For, first, it is impossible for there to be things that are good and are simply and in themselves entirely evil (for we have shown that any thing is good in itself); and, second, a thing cannot be evil because of the natural perfection owed to it. Whatever in it falls short of such perfection, or whatever it has that is directed against such perfection, cannot be natural to it, since it would have to be taken to be opposed to the perfection owed to it. Hence, no thing can be by its nature evil in itself.

From this principle, the church fathers have further concluded that evil in the literal sense, or malice (which makes us call something evil), is not a thing, or positive form, nor again is it a mere negation, but is rather a privation of the perfection there should be in a being. For, in the first place, every positive thing is good, as has been said. And in the second place, a thing is not evil in virtue of not having a more excellent perfection, if this is not due to it; if that were so, every created thing would be evil in virtue of not having the perfection of the creator. . . . [18]

Form, Essence, Nature

The metaphysical form, in the strict sense, which is the form of the whole, is nothing else than the entire essence of a substantial thing,

17. Disputation 10, section 1, §15; cf. Fourth Meditation, AT VII 55; CSM II 38.
18. Disputation 11, section 1, §§2, 3; cf. Fourth Meditation, AT VII 55; CSM II 38.

which we call the whole nature of the thing. It is not called a form insofar as it especially exercises the proper causality of a form, but because essentially and through itself it constitutes the nature of the
thing. . . . In the case of man, for example, this form of the whole is said
to be humanity, which, since it consists of the matter and form of man,
indicates the whole essence of man; for whatever a man has in addition
to his humanity is not part of the essence of man. . . . Hence, this form
in immaterial things can be nothing else than their essence. In material
things, however, the metaphysical form differs from the physical and
partial form of the whole, as is clear from the common usage of these
terms, and from the very distinction between a physical and a metaphysical form. The difference consists in the fact that the form of the
whole indicates the entire nature composed of matter and form, while
the physical form indicates only the formal part; hence, the metaphysical form, even in the case of physical things, indicates their total
essence. As we have shown in discussing material substance, matter is of
the essence of such substance; hence, a composite nature of matter and
form is its total essence. . . .

That the metaphysical form should most properly be called the "nature" is shown first by usage. For we attribute to God a divine nature,
to intellectual beings an angelic nature, to human beings a human nature, and so on. . . . Again, each thing by its nature possesses what
makes it such and such a thing, and what essentially distinguishes it
from other things; hence, the nature of a substantial thing, quite adequately, if I may so put it, is itself the whole form whereby it is essentially such and such a thing. Finally, the term "nature," as is commonly
reckoned, indicates the category with respect to something's function-
ing, and differs from an essence only insofar as the term "essence" is
taken from the order of being, while the term "nature" is taken from
the order of operating. Nature is said to be what, as it were, brings
something to birth, and so it is said that nature is not idle, but is the
producer of things, and does nothing in vain, and so on. Hence, the
theologians too say that faculties and operations are multiplied when
natures are multiplied. But the first and adequate chief principle of operations in each thing is its essence, as is manifest in immaterial things.
In material things, the form seems to be the principle of operation,
which is the formal and active principle; yet since the matter is in some
way a cooperative cause in its kind, especially with respect to natural
and intrinsic motions or actions, I therefore said that the essence is
the first adequate and radical principle of each thing. Hence the es-

sence itself and the form of the whole is the same as the nature of each thing.[19]

Essence and Existence

In created things, existence and essence are distinguished either as entity in actuality as opposed to in potentiality, or, if both are taken in actuality, the distinction between them is merely a distinction of reason with some foundation in reality; such a distinction will suffice to enable us to say absolutely that it is not of the essence of a created thing to exist in actuality. In order to understand this distinction, and the locutions that are based on it, we should suppose (which is most certain) that no entity apart from God has its being, as a true entity, from itself. To remove any ambiguity, let me add that being in potentiality is in fact not being, but nothing, and with respect to a thing capable of being created implies merely the lack of contradiction, or logical possibility. We say therefore of a true actual entity, either that it is an entity of essence, or of existence; for there is no entity outside of God, except by God's productive power. Hence, nothing outside God has its being from itself, since the term "from itself" implies not having it from another; that is, it implies such a nature that it has actual being, or rather is an actual entity, in virtue of the efficient power of another.

From this we may gather in what sense it is a most true saying that actual existence pertains to the essence of God, and not to the essence of a created thing. For indeed it belongs to God alone, from the power of his nature, actually to exist, independently of the efficient power of another; a created thing does not have this power. . . .

From this it also comes about that our intellect, which can abstract those items which are not separate in the thing, can conceive of created things in abstraction from their actual existence. For since they do not exist necessarily, there is no contradiction in conceiving their natures in abstraction from any efficient power, and consequently from actual existence. . . . In this way we have of conceiving things, it happens that in a thing thus conceived in abstraction from actual being, something is considered as entirely intrinsic and necessary and, as it were, the first constitutive nature of the thing that is so conceived; and we call this the essence of the thing, since it cannot be conceived without it. The pred-

19. Disputation 15, section 11, §§3, 4; cf. Fifth Meditation, AT VII 64; CSM II 45.

icates that derive from this nature are said to belong to it entirely necessarily and essentially, since without them it can neither be, nor be conceived, although in reality they do not always apply to it, except when the thing exists. Conversely, its actual existence, or its being an actual entity, is something we say is not part of its essence, since such actual existence can be abstracted from the said concept, and could in fact not apply to the created thing so conceived. All these things are quite otherwise in the case of God, for, since he is a being that is necessary from itself, he cannot be conceived through the mode of potential being, but only of actual being; hence, actual existence is truly said to be of his essence, because actual existence belongs to him necessarily, both in reality and in every true objective concept of the deity.[20]

A Priori Proofs of God

As far as the second way of proving the truth in question [i.e., an a priori proof of God's existence], the position is that simply speaking it is impossible to demonstrate the existence of God a priori, since in the first place God does not have a cause of his existence by means of which his existence might be demonstrated a priori, and, in the second place, even if he did have such a cause, God is not known by us so exactly and perfectly as to enable us to reach him, if I may so put it, from his principal properties. This is what Dionysius meant when he said in the *Divina nomina*, chapter 7, that we cannot know God from his own nature.

In spite of this, we are nonetheless able, once something has been demonstrated of God a posteriori, to make use of one attribute of God as the basis for providing an a priori demonstration of another – for example, we might use his immensity to reach conclusions about his immutability in respect of place. I am supposing that a distinction of reason [a conceptual distinction] between attributes is sufficient for reasoning a priori in the human manner.

In this manner then, we may say that once we have demonstrated a posteriori that God is a necessary being, who exists from his own nature, from this attribute it may be demonstrated a priori that apart from him there cannot be any other being that is necessary and exists from its own nature; and consequently the existence of God can be demonstrated. You may object that this implies that God's existence can be demonstrated

20. Disputation 31, section 6, §§13–15; cf. Fifth Meditation, AT VII 66.

from a knowledge of his essence [*quidditas*] (since the essence of God is that he is a being who is necessary and exists from his own nature), yet that such reasoning involves a plain contradiction, since the question of essence already presupposes the question of existence (as Saint Thomas correctly observed in [*Summa theologiae*] part I, question 2, article 2, reply to the second objection).

To this I reply that, formally and strictly speaking, God's existence is not demonstrated through the essence [*quidditas*] of God as such, which the argument correctly establishes; rather, from a certain attribute which really is the essence of God, but is conceived by us in a more abstract fashion, as a mode of a noncaused being, another attribute is established, and hence it is inferred that this being is God. Hence, to enable us in this way to reach the conclusion of the existence of God based on the concept of God, it is supposed that a proof has already been supplied that there is a certain being that is necessary through itself, namely a proof starting from its effects, and based on a denial of an infinite regress. And thus, the first thing that is proved of this being is its existence, next that it has an existence that is intrinsically necessary, then that it has an existence that is unique in such a manner and way of being, and hence that it is God. And in this fashion, the question of existence is in a certain way determined before the question of essence.

However . . . these questions cannot be entirely separated in the case of God, since, first, the existence of God is the essence [*quidditas*] of God, and, second, the properties of this existence, by which it can be shown that the existence in question is proper to God, constitute, as we may put it, the very quiddity and essence of God.[21]

Quantity, Extension, and Material Substance

Before we inquire into the essential definition of continuous quantity, and the distinction between its various kinds, we must suppose it to be a true and real entity, which we cannot explain more aptly than by unfolding the distinction between it . . . and the quantity of mass which we find in bodies and call "quantitative body." . . . The view that quantity is to be really distinguished from substance must be adhered to; for although it cannot adequately be demonstrated by natural reason, the principles of theology convince us it is true, especially in the light of the

21. Disputation 29, section 3, §§1–2; cf. Fifth Meditation, AT VII 66ff.; CSM II 45ff.; First Replies, AT VII 120; CSM II 85.

mystery of the Eucharist. And our natural reason itself, when thus en-
lightened, understands that this truth is more consistent with and in
conformity to the very natures of the things in question. The primary
argument for this view is that in the mystery of the Eucharist God has
separated quantity from the substances of the bread and the wine, conserving the quantity and turning the bread and wine into his body and
blood; now this would not be possible unless quantity were in its real
nature distinct from substance. It is quite impossible to invoke a modal
distinction here, since substance cannot be a mode of quantity, as is self-
evident; so quantity would have to be a mode of substance; and yet a
mode is not separable from the thing of which it is a mode in such a
way that it could exist without it. . . . Hence, quantity is not merely a
mode but a thing distinct from a substance. . . .

There is a natural necessity behind this view of quantity as a thing
distinct from corporeal substance and its qualities. We see in material
substance that many things that are in themselves extended are so conjoined among themselves that they interpenetrate, and exist at the same
time in the same space without any mutual antagonism. Again, we see
one corporeal substance, or one whole part of the same body, resist the
entry of another into the same space, so as to make interpenetration
impossible; hence, it is necessary that this effect and this resistance come
from something that is distinct from substance and its qualities, since
these alone do not have such a contrary tendency. . . .

It may be said that the natural aptitude that a body has to occupy
and fill a place with its extension is simply the very wholeness of material
substance itself, and that for this thing to be called a substance adds no
real thing to it, nor any real mode distinct from the nature of the thing,
but merely something in accordance with our own definition and way
of conceiving it. It is called quantity insofar as it is apt to occupy an
extended place, and that extension of which it is capable, or that aptitude
with respect to local extension, is called quantity; and this distinction of
reason suffices to set up various ways of talking about quantity (as happens in the case of duration, and time, and so on). . . . Yet the objection
to this line of thought is what would follow from it, namely that the
body of Christ in the Eucharist would lack its quantity. . . . [22]

22. Disputation 40, section 2, §§1, 8, 11, 13, 16, 17; cf. Sixth Meditation, AT
VII 78; CSM II 54.

Modal versus Real Distinction

A mode is not strictly a thing or entity, unless we take "entity" in the broadest and most general sense of whatever is not nothing, But if we take an entity to be that thing which, from itself and in itself, is something, such that it does not need in any intrinsic and essential way to be always joined to something else, but is either not capable of being united to another, or at least cannot be united except by some intermediate mode that is distinct from itself by the nature of the thing, then a mode is not strictly a thing or entity. Its imperfection is most clearly shown from the fact that it must always be joined to another thing. . . . A mode includes so intimate a conjunction to the thing of which it is a mode, that it cannot, by any power whatsoever, be without it. . . . Hence, there is much less of a distinction between a mode and a thing than between two things. . . .

If we are talking of inseparability in respect of the infinite power of God, there is great force in the argument that items which are compared in this way and which cannot be conserved in separation from each other, are only modally distinct. The reason for this is that if one of the two terms is such that it cannot, even through the absolute power of God, be conserved without the other, this is a great argument for its being only a mode and not a true entity. For if it were a true entity, it could not have such an intrinsic dependence on another entity that God could not make up for it by his own infinite power; hence, such a state of affairs can only arise from the fact that the term in question is, in its intrinsic essence, not an entity, but merely a mode.[23]

Is the Soul a Complete Substance?

You may say that on my view [that the soul is not a complete substance] not even a separate drop of water will be a complete substance, since, although it is not actually a part of something, it is still apt to be a part, which is enough for the definition of an incomplete substance. For a rational soul, even when separated, is an incomplete substance, since, though it not does actually make up a whole, it is of itself apt to be a part. But I reject the comparison; for a separate drop of water is not in a positive sense, if I may so put it, a part, even in virtue of aptitude, but

23. Disputation 7, section 1, §§18, 19, and section 2, §8; cf. Sixth Meditation, AT VII 78; CSM II 54.

is merely so in a negative sense; for in virtue of its nature it does not require to be joined to another portion of water. It has in itself the entire essence of water, and has its own proper subject and intrinsic term, though there is no contradiction in its being joined to other water; and hence, so long as it is not so joined, it retains the status and denomination of a complete substance. In the case of the soul, the matter is quite otherwise; for even when separate, it is a part in respect of positive aptitude and nature, and not merely in virtue of there being no contradiction in its being joined to something else. It is not a part in the sense of something whole in itself but is essentially a part, and has an incomplete essence, which is by its own nature ordained to make another essence complete; hence, it is always an incomplete substance.[24]

24. Disputation 33, section 1, §11; cf. Sixth Meditation, AT VII 78; CSM II 54; Fourth Replies, AT VII 219; CSM II 155.

FIVE

Pierre Charron, *Wisdom*
[*De la sagesse*, 1601]

Introduction

Pierre Charron (1541–1603) was a lawyer-turned-theologian who was also a brilliant preacher. He served as vicar-general of Bordeaux from 1576 to 1593, and during that period came into contact with Montaigne, whose influence on him is evident. Charron lived during a time of intense religious wars, which he regarded as the playing out of uncontrolled passions. His *De la sagesse* (*Wisdom*) fits in with this preoccupation. It originally appeared in 1601 in Bordeaux. A revised edition was published in Paris in 1604, and the text for the present translation is that of the latter edition (Paris: Librairie Arthème Fayard, 1986).

Wisdom is a long work, in three books. Book I is a sixty-chapter account of the "parts" of human nature, including the body; the soul, the spirit, or mind; and the various passions. (The account of body, mind, and spirit does not look forward in any significant way to Descartes.) Book II is a general account of wisdom and how to achieve it; and book III considers wisdom more specifically in relation to the four virtues of prudence, justice, courage, and temperance. There are important connections between Charron's books I and III and Descartes' writings on ethics and the passions in the *Discours* and the *Passions de l'âme*. There are connections between all three books and Descartes' own remarks about wisdom in the preface to the French edition of the *Principles of Philosophy*. But the early chapters of book II have been chosen here for their connections to Descartes' *Meditations*.

Book II, chapters 1 and 2 have a bearing on Descartes' First Meditation. Charron speaks of the need to make oneself empty and clear, like a white sheet, so that one can receive the stamp of wisdom. This anticipates the end result of the process by which Descartes tries to attack the accumulation of beliefs he has received from his own experience or education. What Charron thinks one should empty oneself of is erroneous popular belief and one's own passions. One does this partly by the use of judgment (chapter 2) – a faculty for staying noncommittal and open-minded about practically everything: everything except divine truths, which one rightly abandons oneself to without second thoughts. Judging properly means being prepared to discover that there are reasons against what one believes, even when one has looked for such reasons and not found them. Again, good judgment involves connecting reasons for one's beliefs to the "natural and universal." Charron and Descartes may have less in common when it comes to suspension of judgment and the resolution to stay open-minded in view of the variety of human belief and practice, but this material provides an interesting example of a thoroughgoing form of skepticism, to be contrasted with Descartes' purely methodological use of doubt.

[TS]

WISDOM

Book II, Chapter 1:
On Avoiding and Freeing Oneself from Popular Errors and Vices and the Passions

First Disposition to Wisdom

For the first lesson and instruction in wisdom, one requires knowledge of oneself and the human condition, because the starting point in everything is a good knowledge of the subject one has to do with, so that one handles it in such a way as to bring it to perfection. This is already established: it is the subject of book I. We can only say here as a sort of summary of what has gone before that the man who aspires to wisdom has, above all, to know himself and every man well: that is the true science of man. It is very useful, an important study, fruitful, and effective. . . . But let's put down as the first rule of wisdom the fruit of this knowledge, so that the end and outcome of book I can be the beginning and point of entry of book II. The lesson of book I is that one should keep and preserve oneself from the contagion of the world, of others and oneself. There are two maladies we suffer from, two obstacles to wisdom, the one external – popular vices and opinions, the general corruption of the world; the other internal – our passions. One sees immediately how difficult it is to protect ourselves against these things. Wisdom is difficult and rare; the greatest and almost the only means we have of achieving it, if we want to have access to it, is that we have to free ourselves, extract ourselves from a miserable double captivity – public and private – that we are subjected to by others and ourselves. Once wisdom is gained the rest will be easy. Let us consider each of these maladies in turn.

To take the external first, we have just now very fully described how people naturally behave – the strange humors of the crowd and common people – and it is quite easy to see what these can give rise to. What can be deliberated about, judged, resolved; what can be said or done correctly, when the people around us are dedicated to vanity, are envious, malicious, unjust, without judgment, discernment, or moderation? For example, (by representing human misery) we have also reported and accounted for several great faults generally committed by the world, in judgment and in will; from this it is clear that everything is done in error and vice. All of this is in accordance with what the wise say: that the worst part is the greatest, that of a thousand not one is good, that the number of follies is infinite, that contagion is very dangerous in a crowd.

In this way, they are advising us not only not to be deceived, but also to keep ourselves free of popular opinions, designs, and affections, as if they are all base, weak, undigested, impertinent, and often enough mistaken or at least extremely imperfect; but also, above all, to avoid the bog – that is to say, the company and conversation of the mob, insofar as one can never join in without ending up damaged and worse off. Associating with people can infect one, and is very dangerous even to the wisest and firmest of all; for who can stand the strain and burden of the vices coming with so great a crowd. A single example of greed or decadence does a lot of harm; the company of a man of delicacy makes those who live with him go soft. A rich neighbor inspires our covetousness; the debauched and corrupted person makes an impression by his way of talking and reproduces his vice. . . . It is solitude, so much praised by the wise, that serves to unburden the soul of all popular vices and errors, rid it of this confusion and captivity, and restore it and make it free.

The other malady and impediment to wisdom that one must guard against, one that is internal and thus the more dangerous, is the confusion and captivity of one's passions and tumultuous affections. One must rid oneself of these, so as to become empty and clear, like a white sheet. Only then can one receive the coloration and stamp of wisdom against which the passions struggle. Which is what the wise say – that it is impossible even for Jupiter to love, to hate, to be touched by some passion, and to be wise all at the same time. Wisdom is the rule of our soul by measure and proportion; it is equability and gentle harmony of judgments, volitions, customs – a lasting health of our mind. The passions in contrast are no more than leaps and flights, sallies and violent or bold motions: feverish comings and goings of madness.

In the preceding book we described the passions well enough to have a horror of them. The general remedies and means of ridding oneself of them and getting the better of them . . . are many and varied, good and bad; and it is without counting on the goodness and felicity of nature, so well fashioned and seasoned, that we make ourselves calm, serene, free and clear of the strong passions and violent motions, that we keep ourselves whole, firm, and assured against the passions. Indeed, this would not be a remedy for the malady but an avoidance of it altogether, a sort of true health. As to remedies, we can distinguish four.

The first, unwholesome and hardly praiseworthy, is a stupor and insensibility that makes us numb to everything, a brute apathy of low souls, entirely flattened out, or else a calm sensibility that seems healthy but in fact is not, because there cannot be wisdom and constancy where there is no awareness, feeling, or activity, and so it is temperament rather than virtue. Rather than being a cure for the illness, it is a sort of deadening of it. Nevertheless, it is less bad than knowing, feeling, and letting oneself become a glutton and be vanquished. . . .

The second "remedy" is no more a cure than the illness itself, though it is employed more often: it is to suppress and smother one passion with another that is stronger, for the passions never balance out one another equally: there is always a dominant one (as in the humors of the body), which rules and consumes the others. And we often attribute most falsely to virtue and wisdom what has nothing to do with it and comes from passion; but it is already a gain for some people if the passions that get the better of them are not the worst.

The third remedy and a good one (even if not the best) is prudent and practicable. It is to flee, to hide, to take cover, and to avoid any circumstances that prick, arouse, or heat up the passions. This is the art by which one takes precautions and makes oneself insensitive to the passions by warding off their advances and keeping oneself from feeling them. Like the king who himself smashed the fine and costly dinner service he was given so as to eliminate early any possibility of anger with anyone else for breaking it. The saying appropriate to these people is "lead us not into temptation."[1] By this remedy those who get heated when they play do not play at all; honorable people who are quick to anger flee contentious altercations, stifle the first stirrings of emotion. When one is already involved it is far from easy to extricate oneself wisely and discreetly: we have matters under control when we take charge of them early: once they have gotten complicated and heated, it is they that take over and carry us away. "The passions are much easier to avoid than to moderate,"[2] because everything is tender and weak at birth. . . .

The fourth and best of all remedies is a lively virtue, resolution, and firmness of soul by means of which one foresees and confronts things without trouble; one struggles and fights against them. It is a strong, noble, and glorious imperturbability, quite different from the first sort we considered, which we said was base and stupid. But to form and acquire this virtue nothing is more useful than the previous discourses. Discourse is the master of the passions; foresight strengthens the soul and renders it hard, keen, and impervious to whatever would subdue it. The right way to quieten and soften the passions is to know them well, examine and judge what powers they have over us and what powers we have over them. But the best remedy by far is not to succumb and not to let oneself be carried away by opinion, which is what stirs up and inflames the passions, and is, as has been said, false, foolish, flighty, and uncertain – the guide of fools and the common people; instead, one should let oneself be guided sweetly by nature and reason, mature, solid, and considered – the guide of the wise. Of this more later.

But of all the passions, one must very carefully guard against and deliver oneself from egoism: the presumption and mad love of self, plague of man, chief enemy of wisdom, true gangrene and corruption of the soul, by which we adore ourselves and remain so content with ourselves that we listen only to ourselves and believe only ourselves. Now, we cannot be in worse hands than in our own. It is a nice saying,

1. "Ne nos inducas in tentationem."
2. "Excinduntur animo facilius, quam temperantur."

originally from the Spanish language: "O God, save me from myself!"
This presumption and mad love of self comes from not knowing the
self, its weakness, its slightness, and this as much in relations with the
infirmity and misery of humanity in general as in relation to one's own
and personal weakness. A man with a grain of this madness will never
become wise. Good faith, modesty, the serious and willing recognition
of one's insignificance are a great testimony to a good and healthy judgment, a good will, and an aptitude for wisdom.

Book II, Chapter 2:
Universal and Full Freedom of Mind in Judgment
as in Will

Second Disposition to Wisdom

The other disposition to wisdom, which follows from the first, and
which delivers us from internal and external captivity and confusion, that
is, from the effects of the passions on the one hand and the influence
of the mob on the other, is a full, complete, generous, and noble double
freedom of mind, namely, freedom of judgment and freedom of will.
Judgment consists in the first place of considering, judging, and examining all things – without being tied or committed to any. It is to stay
free, broad-minded, open, and ready for anything. This is the high point,
the hallmark of the wise and able man, but which not all are capable of
understanding or acknowledging, still less of practicing. And this is why
we must establish it here in the face of those who are incapable of
wisdom. . . . And first of all, to prevent any misunderstanding, we will
explain these words and give them a precise sense. There are three
things that sustain, conserve, and maintain one another, and these are
to judge everything; to avoid being wedded or tied to anything; and to
remain broad-minded and open to everything. By judging we do not
mean resolving, affirming, or determining: this would run counter to the
second of our three precepts – not to tie oneself to anything. Rather,
we mean to examine, to weigh, to balance reasons for and against in
every way, to assess their weight and merit, and thus to search for truth.
Again, not to attach or wed oneself to anything is different from stop-
ping and standing still, gaping, ceasing to act, and proceeding to required actions and deliberations; because in the external and common
actions of life and in what has an ordinary use one should conform to

and accommodate common practice. Our rule has nothing to do with the public sphere and with action, but rather with the interior, with thought, and with internal and secret judgment. In what is internal and secret I advise that one hold on to what seems most likely, honest, useful, convenient, but without any determination, resolution, or affirmation, or any condemnation of adverse or different opinions and judgments, whether new or old. In addition, one should remain ready always to receive a better if it appears, not to find fault if anyone quarrels with or challenges what we think is best – indeed to desire it. This is the means to exercise the first precept, which is to search for truth. These three things, I say, maintain and conserve each other, because whoever judges well and without passion about everything finds likelihood and reason everywhere, which prevent him from making up his mind, lest he be caught out by his judgment about which he remains undecided, indifferent, and universal; on the other hand, whoever reaches a conclusion no longer judges; he stops himself and acquiesces in what he holds, is partisan and particular. Of the three things, the first goes against the foolish, the simple, the weak; the second against the opinionated; and the third against both of the foregoing, who are particular. But all three are practiced by the wise man, modest, discerning, temperate, seeker after truth, and true philosopher. It remains to add to this explanation of our proposition that by "anything" and "everything" (for it says judge about everything but do not be certain of anything) we do not mean the divine truths which have been revealed to us, which we have to receive simply and with all humility and submission, without entering into discussion or dissection. There it is necessary to bow one's head and allow one's mind to be restrained and taken captive: "subjecting the intellect to the obedience of faith."[3] But we do mean everything else without exception.

This simple explanation will perhaps only be enough for a balanced mind, to receive the rule of wisdom, but I see around me a host of people who are vain, decided, and positive, and who want to rule and command other men. Like the previous ones who have sworn themselves to certain principles and committed themselves to certain opinions, they want all the others to do the same and in this they go against this noble freedom of mind. It is necessary to enlarge on each of these points and their parts in order.

3. "Captivantes intellectum ad obsequium fidei."

To Judge All Things

The first is to judge everything, as befits the wise and whoever possesses a mind. As one of the leading sages says, "a spiritual person judges all things and is judged by none."[4] The true role of man, his most proper and natural function, his most apt employment, is to judge. Why is a human being able to discourse, reason, and understand? Why has he the mind to, as they say, build castles in Spain, and to feed himself with foolishness and vanity, as most people do? "Who ever had eyes of darkness?"[5] Surely so that he perceives, understands, and judges everything: that is why he is properly called the magistrate, superintendent, and controller of nature, of people, of the works of God. To wish to deprive him of this right is to wish that he were no longer human but beast; but whoever judges singularly, excellently, is a wise man. Again, if not to judge is to go against the simple and proper nature of man, what of the wise man who is as far above the common run of men as man is above the beasts? It is therefore astonishing that so many men (I do not mean the feeble or the idiotic who haven't the means of exercising it) . . . renounce and deprive themselves knowingly of this right and authority that is so natural, so just, and excellent by examining nothing, judging nothing, receiving or approving of anything that comes along, either because it is good to look at, or because it is in fashion. . . .

When among a thousand lies there is only one truth, a thousand opinions of the same thing only one of which is correct, why should I not examine them with the one tool – reason – which is the best, the truest, the most reasonable, most honest, useful, and convenient? Is it possible that with so many laws, customs, opinions, and manners different from and contrary to ours in the world, only ours are any good, that the rest of the world has made a mistake? Who would dare to say so? And who doubts that others would not say the same things of ourselves? Who of those who condemn others, if they have been born or brought up elsewhere, would not find them better and prefer them to the ones they now suppose to be the only good ones, simply because they are used to them? Well, to anyone so foolhardy as to say it, I reply that the rule of judging everything is at least good for everyone else, in that they will judge and examine everything, and in doing so they will find our ways the best! Above all, then, the wise man will judge everything. Noth-

4. "Spiritualis omnia dijudicat et a nemine judicatur."
5. "Quis unquam oculos tenebrarum habuit?"

ing will escape him. He will put everything on the table and in the balance. To allow oneself to be led like a buffalo is to go over to the side of the profane and the beasts: I am happy to live, to speak, to behave as others do in the manner of the common people, but not to judge like the common people. Indeed, I want to judge the common people. What will the wise and holy person have over the profane one if he makes his mind, his leading and outstanding faculty, the slave of the common run of men? The public, the common people, can content themselves that we will conform to their practices to all appearances. But what have they to do with my interior, with my thoughts and judgments? They can control my hand and my tongue as much as they want, but not my mind. That has another master. No one can take away the freedom of the mind. To wish to do so is the greatest tyranny of all. The wise man will protect himself from it both actively and passively, maintaining his own liberty and not disturbing that of others.

In enjoying this right to examine all things, the wise man will often find that the judgment and the hand, the mind and the body, come into conflict, and that he will behave in one way for the outside world and judge otherwise internally – play one role before the outside world and another in his mind. He will find that he has to do so to be just. The general saying, "everyone is a player on a stage,"[6] is best and truly understood in relation to the wise man, who is not inwardly as his external behavior would suggest. If he were to outward appearance as he was inside, he would not be able to give or to receive; he would come into conflict with too many people; on the other hand, if he were on the inside as on the outside, he would no longer be wise; he would judge badly and would be corrupted in his mind. He must do and behave outwardly for public respect and offend no one, in accordance with the law, custom, and rites that the country observes and requires; and inwardly he must judge things as they are, according to universal reason, which will often lead him to condemn what he does outwardly. . . .

If someone says that I have judged badly in these cases and that, generally, to be given the liberty to judge all things is to run the risk that the mind will wander and get lost, becoming infatuated and stuffing itself with foolish and false opinions, I say to the first point, which touches me particularly, that it is very likely that I have gone wrong in the cases I have considered, and that it is very rash to accuse anyone, for this is to pretend to know where and what the truth is, and who

6. "Universis mundus exercet histrioniam."

does know it? Besides, not to find the truth is not to judge badly; to judge badly is to weigh or balance or size up badly, in short to examine reasons badly, or incorrectly to reduce them to a natural and universal first principle, and still, even if one does these things well, it does not follow that the truth has been discovered. To speak plainly, I am not certain of any of it. If it is not shown, if it can be shown by other contrary and more powerful reasons, then so be it. Reasoned objections and contradictions are the best means of exercising the office of judgment. I only had these opinions while waiting for you to relieve me of them and provide me with better. But to go deeper and consider the danger in this liberty apart from what has already been said and what will be gone into more explicitly in the third lesson of wisdom, the rule one must follow in judging and in all things is natural and universal nature – reason – in following which one can never go wrong. This is the other aspect of that judicious liberty which we are going to treat of at length, and which will deal with the supposed danger.

To Be Indifferent to Everything

The other aspect of this noble liberty of mind is an indifference of taste and a suspension of decision and resolution, by which a man considers all things coolly and without passion. The wise man does not set himself against others, does not judge, tie, or obligate himself to anything, keeping himself ready to receive the truth or the most plausible thing that appears to him, and saying in his internal and secret judgment what the ancients said in their external and public ones, that is, it seems thus [*ita videtur*]; that side seems very apparent; so that if someone takes issue and contradicts him without getting carried away, he is ready to listen to reasons on the other side, and to receive them, finding them stronger and better, and whatever his current opinion is, he thinks there is or might always be a better one, only one that has not yet come to light. This suspension is founded primarily on those propositions that are so well praised among the wise, namely, that nothing is certain, that we know nothing, that there is nothing in nature but thought; nothing certain but uncertainty, *solum certum nihil esse certi, hoc unum scio quod nil scio*: that everything can be disputed, that we do nothing but search, inquire, and feel out different appearances, "We know nothing, but merely have opinions about what is probable,"⁷ . . . that everything has two handles

7. "Scimus nihil, opinamur verisimilia."

and two faces, that there is reason everywhere, that nothing lacks a contrary, it is of lead, it folds, turns, and accommodates itself to anything we like. In short, it is the doctrine and practice of all the greatest sages and most noble philosophers, who expressly professed not to know, to doubt, inquire, and search. . . .

I will say here that I had the phrase *Je ne scay* [I do not know] engraved on the door of the little house I had built for me in Condom in 1600. But one is always expected in the end to submit to certain principles, which is an unjust tyranny. I admit that one uses them in all judgments, but those who say that one cannot help doing so I strongly and firmly oppose. Who in the world has the right to command everyone and lay down the law to everyone, subjugate minds, and give principles that are no longer able to be examined, that cannot be denied or doubted, except God, the sovereign spirit and principle of the world, who alone is to be believed because he says something. Everyone else is subject to examination and opposition, and it is weakness to submit to them. If I am expected to submit to principles I will say, as a vicar would say to his parishioners or one of our princes to his sectaries in matters of religion: first agree among yourselves about these principles, and then I will go along. For there is so much doubt and dispute as to principles and as to conclusions as to theses and as to hypotheses, and there are so many sects, that if I join one I shall offend another. They say also that it is a great misery never to be able to resolve a question, to remain in doubt and perplexed, seeing how difficult it is to stay in that state for long. They are right to say it, as they feel it within themselves, but that is for fools and the feeble. . . . To wise people who are modest and restrained, it is, on the contrary, the surest way, the happiest state of mind, which is always firm, straight, unbending, and which enables people to stay free and self-possessed: "By this we have greater liberty and freedom, for our power of judgment remains intact."[8] It is a very gentle, peaceful, and pleasant state in which one never fears going wrong or miscalculating, and where one is sheltered and out of any danger of participating in the errors produced by human fantasy. In short, it is to be at rest, with peace of mind, far from the confusion and vices which come with the believing in the knowledge we think we have of things – that way goes pride, ambition, immoderate desire, opinionatedness, presumption, love of novelty, rebellion, disobedience. . . .

8. "Hoc liberiores et solutiores sumus, quia integrea nobis judicandi potestas manet."

What is more, nothing is of greater service to piety, religion, and divine action than indifference. So far from interfering with them, it promotes their generation, propagation, and conservation. Theology, even mysticism, teaches that to prepare our soul for God and the entrance of the Holy Spirit, one has to empty it, clean it, pluck it, and render it bare of all opinion, belief attachment – turn it into a white sheet dead to itself and to the world, so as to allow God to live and act there, drive out the old owner so as to establish the new one, "purify the old wine, and cast off the old man."[9] From this it appears that to plant and grow Christianity among a violent and faithless people, such as one finds today in China, it would be a fine technique to begin with suggestions and persuasion. All the knowledge of the mob is nothing but vanity and illusion: it is torn and hounded by fantastic opinions concocted in its own head. God has indeed created man to know the truth, but he cannot discover it by himself, or by any human means. It is necessary for God, in whom it resides, and who has given man a desire for it, to reveal it, as he has done. But to prepare oneself for revelation, one has to have renounced and driven out all the opinions and beliefs that the mind has already taken in and present the mind blank, naked, and ready. Having accomplished this and turned men into academics and Pyrrhonists,[10] it is necessary to take the principles of Christianity as heaven-sent; brought by the perfect ambassador of God, authorized and confirmed in its time by marvelous proofs and authentic testimonies. That is how this innocent and honest suspension and emptiness of resolution is a great aid to real piety: not only to receiving it, as I said just now, but to conserving it, because with it there will never be any heresies or divided, slanted, and extravagant opinions. An academic or a Pyrrhonist will never be a heretic: the two things are opposites. But someone might say that he will also never be Catholic or Christian either, because he will also be neutral and hold himself in suspension with respect to these things as with the others. But this is to misunderstand the saying that there is no suspension and no room for judgment, no liberty even, in what concerns God. It is enough for him to engrave what he wills [on the mind].

Universality of Mind

After these two things, to judge everything and to suspend judgment, there is in the third place that universality of mind by which the wise

9. "Expurgate vetus fermentum exuite veterem hominem."
10. That is, systematic doubters.

man casts his eye round the whole universe. He is a citizen of the world like Socrates. He embraces with affection all of mankind. He is at home wherever he goes, sees like a sun, with a firm and detached uniform gaze, as if from some high vantage point, all the changes, differences, and vicissitudes of things, without being affected himself, keeping himself always to himself. He thus has a godly bearing, and this is the highest privilege of a wise man – to be the image of God on earth. . . . The handsomest and greatest minds are the most universal, as the lowest and flattest are the most particular. It is foolish and weak to suppose that everyone else must think, act, or live as one does in one's village or country, and that the peculiarities of this place affect and are common to the rest of the world. If one tells the fool that there other laws and customs contrary to the ones he sees being kept and used, either he will refuse to believe it, calling it a fable, or else he will promptly condemn and abominate it as barbarous, so partial a soul has he, so much is he a slave to the parochial laws and customs that he recognizes as the only ones that are naturally true and universal. They each call barbarous what is not to their taste and usage, and it seems to them that we have no measure of truth or reason but the example and ideas of the opinions and practices of the country where they find themselves. People like that do not and cannot judge, are slaves of what they hold on to. They are so caught up in acquiring opinions that they can neither undo nor renounce them. Partiality is the enemy of liberty and mastery. . . . Whoever is tied to one place is banished from and deprived of all others. The sheet dyed one color is no longer capable of taking on any other, while the white sheet can take on all of them. . . . We must free ourselves from this brutality and present to ourselves, as a sort of picture, this great image of our mother nature in its complete majesty, noting in it a kingdom, an empire, the whole visible world . . . and read there a general and constant variety in everything, in all things: humors, judgments, beliefs, customs, laws. . . . In this way one learns to know oneself, to wonder at nothing, to firm up and determine oneself, and to avoid being taken aback by anything new or strange. To obtain this universality of mind only four or five points need to be borne in mind:

The great inequality and difference of men in nature, form, composition . . .
The great diversity of laws, customs, manners, religions, opinions . . .
The diverse opinions, reasons, and sayings of philosophers concerning
    unity and plurality, eternity and temporality, the beginning and end,

duration, continuity, the ages, states, vicissitudes of the world and its
parts . . .

There are many worlds, so many, in fact, that there is nothing truly
unique in this world. First, all appearances are multiple in number, so
that it is not probable that any of God's works is without a counterpart,
and that everything is used up in a given individual. At any rate, theology
tells us that God can make many or infinitely many worlds; if he could
not make more than the visible world, his power would be finite, because
this world is finite. We see from the discovery of the New World, and
the West and East Indies, that all the ancients were mistaken, since,
being unaware of the Antipodes, they thought they had mapped all of
the habitable world and had a complete cosmography except for a few
out of the way islands; but we find that there is a world quite like our
own all on terra firma, inhabited, civilized, divided into different realms
and empires. These are adorned with towns which have surpassed in
beauty, greatness and opulence all of those in Africa, Asia, and Europe,
several thousand years ago; and who doubts that some years from now
we will discover others? . . .

Second, the zones that were ignorantly thought to be uninhabited
because they were much too hot or cold are in fact densely populated.

Third, in these new worlds nearly all of the things that we value so
highly here, and which we like to think were revealed to us first of all
and sent from heaven, were commonly observed thousands of years before we had any inkling of them. . . . From all of these discoveries we
readily conclude that this great body which we call the world is not what
we think and judge it to be, neither as a whole nor in its parts; that it
is not always the same, but is in perpetual flux and reflux; that nothing
is said, maintained, or believed at one time and place that is not also
said, maintained, and believed – and also contradicted, reproved of, and
condemned – elsewhere; that human nature is capable of everything;
that the world continues true to type – at times the same, at times
different; that everything is contained in the course and cycle of nature,
subject to birth, change, ending, and variation of time, place, climate,
air, territory. And from these conclusions we learn to be wedded to
nothing; to swear to nothing; to wonder at nothing; to trouble ourselves
about nothing; but that whatever happens, whether we cry, storm, or
order it about, nature will always take its course. . . . That is enough
about the perfect liberty of judgment formed of the three elements of
judging everything, judging nothing, and being universal.

Liberty of Will

The other liberty, which is of the will, is even more to be recommended to the wise man. We will not speak here of free will in the way the theologians do; we will only say that the wise man, in order to keep himself calm and free, has to manage his will and his affection; that is, by not indulging them except on the few occasions when it is necessary to do so (and these are few in number, if we are right), and never with violence or sharpness. In connection with which, it is necessary to take issue with (or, to speak more politely, to explain and better understand) two widely held and plausible opinions. The first teaches one to be quick and willing in the service of others, to forget oneself for others, and principally for the majority, at whatever cost to the individual. The second calls for acting courageously, with feeling, zeal, affection. Whoever fails to behave in accordance with the first opinion is accused of having no charity; whoever fails to act on the second is suspected of being cold, of lacking daring, and of being no true friend. . . .

But these opinions, badly understood and poorly taken like so many others, are invitations to much injustice, confusion, suffering, and pain, as can be seen in those who allow themselves to be exploited by others. Not only do they let themselves be taken advantage of, but they meddle in everything, as much as in what does not concern them as in what does, in big as well as small things, and often for no other reason than to interfere and fuss, "in business there's always something to be busy about,"[11] not being able to hold or stop themselves, as if they had nothing to do with themselves or nothing to look after, and, for lack of their own internal and essential business to mind, they had to find and interfere in other people's. They are careful or thrifty with their money, but free with their soul, life, time, affection, and will, of which things only their care with money is useful and praiseworthy. And when they dedicate themselves to something, it is with such an extreme passion and violence that they no longer belong to themselves but undertake and plunge into everything else. The powerful ask such people to work themselves up and kill for them, and use promises and great pretenses to make them come to that point. They often find fools who believe them; but wise people give them a wide berth.

The person who dedicates himself to causes in this way is unjust, disturbs the state, and drives away the peace and freedom of the mind.

---

11. "In negotiis sunt negotia causa."

He does not know what he owes to himself and how many duties a person requires of himself. In wishing to be officious and at the service of others, he is importunate and unjust to himself. We all have enough business in and with ourselves without losing ourselves outside and giving ourselves to everyone. One must keep to oneself. Whoever wants to give up living honestly safely and happily to serve others is poorly advised and takes a bad and unnatural position. Only a few things should command one's affection and loyalty, and these should be just.

Second, this raw intention and passionate enthusiasm disturbs everyone, and interferes with the business to which one is so fervently given. As with undue haste, overdone solicitude trips itself up. . . . Again, in being carried away with fervor one encumbers, embroils, and gives oneself up to indiscretion and injustice, bringing hardship to others and suspicion to others, feeling impatience when things go against one or are delayed or are not as one would have wished, "excessive haste serves all enterprises badly."[12] This goes not only for serious matters but also for vain or frivolous ones, such as play, where to be carried away by too much of a will to win gets one into trouble. To behave with moderation in all things is always to feel comfortable, to avoid annoyance, to carry on more profitably, securely, and happily. . . .

Third, this violent and harsh enthusiasm infects and corrupts judgment itself, because taking one side and wishing it to prevail drives people into factions, leaving one to praise or to ascribe illusory qualities to the side one supports and to direct false accusations against those one opposes. It is to interpret all events and portents as it suits one to. Must all those who support the other side be that wicked? Must all the vices inhere in them? Must all those who find something good in them or say something good about them be suspected of being on their side? For the passions to get the better of the will is bad enough, but for them to take over the judgment is too much. Judgment is the final and supreme element of our nature that must always maintain its authority. . . .

To handle things properly in this area one has to remember that the main duty we have, and the most legitimate one, is to see to our own conduct. That is why we are here, to keep our peace and freedom. And to do this then it is important above all merely to lend ourselves to others, but to give ourselves only to ourselves; to take things over, but not take them to heart; take charge of them rather than be taken over

12. "Male cuncta ministrat impetus."

by them; to care about things rather than rave about them. Attach yourself to them and take hold of them only loosely, but always take hold
of yourself to yourself. This advice does not diminish in any way our
responsibilities to the public, to one's friends or one's relations. The
wise person has to be helpful and charitable; has to be useful to others
[and the world], and to do this he must contribute by carrying out public
duties and offices. "Know that he who is a friend to himself is a friend
to all."[13] But I ask for a double moderation and discretion: first, not to
concern oneself with everything that comes along but only with what is
appropriate and necessary (and that does not go very far); second, that
it be done without violence and disturbance. . . .

For the rest, it is important to distinguish and separate ourselves from
our public charge. Each of us plays two roles and is two persons: the
one apparent and extraneous; the other real and essential. One has to
tell the skin from the shirt. The able man will discharge his burden well,
and will not let himself be taken in by stupidity, vice, or wrongdoing.
He'll make use of it, as it is in use in his country, and when it is useful
to the public or perhaps to himself. The world lives that way; one should
not waste anything; one has to make use of the world as one finds it,
nevertheless considering it as something foreign to oneself.

13. "Qui sibi amicus est, hunc omnibus scito esse."

SIX

Eustachius a Sancto Paulo, *A Compendium of Philosophy in Four Parts*

[*Summa philosophiae quadripartita*, 1609]

Introduction

First published in Paris in 1609, then 1614, with subsequent print-ings in several European cities, including Geneva (1638) and Cam-bridge (1640), this comprehensive manual was a widely used text-book in the first half of the seventeenth century, and was praised by Descartes as "the best of its type ever produced."[1] At one time Descartes planned to have it reproduced alongside an exposition of his own philosophical system (later issued as the *Principles of Philos-ophy*), in order to show how his own position compared with ortho-dox Scholasticism.[2] Eustachius a Sancto Paulo (Eustache Asseline) belonged to the Feuillants, a Cistercian order, and was professor of philosophy at the Sorbonne. He died in 1640.

The *Summa* is in four parts (the subtitle reads "Concerning Di-alectic, Morals, Physics, and Metaphysics" [*De rebus dialecticis, mor-alibus, physicis, et metaphysicis*]) and each part is subdivided into pro-gressively smaller sections: part, treatise, discourse, question. These divisions are common to all editions, and the appropriate references are supplied in square brackets after each extract included here. The page references in parentheses are to the 1640 Cambridge edition (to be found in the Bodleian Library, Oxford) on which the present translation is based. The titles or headings preceding each extract are generally those supplied by Eustachius himself, though some have been modified for the purposes of this anthology. In order to give an idea of the range and scope of the *Compendium*, an abbre-

1. Letter to Mersenne, 11 November 1640, AT III 232; CSMK 156.
2. Ibid.

viated table of contents for the complete work is supplied first, followed by individual extracts from throughout the work, chosen for their relevance to Cartesian themes.

[JC]

A COMPENDIUM OF PHILOSOPHY

Part One: Dialectic or Logic
Preliminary questions
  1. What is dialectic (art or science)?
  2. Its subject matter
  3. Is dialectic theoretical or practical?
  4. Its necessity for the other sciences
  5. Its divisions
First Part: What concerns the first operation of the mind
  Preface: The operations of the mind and the tools of discourse
  Treatise I: The terms of dialectic
  Treatise II: The five universals
  Treatise III: The categories
  Treatise IV: Definition
Second Part: What concerns the second operation of the mind
  Treatise I: The enunciation or proposition
  Treatise II: Method
Third Part: What concerns the third operation of the mind
  Treatise I: The syllogism in general
  Treatise II: The figures and modes of syllogisms
  Treatise III: The three main types of syllogism

Part Two: Ethics
Preliminary questions
  1. What is moral philosophy? Is it truly a science?
  2. What is the subject of moral knowledge?
  3. What are the chief divisions of moral philosophy?
First Part: Blessedness
  Treatise I: The good and the end
  Treatise II: Felicity
Second Part: The principles of human action
  Treatise I: The internal principles of human action
  Treatise II: The external principles of human action

Third Part: Human actions themselves; the passions, virtues, and vices
  Treatise I: Human actions
  Treatise II: The passions of the soul
  Treatise III: The virtues and vices

Part Three: Physics
Preliminary questions concerning natural philosophy
  1. Is physics truly a science?
  2. What is the object of physics?
  3. The order to be observed in dealing with this part of philosophy
First Part: Natural bodies in general
  Treatise I: Principles
  Treatise II: Causes
  Treatise III: The common properties of natural things
Second Part: Natural inanimate bodies
  Treatise I: The world and the heavens
  Appendix to Treatise I: A brief schema of geography
  Treatise II: The elements
  Treatise III: Mixed bodies
Third Part: Animate bodies
  Treatise I: The soul in general
  Treatise II: The vegetative soul
  Treatise III: The sentient soul
  Treatise IV: The rational soul

Part Four: Metaphysics. Concerning Abstract and Spiritual Things
Preliminary questions
  1. The nature of metaphysics
  2. Its object
  3. The principal functions of metaphysics
  4. The order to be observed in pursuing this part of philosophy
First Part or Treatise: The nature of being
  Division 1: The concept of being
  Division 2: The common nature of being and its relation to lower
    orders
Second Part or Treatise: The principles of being
  Division 1: The principles of complex being
  Division 2: The principles of noncomplex being, essence, and ex-
    istence

Third Part or Treatise: The properties of being
  Division 1: The properties of being in general
  Division 2: The simple properties of being
  Division 3: The complex properties of being
Fourth Part or Treatise: The divisions of being
  Division 1: Substance and accident in general
  Division 2: Created spiritual substance, or intelligences
  Division 3: Uncreated substance, namely God

Part One: Dialectic or Logic

The Operations of the Mind

... It is agreed that the operation of the mind is generally speaking a cognition elicited by the intellect. For the human mind reaches to the perfect knowledge of things in three cognitive steps. First of all, it intuits the things presented to it by a kind of simple vision, without any affirmation or denial. Next, it compares these things and separates them out, and either assents to them by affirming or dissents by denying. Finally, from the many things thus collected together it infers something distinct from them by a process of reasoning or argument. Of these three operations of the mind, the first is called simple apprehension, the second judgment or enunciation, and the third discourse or argument. ... [3]

Confused versus Distinct Understanding

The simple apprehension of the mind is of two kinds, the first confused, the second distinct. The first involves the bare understanding of what a word means; the second involves not merely an understanding of a word but a clear and distinct conception of the nature of what is signified. The first may be said to be the apprehension of a word or a term, the second of a nature and essence. The former is shared by everyone who is familiar with language, including common people and peasants; the latter is found in the wise, who have explored the natures of things. ... [4]

3. First part, preface (p. 12).
4. First part, treatise I (p. 14).

The Categories; Grades of Being

It is certain that there must be as many categories as there are most general kinds of things. There can be some doubt as to how many these are, and the ancient philosophers have different views. But it is agreed by all the Peripatetics, who follow Aristotle, that there are only ten highest kinds, and hence that there are ten predicables or categories. The ten highest kinds are as follows: substance, quantity, quality, relation, action, being acted on, place, time, position, and disposition. In the entire realm of things, there is nothing, whether substantial or accidental, that does not belong to one of these. That the number of these most general kinds is ten is inferred from the various questions that may be put concerning some particular. First, we may ask *what* it is, then *what quantity, what kind,* what it is *related* to, what it *does,* what it *has done to it, where* it is, *when* it is, in what *position* it is, and what *disposition* it has. . . .

It should be noted that these ten supreme kinds, though they are true and real, are not called "entities" in the same way, since they do not have an equal share in being: some are more properly said to be entities than others. For example, a substance is said to be more properly an entity than any accident, since no natural power can enable accidents to exist unless they inhere in or belong to a substance. Or again, among accidents, quantity and quality have more right to be considered entities than the remaining categories, which generally follow from them. For example, relations arise partly from quantity and partly from quality; action and passion arise from active and passive powers, which are qualities, and so on. . . . [5]

[*Genuine versus Spurious Entities*]

In order for anything to be assigned to the set of categories directly and in its own right, certain conditions must be met. The first is that it be a true and real entity. This condition excludes fictitious and impossible entities, such as a *goat-deer* and such like. It also excludes entities of reason that only exist objectively in the intellect, such as *being defined, being divided,* and so on, as well as negations and privations, which are formally nothing, such as *nonbeing, blindness,* and so on. The second condition is that it be an entity in its own right, that is to say, having a

5. First part, treatise III, discourse 1, question 2 (pp. 45–46).

single nature and essence. This condition excludes accidental entities, which are unities only by aggregation, while absolutely speaking they are a plurality – such as *an army, a state*, and *a republic*. Artificial things like a *house* and a *stool* are also excluded, since they are made up of many things assembled by human industry. The third condition is that the thing be finite, that is, of finite perfection and essence. This condition properly speaking excludes God alone, who alone is infinite in perfection and essence; for he contains every perfection not just of substance but also of quantity, quality, and the other entities, in a far nobler manner than is the case in other things, since he cannot be circumscribed by the limits of any category. It is not the same with infinite quantity, if there is such a thing; for though this may be infinite in extension, it is not infinite in perfection and essence; any perfection or essence it can boast relates merely to quantity, and hence there is nothing to prevent this kind of infinity from being placed in one of the categories. The fourth condition is that the thing be an entity that is complete in its own grade and in terms of the status that defines it. This condition excludes, first of all, differences, whether generic or specific; then, parts which go to make up a whole, such as *a head, a chest*, and so on; next, *matter and form*. But genera are not excluded, for even though a genus may be part of a species, and in this respect something incomplete, nevertheless insofar as it is something universal and distinct from the lower species that make it up, it is, in terms of the status that defines it, something complete in its kind, and in nature prior to the species. The fifth condition is that anything universal that is placed in a category should be univocal. This condition excludes homonyms and analogues; the purpose here is to remove all ambiguity and confusion in things. For the categories were set up in order to make it easier to distinguish all things.[6]

Quantity, Form, and Figure

... The formal definition of quantity is one thing, the definition of form or shape [*figura*] another. Hence the same numerical quantity may change its shape, as is clear in the case of wax. Now quantity comes from matter, but shape or external form comes from the inner substantial form. Hence the natural shape of a man differs from that of a lion and so on, though there may be the same quantity [of matter] in each of them. It is clear from this that something's form or shape is to be

6. First part, treatise III, discourse 1, question 3 (p. 48).

formally distinguished from the quantity it has. However the same external composition may equally well be called *external form* or *shape*, though philosophers prefer to use the term *forms* when speaking of those which are natural and physical, while they talk of figures when referring to those which are intelligible or mathematical.

A figure or form may thus be divided into a physical or natural form, or a mathematical, or abstract and intelligible form. There is one natural form belonging to inanimate bodies, and another to animate bodies; and again there is one for plants, another for animals, and another for men. In the case of mathematical forms, some are imperfect or inchoate, others perfect or complete; and in each kind a form may be linear, plane, or solid. There are various kinds of all these, which you may ask the mathematicians about.[7]

Essential Definition

... Some maintain that in the realm of physical and material things, the *genus* is always taken from the matter, and the *differentia* from the form. Others take the more correct view that we are using a kind of analogy when we say the genus corresponds to matter and the differentia to form; it remains true that each part, namely the genus and the differentia, is taken from the entire composite, insofar as in comparison with other things it is found to have some points of agreement and some of difference. For example, we should not think that *animal,* the genus to which man belongs, is taken from body alone, while *rational* [the differentia] comes from the soul alone. Rather, each comes from the entire composite, insofar as man when compared with other animate things agrees with them in respect of being an *animal,* and differs from them through the distinguishing characteristic of being *rational.* It is certain that man is not an animal in virtue of his body alone, since his soul is itself the principle of life and sensation; nor, on the other hand, is man said to be rational, as we understand this term, in virtue of the soul alone, since in our earthly life the process of ratiocination requires the presence of corporeal images [*phantasmata*]. . . . [8]

Truth and Falsity

Truth and falsity are found in different ways in three categories, namely in things, which are their basis, in the intellect as in a subject, and in an

7. First part, treatise III, discourse 2, §3, question 6 (p. 70).
8. First part, treatise IV, question 2 (p. 89).

assertion or verbal proposition, as signifier. The things we know are rules and norms of that truth which is found in our intellect, and the verbal proposition is the interpreter of that truth. From this we may understand that truth, like falsity, is more properly in the intellect than in things or in words; and hence truth is properly defined as conformity of the knowing intellect with that which is known. This conformity is a relation of assimilation or adequacy of the intellect to the thing which is understood; and falsity is a deviation of our intellect from the truth of the thing known. Thus, propositions are said to be true or false not because they do or do not conform to our cognitions, but because they do or do not conform to the thing known. It can happen that a proposition is in conformity with our conception but is absolutely false, as when someone thinks that an angel is corporeal and asserts the proposition "an angel is corporeal"; such a proposition will conform to his knowledge, and yet will be absolutely false, because it does not conform to the thing known – for an angel, in reality, is not corporeal. Similarly it can happen that a proposition does not conform to our knowledge and yet is absolutely true, as when someone says, against his own belief, that an angel is a spirit; even though he supposes that the thing is not really so, the proposition will be true, since this is how it really is. Again, since words are signs not only of the things signified, but also of concepts, verbal propositions, if they are sincere, are indicators of truth or falsity in the intellect, so that when the conception is true, the proposition is true, and when it is false, the proposition is false. . . . [9]

Method

. . . In any science, there are two principal things to be considered, namely the objects of the inquiry and the means that are generally used to explain those objects. And the objects of inquiry may be compared among themselves, or the means among themselves, or finally the means with the objects of inquiry. Hence there is a triple order to be observed in any science. First the many objects of inquiry must be compared among themselves, and what are prior must be expounded earlier, and what are posterior, and incapable of being understood without what has gone before, should be explained later. Second, the means should be compared among themselves; and when there are many means to prove a given result, those which are closer to the thing to be proved should be dealt with in an earlier place, and those which are more remote in a

9. Second part, treatise I, discourse 1, question 4 (pp. 96–97).

later place. Third and finally, the means must be compared with the objects of inquiry, the order to be observed here designed to ensure that the prior means correspond with the prior objects of inquiry, and the posterior means with the objects which are posterior.... [10]

The Legitimate Principles of Demonstration

The *principles of demonstration* means the assumptions or premises from which a necessary conclusion is deduced.... [In the course of the *Posterior Analytics*, Aristotle mentions eight conditions that such principles must meet, namely] that the principles must be true, immediate, better known, prior to and causes of the conclusion, necessary, appropriate, and eternal.... With respect to the third condition, the premises must be *better known*, that is more manifest, than the conclusion – not as far as we are concerned, but in accordance with the nature of the thing itself. For something may be said to be better known than something else in two ways, either by nature, or to us. Aristotle wants these principles to be better known both by nature and to us, and there are only a few principles of this kind, apart from a number of general axioms that are the first principles in every kind of science. The rationale for the condition is that when the conclusion has to be known through the principles themselves, the principles must surely themselves be better known. For as Aristotle says, if something is of a certain kind, that on account of which it is of such a kind must be even more so. The principles are said to be better known than the conclusion not because they are truer in themselves, but because they are more evident; that is, they possess more perspicuous truth; and hence they are more certain, and the intellect assents to them more firmly. This is not because the intellect has more respect for them than it has in the case of other matters of which it is assured (for in all these cases alike there is no fear of error), but rather because it sticks more resolutely and constantly to truths that are better known and more evident.... [11]

Science, Opinion, and Faith

... We may ask how demonstrative science is related to opinion and faith. The three are alike in being capable of truth (they differ here from error, which can never be true), but with this difference – namely, that

10. Second part, treatise II, question 2 (p. 107).
11. Third part, treatise [III], discourse 1, question 3 (pp. 134–135).

science is a state which is always true, while opinion and faith can be false. Then again, science and opinion rely on reason (science on necessary reason, opinion on probable reason), while faith relies on authority alone. Faith is a condition that has two aspects, one directly implanted, and called divine faith, and the other acquired, and called human faith. The former is always certain like science, because it depends on divine authority, which can never deceive or be deceived; but the latter can be doubtful, like opinion, because it depends on human authority, which can both deceive and be deceived (and hence some do not distinguish this doubtful kind of faith from opinion, though they are probably not correct here). Faith depends on two principles, namely that what is believed is said to be true, and that the person who is believed is veracious. When both conditions are met, faith is said to be evident testimony, but when one of the conditions is not met, it is said to be nonevident testimony. But it is of the nature of faith that it is always nonevident in respect of the thing that is the object of the testimony, or which is believed; for if the thing believed or testified to were itself evident, that is, if its truth were manifest in itself, it would not be believed but known. Now the three conditions are distinguished in terms of their objects, insofar as science relates to something that is necessary in virtue of its cause, while opinion relates to something that is probable by reliable signs, and finally faith relates to something testified to by authority. And hence the three are distinguished in virtue of their corresponding acts: by science we know, by opinion we conjecture, and by faith we believe. But it may happen that we have science, opinion, and faith with respect to the same thing, although the means we employ are different. It will be science if the thing is demonstrated by necessary reason, opinion if it is inferred merely by probable reasoning, and faith if it is believed because of the authority of the testifier. Hence these three conditions can all be present in the same intellect with respect to the same thing, although the corresponding acts cannot be exercised simultaneously and at once. . . . [12]

Part Two: Ethics

The Aim of Philosophy

The end of all philosophy is human happiness, for in the eyes of the ancients nothing was a greater spur to philosophizing than the aim of

12. Third part, treatise III, discourse 1, question 4.

becoming more blessed than other men. This happiness was taken to consist partly in the contemplation of the truth, and partly in action in accordance with virtue. Hence in addition to the contemplative sciences there must be some science that provides an account of what is right and honorable, and instructs us in virtue and moral probity. This science is called ethics, that is, moral learning, or the science of morals, and is traditionally reckoned as one of the chief parts of philosophy.... [13]

Is All Appetition Directed Toward the Good?

... If the will could incline to evil under the description evil, then evil qua evil could actually be an object of appetition, which is plainly absurd; for the very description of something as evil removes the favorable aspect, and when this is removed, the possibility of being an object of appetition is also removed – such a possibility arising from some favorable aspect or some connection with the good. So if evil as such is not a possible object of appetition, it is unintelligible that it could be sought as such by the will. If you object that the will is free with respect to good and evil, and hence that it can pursue not only good qua good, but also evil qua evil, I answer as follows. The freedom of the will with respect to good and evil is not a *liberty of contrariety*, as if it could positively incline by its appetition toward plain contraries, namely toward good and evil as such; or as if it could by contrary actions incline to the good and also to the evil (for example seek the good and at the same time repudiate the good as such, or repudiate the evil and at the same time seek it as evil). It is, rather, a *liberty of contradiction*, insofar as it can either will or not will a good, or either reject (or actually repudiate) an evil or not reject (or actually repudiate) it. In other words, the will's freedom with respect to both good and evil consists in the exercise of an act, since in connection with good and evil it has the power to exercise or to suspend a given act.... [14]

Does the Intellect Move the Will, or Is It Moved by It?

The intellect is said to move the will, since there can be no action of the will unless, as a precondition, there is a prior action of the intellect. Now this alone would not be enough to enable us to say the intellect

13. Preface (p. 1).
14. First part, treatise I, discourse 1, question 3 (p. 9).

moves the will. But in addition, and most importantly, the intellect, by its antecedent awareness of an object or a goal, is the cause that makes such and such an act of will ensue. . . . We say, then, that the will is moved by the intellect insofar as the *form* [*species*] of its action is concerned, since the intellect proposes to the will an object from which the acts of will take their form, as from an external formal principle. . . .

However, with respect to its *exercise*, the intellect is moved by the will in its free acts. For we all experience that we can apply our mind to learning something at one time, and can withdraw it again, when we wish. Moreover, the principle of action, and hence of understanding, is an end, since every agent operates for the sake of an end; yet the good in general, wherein lies the rationale for the goal of every human action, is an object of the will. Hence, it belongs to the will to move other faculties of the soul, including the intellect, to their respective acts. . . .

You may object that the will seeks nothing but what is represented by the intellect; yet if the intellect, in order to produce its own actions (and propose something to the will) has itself first of all to be moved by the will, then the acts of the will and the intellect would stretch back in an infinite regress. . . . The answer is that there are acts in the eliciting of which the intellect is not moved by the will, and hence not every act of the intellect is preceded by an act of will. In the regress just mentioned, we must reach some act in respect of which the intellect is moved not freely, but necessarily, simply by the object, with the aid of the imagination alone; hence, there is no need for the concurrence of the will in such cases. . . . [15]

The Nature of Free Choice

. . . What is free choice [*liberum arbitrium*]? The very term signifies some act of reason commanded by the will (for to "choose" [*arbitrari*] is nothing else but to deliberate about something, or to make a probable judgment about it). Nevertheless the term is commonly used by philosophers and theologians to signify a human power or faculty of choice, namely the will itself, insofar as it is free with respect to its acts. . . . How does free choice differ from the intellect and the will? It is really the same as the will, as Saint Thomas establishes (*Summa theologiae*, Ia, question 83, article 4), since willing and choosing belong to the same power. . . . But there is a distinction to be made in terms of its formal

15. Second part, treatise I, discourse 1, question 1 (pp. 20–21).

concept, insofar as the will qua will extends to more objects than free
choice, namely to certain acts that are not free, and hence outside the
scope of free choice. Now the will is really and formally distinct from
the intellect, while free choice is really the same as the will; hence, it is
easy to see that free choice is distinct from the intellect not merely
formally but in reality. To make it clear how free choice nevertheless
depends on the intellect or reason, you must know that free choice can
be viewed in two ways – as indeed can the freedom of the will – first,
as a power or disposition and, second, as an act or exercise. If it is
considered in the first way, it depends in no way on the intellect, but
only on God the Creator, who to his greater glory endowed rational
creatures with this principle of free action. But if it is considered in the
latter way, it clearly depends on the intellect or reason; for the faculty
of freedom cannot actually be exercised unless some judgment of reason
comes first – hence the term free *choice*. It is in this sense that Saint
Thomas says that free choice is a faculty belonging to each of the two
powers, namely reason and will; it is dependent for its exercise on both
powers (Ia IIae, question 1, article 2). The Angelic Doctor also proves
that man has free choice from the fact that he acts from judgments of
reason that are free, or in no way determined to one result (Ia, question
83, article 1); this is because of the indifference of reason with respect
to contingent matters or particular objects of action. Such judgment is
not found in the beasts.[16]

Part Three: Physics

The Object of Physics

. . . The object of physics, properly speaking, is a natural body, insofar
as it is natural. I say a *body* not an *entity* or *substance*, because each thing
should be explained in terms of its nearest genus; hence it is more appropriate to say man is a rational *animal* than that he is a rational *entity*
or a rational *substance*. I say *natural*, not *mobile*, because it is more fitting
to explain something by its differentia than by a property; hence it is
better to say man is a *rational* animal than that he is an animal that gives
rise to laughter. Now natural is the proper differentia of the object of
physical study [*physiologia*], while mobile is simply a property. Hence
something is mobile because it is natural, but not vice versa. I add "in-

16. Second part, treatise I, discourse 1, question 4 (pp. 24–50).

sofar as it is natural" to prevent your supposing that a natural body comes under physics irrespective of the way we consider it. If we consider it as something *capable of being healed*, it belongs to medicine; if we consider it as an *entity*, it belongs to metaphysics. It belongs to physics insofar as it contains the principle of motion and rest. We call this a "natural body" – something that has a dual nature, namely matter and form – for these are called the principles of motion and rest.... [17]

Matter and Quantity

... The first property of matter is that it has quantity. Quantity is a property of matter to such an extent that it belongs to it of itself and first of all; and secondarily, in virtue of it, it belongs to the whole natural composite [of matter plus form]. Moreover form, whether substantial or accidental, cannot be received by matter except through the mediation of quantity. From this we may understand that quantity and matter have the same duration, and that the former was produced or created along with the latter, especially since we see that no agent can produce quantity from the potentiality of matter alone. Hence, just as one and the same piece of matter can undergo various forms in succession, so one and the same quantity may endure in all these forms (and sometimes indeed there are changes in the very nature of the matter, as happens in the most revered sacrament of the Eucharist).... [18]

Efficient Causation

An efficient cause is very well defined by Aristotle in book II, chapter 3, of his *Physics* as "that from which comes the first principle of motion or rest." The sense of this account is that an efficient cause is that *from which* something exists or comes into being. Moreover it is the first or most important principle, not indeed in the sense of something simple or inherent, as a form is, but as something whole and complete which acts to produce the change or cessation of motion that comes about in the subject (which is generally separate from it). From this it is clear that Aristotle means to give a definition of an efficient cause construed as the principal and total physical cause, insofar as it acts transeuntly, not immanently. Such a cause is said to be the principle not merely of

17. Preliminary questions, 2 (p. 112).
18. First part, treatise I, discourse 2, question 4 (p. 122).

motion but also of rest, since just as some things are moved by an efficient cause, so others are brought to rest by the same cause. . . . [19]

The main properties of an efficient cause are as follows. (1) If the efficient cause is there, the effect occurs (this should be understood of an efficient cause insofar as it is an actual cause). (2) The effect is weaker in proportion as it is more remote from the cause that produces or conserves it, and contrariwise it is stronger in proportion as it is nearer. (3) The efficient cause acts more strongly on matter that is nearby than on that which is further away. This last is true if other conditions are equal; for it sometimes happens that a cause can act more strongly on material that is further away (e.g., the Sun generates much more heat on the ground than at high altitudes, which are nearer to it). (4) An efficient cause acts by contact – either by contact of position, as when the cause is touching the actual subject it is working on, or by virtual contact, as when it propagates its force to the subject via some interposed medium. . . . (5) An efficient cause produces something similar to itself; this is to be understood as covering "univocal causation," where the cause is the same kind as its effect. It can be extended to cases of "equivocal causation," where the cause does not produce something similar to itself in form, but produces something virtually similar, since equivocal causes contain in an eminent and virtual manner the forms of their effects. Moreover, the axiom is to be understood as covering causes that are proximate causes and causes in themselves, not causes that are instrumental and accidental, which do not produce effects like themselves.[20]

How the Infinite Can Be Known

. . . Can the human mind encompass in thought a thing that is infinite? Since some concepts of the mind are distinct, and others confused, and some things can be known in a moment, others in time (and time may be finite or infinite), this question cannot easily be solved except by making some distinctions. If we are talking only of confused conception, it is certain that the infinite can be known in this way by a created intellect. But if we are talking of a distinct conception, and one that occurs in a moment, or infinite time, there is a greater problem. We think, however, that the infinite cannot be known in this manner by a

19. First part, treatise II, discourse 2, question 3 (p. 140).
20. First part, treatise II, discourse 2, question 5 (pp. 142–143).

created intellect, at least by means of its natural powers. The reason is clear: the strength of the human intelligence, and even the intellect of an angel, is finite, and hence what falls within its express awareness is necessarily finite. This is confirmed by the fact that the greater the thing that is conceived in the mind, the greater force of intelligence is needed; so if something is infinite, it will require infinite force of intelligence. But we need not deny that it seems very probable that a human mind can be so augmented by supernatural power that it may in this way be able to intuit the infinite clearly, and even embrace or comprehend it (though such an augmented mind is infinite only in one respect). Finally, if we are talking of a distinct conception taking up infinite time, it seems there is nothing absurd in supposing that all the individual parts of something infinite could be conceived in this way. Thus, if the world had existed for an infinite time, and the heavens had undergone their movements all this time, an angel existing for an infinite time could have taken note of all the individual revolutions of the heavenly bodies.[21]

The Animate Body

... The soul is the principle of all the faculties and operations that are found in an animate body as such. Hence, whatever can be said of an animate body can be referred to the study of the soul as the essential principle of an animate body. Now every soul is the form of a living body and, hence, like the other forms, just part of the whole composite [of form and matter], so that it cannot provide us with complete knowledge. Nevertheless, the kind of form that it is makes it very distinct from the others, since it requires a more noble object, and operates in a way that is far nobler than all the others. And hence the consideration of the soul has become a special branch of physics, starting from Aristotle, who before descending to the more specialized study of living things (in the books called the *Progression of Animals*, the *History of Animals*, the *Parts of Animals*, and the *Generation of Animals*, and also in the treatise on plants) provided a general treatise concerning this very principle of life, namely the soul, in his three books of the *De anima*; to this may be added the short book called the *Parva naturalia*. Our task is to consider the soul in general, and also in its three types, namely the vegetative, sentient, and rational. . . .[22]

21. First part, treatise III, discourse 1, question 6 (p. 153).
22. Third part, preface (p. 247).

Is the Soul the Actuality of the Whole Body or Only of a Part of It?

This question relates principally to the sentient soul in animals and especially the rational soul in man (for it is agreed that the vegetative soul in plants is equally diffused through all the parts of the plant's body). We may ask whether it has a special seat in the body, in such a way that it is present in the other parts of the body merely as a power, not as a substance. Thus some suggest it is in the heart (as do most of the church fathers), some in the brain (as do the Platonists), not to mention other subtle views of lesser authors. In fact we must follow Aristotle in holding that no special seat is assigned to the soul by nature, but it is diffused through the entire body, in such a way that it is the actuality not of one determinate part, like the heart, brain, or liver, but of the entire organic body; it truly actuates and informs the body in all its parts. This is proved firstly from Aristotle's very definition of the soul as the actuality of an organic body, not a part of it. Second, in *De anima*, book II, chapter 9, and in *Metaphysics*, book 4, final chapter, separated parts of animals are said to have their names equivocally and not properly and essentially (thus a severed arm is said to be a human arm only in an equivocal sense); and this would not be true unless before they were separated these parts were informed by one and the same soul. Finally, if the soul resided solely in the heart, for example, only the heart would be said to be truly and essentially animate – which would be most absurd.

However, although the soul is substantially united to the whole body as form to matter, this is not true in respect of all its faculties and operations; for some faculties and operations of the soul occur in the brain, others in the heart and so on. . . . The fountain of life, however, is especially in the heart, according to the probable opinion of Aristotle. For the heart is the first thing to live and the last to die, whereas more noble operations of the soul depend mostly on the brain.[23]

Is Every Soul Indivisible?

It is sufficiently established by experience that the souls of some living things, such as plants and imperfect animals, can be cut or divided. Thus we see a branch from a tree grow and produce leaves even when cut off; and each of the two halves of a lizard which is cut in two are capable of animal motion of a sort and are thus alive. The only explanation for this

23. Third part, treatise I, discourse 1, question 2 (pp. 249–250).

is that the soul of these living things is quantitatively divided, and after the division it still resides in the severed parts.

But the rational soul is indivisible or unextended, as is adequately proved not just by reason but also by faith. It is an article of faith (supported by reason) that the soul of man is immortal and spiritual; and it could not be spiritual or independent of matter, and hence could not be immortal, unless it were unextended and indivisible. So it follows that it contradicts both faith and reason to say that the intellectual soul is extended. . . . [24]

The Five General Kinds of Power in the Soul

Aristotle in the *De anima*, book II, chapter 3, lists five general powers of the soul or of living things, namely the powers of growth, sensation, locomotion, appetition, and understanding. The basis for this legitimate distinction comes from the objects with which the operation of living things is concerned. Either that object is the body conjoined to the soul, or it is something separate. The power of growth has to do with the body conjoined to the soul, since it is occupied in the digesting and processing of food. This power of generation is related to this; it is concerned with the combined object, since it produces seed, which arises in the living creature from a superabundance of food. The other powers are concerned with a separate object, either in such a way that they have its image within them (an image that relates to the sensitive power if it is received into the organic body, or else to the intellectual); or in such a way that they tend toward it either as an end or as a terminus of motion. In the former case it is the appetite, whose nature is to incline to the good, and hence to an end; in the latter case it is the locomotive power. These five are the general powers of living things. . . . [25]

In What Subject Do the Faculties of the Soul Reside?

There can be no doubt of the answer in the case of the faculties proper to the rational soul, namely the intellect and the will. Since these are spiritual, and do not need an organic body, they reside in nothing else but a spiritual subject, namely in the rational soul itself. Our question here concerns the faculties assigned to the level of vegetative activity

24. Third part, treatise I, discourse 1, question 10 (p. 258).
25. Third part, treatise I, discourse 2, question 1 (p. 259).

and sensation, and which are called organic because they need organic bodies. Are they in the soul alone, or the body alone, or both? . . .

Our conclusion is that the organic faculties do not inhere in the soul, but in the body alone. The proof is as follows. Since the operations of the vital faculties, of whatever kind, are immanent, it is necessary that the faculty should reside where the operation occurs. Yet the operations do not occur in the soul but in the body itself – for example, growth, nutrition, vision, and so on. Hence it is necessary that the faculties of growth, nutrition, vision, and all the others, both vegetative and sensitive, should belong not in the soul but in the body. Again, when the body or a bodily organ is damaged, the corresponding faculty is destroyed, even though the soul survives, which is a sign that the faculty inheres not in the soul but in the body. The truth of our conclusion is also clear in the case of a human being, whose soul, though it is spiritual, can in no way be the object of the faculties under discussion, since they are all corporeal (as is clear from their operations). Hence, though the soul is as it were the principle from which they come, these faculties are brought forth from the body, as from a subject, by the soul itself; they inhere in the body.

Our second conclusion is that the subject of the aforementioned faculties is not the body simpliciter, but the animated body. For as soon as the body is deserted by the soul, all the body's faculties, both vegetative and sensitive, perish. Just as these faculties are brought forth from the body by the soul, so they are conserved in like manner within the body; hence, as soon as the body is deserted by the soul, it is immediately bereft of all these faculties or powers.[26]

Can the Senses Err with Respect to Their Proper Objects?

Since error strictly speaking belongs to the judgment, which cannot in any way reside in sensation, the senses can be said to err only insofar as they may lead astray the superior faculty to which judgment belongs. But it must be noted that the sensible object proper to each sense may be considered in two ways – either under its common aspect (i.e., a white color simply as a color, a shrill sound simply as a sound, a sweet taste simply as a taste, and so on) or else as specific – a white color as white, and so on in the other cases.

This granted, our first conclusion is that the senses never err with

26. Third part, treatise I, discourse 2, question 4 (pp. 263–264).

respect to the objects that are proper to them in the first sense described. The reason is clear, namely that no faculty can escape the limits of its proper object – vision can perceive only what is visible, hearing what is audible, and so on.

Our second conclusion is that the senses sometimes err with respect to the objects that are proper to them in the second way described. Such error generally arises from a defect in one of the three conditions that are required for an object's being perceived as it really is. These three fundamental conditions are as follows: the object must be at a suitable distance; the disposition of the relevant sense organ must be in order; and finally the state of the medium must be appropriate. Thus, as an example of the first, objects that are really gray may appear black because they are at an unsuitable distance; an instance of the second, involving damage to the organ, is that those suffering for eye inflammation may see everything as blood red; and in the third category, involving the medium, those who look through a colored glass see everything tinged with the same color.

Our third conclusion is that the senses err with regard to a common sensible object considered not just in its special aspect but even in its common aspect. That there is such deception concerning common sensibles in their special aspect is shown by many experiences, as when we see the Sun as if it were a foot in diameter, or when we judge that an arc of an enormous circle is a straight line. But that there is deception with respect to the common aspect is also clear from experience, as when we see the Sun as at rest, when in fact it is carried along with an extremely rapid motion; or when it seems to sailors that those standing on the shore are moving, when they are in fact standing still.[27]

The Common Sense

. . . It belongs to the imagination [*phantasia*], insofar as it is called the "common sense," to perform three functions. The first is to perceive not just all sensible objects but all the actions of the external senses that relate to these objects. For when animals perceive that they perceive something with the senses, that they see and hear, and so on, this cognition does not belong to any of the five external senses, since no material faculty can reflect on its own action; it is necessary that such reflective activity should belong to a higher and more common faculty,

27. Third part, treatise III, discourse 1, question 4 (p. 294).

which receives the images not just of external sensory objects but also of external sensory functions. This faculty is nothing else but the imagination considered as the common sense. Its second function is to pick out and distinguish the objects of the various senses; for none of the external senses can do this, because each is occupied only with the specific characteristics of its own proper object – sight with dark and light, and so with the other senses; hence, they say the common sense is, as it were, the arbiter and judge of the other senses. Its third function is to impart to the external senses the power necessary to perform their functions, via the communication of the animal spirits, which it pours forth from itself as from a fountain and as a primary instrument of sensation. Hence, when (as in sleep) there is an obstruction to that pathway in the brain where this power of the common sense resides – the power whereby these animal spirits are sent forth – the external senses must necessarily be out of action. . . . [28]

The Fantasy or Imagination

The fantasy, insofar as it is distinct in its own way both from the common sense and from the estimative faculty and from memory, can be defined as follows. It is the power of the soul whereby we conceive of the external things that have previously been perceived by the common sense, whether they are now present or absent. Its main functions are these. First, to retain for a time the species that have been conveyed through the common sense. Second, by means of species of this kind, to be aware of things presented in this way, even when they are absent. Third, to compare the species perceived by the senses (which have first been received from the external senses, and then brought to it via the common sense), and to divide them up and separate them. From this manifold process, countless species can be formed and conceived, and those endowed with a powerful fantasy have the aptitude and industry to think up many things at speed. Fourth, it rules the animal itself. For as men are led by reason, so the animate brutes are led by imagination; the natural instinct in the brutes does not differ from the fantasy or imagination, insofar as it includes the estimative faculty as well.

It is probable that a fantasy exists in all animate things, both perfect and imperfect, but with this difference. In imperfect creatures, like bees, worms, zoophytes, and so on, the fantasy is also imperfect, and spread

28. Third part, treatise III, discourse 3, question 3 (p. 319).

throughout the body; it is moreover in no way distinct from the common sense and, hence, perceives only things that are present. In perfect creatures, however, it is perfect, organic, and located in a certain part of the body, namely the brain, and is distinct from the common sense in virtue of several functions that are peculiar to it. It is even more perfect in man than in the brute animals, both because it may be said in some way to share in reason, insofar as it is subject to its authority; and also because it can concern itself not only with things to be pursued or avoided, but also with things that relate to contemplation alone. The fantasy in human beings is more powerful in proportion as the brain is more humid, if there is an abundance of animal spirits and provided the humidity is not excessive. This is why those who are blest with native intelligence because of the plasticity of their brain are subject to memory lapses: they find it easy to learn and hard to remember.[29]

Whether the Rational Soul Is Spiritual and Immortal

Even though a Christian may not doubt that rational souls are spiritual and immortal, since the testimony of Holy Scripture, the decrees of the papal councils, and the authority of the church fathers all bear witness to this, and if the immortality of the soul is denied, the fundamentals of the Christian faith are overturned, nevertheless, in order to give greater illumination to faith, and to refute heretics and pagans, it is possible to prove the point by arguments taken simply from physics. And if it is once conceded that the rational soul is spiritual it will be easy to demonstrate its immortality, since it is agreed that spiritual substances are by their nature immortal. We may show that the rational soul is spiritual as follows. The nature of each thing corresponds to its manner of operation, for operation follows essential nature. But the operations of the rational soul are raised above the nature and condition of the body and of matter. Therefore the rational soul is not material and corporeal, but immortal and spiritual. . . . [30]

How the Soul Understands Itself and Its Powers

It is very probable that the soul in this life does not understand itself through its own essence, or by means of an immaterial species of itself,

29. Third part, treatise III, discourse 3, question 5 (p. 321).
30. Third part, treatise IV, discourse 1, question 2 (p. 328).

but rather by the intervention of those intelligible species which it abstracts from the senses. It does this by a reflexive act, and by an inferential process whereby it is led to awareness of itself via perception of other things. For example the soul first forms an intellectual conception of the nature of man in general, and impresses its species on itself through the active intellect, which abstracts this species from its individuating conditions. Then the soul reflects on its own action, and perceives it; and simultaneously it perceives the image or species, and hence the power, by means of which it accomplishes the act in question. Then, since it knows that the species of a common and abstract thing cannot be anything material and bodily, but must be devoid of all matter, and hence can only reside in a spiritual power and incorporeal substance, as in a subject, it finally perceives itself as a kind of immaterial substance endowed with intelligence and reason.

From this it is easy to understand how the intellect, while it is in the body, does not only recognize itself, but also the proper functions and dispositions that inhere in it – namely by inference and by a reflexive act, and by means of species of the things with which it deals in its operations. The soul, or intellect, knows its dispositions through its own acts, since it experiences that it can operate with that ease and swiftness which are proper to a disposition. And from its own actions and dispositions it arrives at knowledge of itself. As far as the will and its acts are concerned, although they are scarcely known by means of a specific impression or species, they are nonetheless perceived by direct cognition. Moreover, that awareness, whether direct or reflexive, which the soul has of itself and its powers is not merely the kind of awareness by means of which we know of something's existence, but amounts to awareness of the thing's essential nature. . . . [31]

How Our Understanding of Some Items Is Prior to That of Others

. . . (1) The intellect knows other things before it knows itself. For direct knowledge is prior to reflexive knowledge, and the intellect knows things other than itself by direct cognition, while it knows itself only by reflexive cognition. (2) The intellect knows material substances before immaterial and spiritual substances. For since nothing is in the intellect that was not previously in the senses, the sooner something is in the senses, the sooner it is in the intellect. Now material substances are in

31. Third part, treatise IV, discourse 2, question 5 (pp. 334–335).

the senses in their own fashion before spiritual substance, since they have a greater affinity with the sensible accidents that impinge on the senses of their own accord. (3) The intellect has knowledge of composite substances prior to knowledge of their parts or differences. For confused cognition comes before distinct cognition, and composite substances are first of all known by a confused kind of cognition, while their parts are known only by distinct cognition. (4) Accidents are known prior to substances. For accidents are generally accessible to the senses, but substances are hidden and not sensible in themselves; hence, they are not so swiftly or easily known. . . . [32]

How a Separated Soul Differs from an Angel

Although souls, when they have departed from bodies, have much in common with the nature of angels, they nonetheless differ in essence, so as to be inferior to angels in respect of the dignity of their nature. In the first place separated souls are distinct from an angel in being parts of a whole, namely a human being. In the second place, separated souls are not whole subjects that are totally and in every respect complete, as are angels. And finally, a soul, even when separated, is always apt to inform the body and to be substantially united with it; but this is not true of an angel.

At this point there arises a difficulty, which must not be overlooked. How is it possible that an angel and a separated soul differ in dignity of essence while sharing the most noble property of understanding? For it seems that there is no essential difference between an angelic and a human intellect, merely a difference in perfection. And if essential properties are held in common, it seems that their principles will correspond, that is, they will be of the same nature and kind. I answer that although we concede that each of the two intellects is of the same kind, it does not follow that their principles are of the same kind; for the property in question does not come from a shared property but from a grade of being that is common to each, namely from spiritual being, which is common to an angel and a rational soul at least in an analogical sense. Similarly, though the faculty of seeing in a horse may be of the same nature as that in an ox (as may be said of the other proper affections of life and sensation), it does not follow that their principles are of the same kind. We may add that it seems to us very probable that the human

32. Third part, treatise IV, discourse 2, question 6 (p. 335).

intellect differs in kind from that of an angel, for even when separated
it always remains apt to be united with the body, and to conduct its
reasoning by means of images, which is not true of an angelic intellect.
Moreover, it is always natural for a human intellect, even when separated
from the body, to use discursive or inferential reasoning, which is not
true of an angelic intellect. There is a difference in the natural light
which is an inherent part of the nature of each.[33]

Part Four: Metaphysics

The Object of Metaphysics

Philosophers differ on this matter. Some maintain that the object of
metaphysics is God, others that it is separate substances, others that it
is substance in general, others that it is finite (or so-called "predicated")
being. All these definitions are too narrow, as will appear. Others extend
its scope too far, when they say that the object of metaphysics is being
taken in the broadest sense, to include both real entities and entities of
reason; yet a true and real science, especially the foremost and queen of
all the sciences, does not consider such tenuous entities in themselves,
only accidentally. So the standard view is far more plausible, namely that
the complete object of metaphysics in itself (for our question is not about
its partial or incidental object) is real being, complete and in itself, common to God and created things. . . . [34]

The Primary Functions of Metaphysics

. . . The first function of metaphysics is to determine the subjects of the
other sciences. For it is its job to scrutinize general kinds of beings, in
order to distinguish the most important classes of being, whose study
belongs to the other lower sciences. Its second function is to supply to
the lower sciences not merely the terms whose employment is necessary
in every division of philosophy, but also the various essential attributes
that are the object of metaphysical consideration. For the nature of any
given thing cannot be explored unless all its essential attributes have
been scrutinized. Its third function is to establish the principles of the
other sciences, and to provide especial guidance in matters that may

33. Third part, treatise IV, discourse 3, question 1 (pp. 343–344).
34. Preliminary questions, 2 (p. 2).

cause trouble, by the assumption of certain very evident principles that are handed down in metaphysics for subduing obstinate and stubborn people. It may be understood from this that all the other sciences come under metaphysics and are in some way subordinate to it.[35]

The General Distinction between a Formal and an Objective Concept

... The concept of any given thing may be taken in two senses, one formal and the other objective. The latter, strictly speaking, is called a "concept" only in an analogical and nominal sense; for it is not truly a concept, but rather a thing conceived, or an object of conception. A formal concept, however, is the actual likeness of the thing that is understood by the intellect, produced in order to represent the thing. For example, when the intellect perceives human nature, the actual likeness, which it produces in respect of human nature, is the formal concept of the nature in question, as understood by the intellect. We say "actual likeness" to distinguish it from the intelligible species, which is the habitual image of the same thing. It may be understood from this that the formal concept is a word that the mind possesses, or the species that it forms of the thing understood. The objective concept however . . . is the thing as represented to the intellect by means of the formal concept; thus, in the example just given, human nature, as it is actually apprehended, is called the objective concept. . . . [36]

Objective versus Subjective Being

... To understand what is meant by "objective being in the intellect," one must note the distinction between objective and subjective being in the intellect. To "be objectively in the intellect" is nothing else than to be actually present as an object to the knowing intellect, whether what is present as an object of knowledge has true being within or outside the intellect, or not. To be "subjectively in the intellect" is to be in it as in a subject, as dispositions and intellectual acts are understood to be in it. But since those things that are in the intellect subjectively can be known by the intellect, it can happen that the same thing can at the same time be both objectively and subjectively in the intellect. Other things that really exist outside the intellect, though they are not subjec-

35. Preliminary questions, 3 (pp. 3–4).
36. First part, discourse 1, question 2 (p. 6).

tively in the intellect, can be in it objectively, as we have noted. But since all these things are real, they have some real being in themselves apart from the objective being in the intellect. There are certain items that have no other being apart from objective being, or being known by the intellect: these are called "entities of reason." ... [37]

First Principles

The first and foremost principle of any science is said to be that which contains the definition of the subject, and the knowable definition of a subject or object is the basis for demonstrating its properties. But it is difficult to arrive at the true definition of any given thing; hence, there are other principles handed down that are better known and more readily available and, hence, far more productive for demonstrative purposes. In metaphysics these are the primary axioms or principles of being, as follows. (1) *It is impossible for the same thing to be and not to be at the same time.* (2) *Anything either is or is not.* These two principles are sometimes expressed in logical terms as the axiom "Nothing can be simultaneously truly affirmed and denied." (3) *Whatever is must necessarily be, so long as it is.* (4) *Whatever has being is true and good and the like.* These are said to be the most general principles applicable to any object. But there are other less common principles that apply to some part of the object of metaphysics, including principles of created being such as, *The whole is greater than its part*, and *If equals are taken from equals the remainders are equal.* ...

If we accept Aristotle's view in book IV, chapter 7, of his *Metaphysics*, the first and firmest of all principles must be such that the force of any demonstration depends in a certain way on its truth and, furthermore, that it gets its firmness from itself. The principle Aristotle cites in the passage mentioned is of this kind, namely, *It is impossible for something to be and not be at the same time.* That this is indeed the first principle is proved as follows. A first principle as such is a principle that enables not only all conclusions, but also all other principles, to be confirmed a priori. Now the principle just mentioned meets these conditions. ... [38]

Are the Essences of Things Eternal?

There are many serious theologians who think the essences of things are eternal, and not capable of being created or destroyed; for they say

37. First part, discourse 2, question 3 (p. 10).
38. Second part, discourse 1, questions 1 & 2 (pp. 15–16).

they have the kind of being that is coextensive with eternity – which they call "essential being" or "quiddity." And from this it follows that things in time come into being and pass away not in respect of their essence but in respect of their existence. But the opposing view is much more probable, namely, that nothing can be, or have any kind of being, unless it is produced or posited outside of its causes. To understand this, note that created things may be conceived to have being in three ways, objective, virtual, and "subjective" or real. The first is being as an object of cognition in the intellect – and in this manner all things that can be produced have already existed in the divine intellect and all artifacts have existed previously in the mind of the craftsman. The second is being within its own causes, which are said to contain its effects virtually; this is how a rose in winter is said to be in a rose garden, and every thing, whatever it may be, has existed from all eternity in the exemplary and effective power of God. The third is being outside the intellect and its causes – being in accordance with true and proper existence.

We say then that the essences of things, and indeed all things, can be said to be eternal in the first two ways, if they are referred to the supreme power of God, who from eternity knows all things and contains them virtually; thus they have existed in God from eternity both objectively and virtually; but neither of these ways of being relates to existence. We deny, however, that the essences of things are eternal, or have eternal being in the third way mentioned. . . . It should be noted, however, that the essences of things, even before they are produced, are truly called real, not because they really exist, or have some real being, but because they are capable of really existing. . . . [39]

Existence in God and Created Things

. . . Existence belongs to God and to created things, but with a difference. For God exists not through existence being added to his nature, but through his very essence (just as quantity is said to be extended through itself). But this is not true of created things, since their existence is accidental to their essence. Hence existence is essential to God, so that it is a contradiction that he should not exist, but existence is not essential to created things, which can either exist or not exist. Hence the divine nature cannot be conceived except as actually existing; for if it were conceived as not actually existing, there would be something missing in its perfection, which is quite inconsistent with its actual in-

39. Second part, discourse 2, question 3 (pp. 20–22).

finity. But the formal or essential concept of a created thing is distinct from its existence. . . . [40]

How God May Be Known by Us

. . . By means of the natural light we can even in this life have imperfect awareness of God, not merely of his existence but even of his essence. For by the power of natural inference we can infer that God is an infinite being, a substance that is uncreated, purest actuality, an absolutely primary cause, supremely good, most high and incomprehensible. All these things belong to God by his very essence and, indeed, uniquely, since they cannot belong to any other being. Hence, when I grasp in my mind an infinite or uncreated being, or some such, I fashion for myself a concept uniquely applicable to God, in virtue of which I have imperfect awareness of his essence. Hence, we can in this life form concepts of God that are unique and proper to him. . . . [41]

40. Second part, discourse 2, question 4 (p. 21).
41. Fourth part, discourse 3, question 1 (p. 57).

SEVEN

Scipion Dupleix, *Corpus of Philosophy*
[*Corps de philosophie*, 1623]

Introduction

Scipion Dupleix (1569–1661) was a historian and pedagogue. He was engaged in the service of Marguerite de Valois, first wife of Henry IV, and became the tutor to her son. He then became the king's historian, in the service of Cardinal Richelieu. As part of the duties of that office, he wrote numerous histories of France and its kings. From 1603 to 1610 he published various parts of an extremely popular multivolume French-language philosophy textbook (*Logic, Physics, Metaphysics, and Ethics*), which he ultimately issued as *Corps de philosophie*. Descartes probably did not read the work. He recalls his own collegiate textbooks as those of various Jesuits – the Coimbrans, Franciscus Toletus, and Antonius Rubius – and when he consulted such philosophy texts later on in life, he read the one by Eustachius a Sancto Paulo and looked over the one by Charles François d'Abra de Raconis. Still, Dupleix offers a good representation of what was commonly known at the time; in doctrinal contents, Dupleix's textbook looks very much like those of Eustachius and de Raconis. Thus, the following selections should be considered as seventeenth-century Scholastic background to Descartes' philosophy. They consist of a complete book from the *Logic*, about science and demonstration (discussing various topics deriving from Aristotle's *Posterior Analytics*); an almost complete book from the *Physics*, about the principles and causes of natural objects: matter, form, privation, and the four causes (deriving from the first two books of Aristotle's

Roger Ariew gratefully acknowledges the invaluable work of Marjorie Grene, who cotranslated the extracts from Dupleix.

Physics); and a selection from the *Physics* and *Metaphysics* about human knowledge, the understanding, and the senses – concerning the question whether knowledge is innate or comes from the senses.[1]

[RA]

The Sixth Book of the Logic, or The Art of Discoursing and Reasoning (1603)

1. Concerning the Subject of This Book

Our soul, which is wholly divine in its extraction, is like a prisoner in the enclosure of this gross matter and human carcass, so that, through its organs, as through a coarse lattice, it does not apprehend the objects of the external senses, except that, however, it does not lose the memory of its origin, but recognizes itself as the daughter of divine Wisdom, to which there is nothing more contrary than ignorance. Our soul stamps us with a natural desire to know with such an insatiable eagerness it can no more be gratified than the inextinguishable thirst of dropsical persons. *We so naturally desire to know and to learn* (said Cicero) *that we believe a thing bad, unseemly, and indecent when it fails and misleads because of its inadequacy.* But insofar as true science consists in knowing things by their proper cause, something ordinarily hidden and unknown to us, this inquiry into it is difficult. Most of what we claim to know lies in an indifferent and often deceptive opinion and belief, which we take from various accidents, rather than in a certain knowledge of things by means of their proper and proximate cause. From this arise so many controversies, disputes, heresies, and wholly contrary sects introduced by various people on the same subject. That is why Socrates, who was held to be the wisest of his time, was satisfied to say that he knew one thing, that he knew nothing. Not that he was ignorant like the common people (for, on the contrary, he was one of the wisest), but by this he intended

1. For more on the relation between Descartes and late Scholastic thought, especially with respect to the metaphysical foundations of physics, see D. Garber, *Descartes' Metaphysical Physics*, and D. Des Chene, *Physiologia: Natural Philosohy in Late Aristotelian and Cartesian Thought.*

to say that humans can only acquire the perfect knowledge of anything whatsoever only through great pain, and that what we commonly say we know consists rather (as I have just said) in opinion, than in a true science. For science is of necessary things, which cannot be discovered in any other way than how they are known and recognized. And the means of achieving this science, this perfect and infallible knowledge, is demonstration, which demonstrates, discovers, and allows us to touch not only the being of the thing, but also the cause of its being; thus it is called by philosophers *the instrument of notification*. It is the sole subject of this sixth book.

2. *What Are Analysis and Analytic?*

Since the matter of which syllogisms is composed is necessary, or probable, or captious and misleading, there arise also three different kinds of syllogisms, demonstrative, dialectical, and sophistical. It remains for us to discuss these in the following three books, beginning in this one with the most worthy and most excellent, that is, demonstration, or demonstrative syllogism, as the only one that is built out of necessary principles, showing us this perfect knowledge of things by means of their proper cause, which we call *science*. This is the richest portion and, as it were, the masterpiece of the part of logic, which, following Aristotle, we have called analytic at the end of the first book, where we postponed the explanation of that word until here. Therefore, before we enter into a lesson on demonstration, let us fulfill our promise.

Analytic (in the same way as *resolutive* in French) is a Greek word derived from *analysis*, that is to say, *resolution*; it is nothing more than a regress or return of a thing to its principles and (to speak more clearly) a dissolution of the pieces of which a thing is composed – so that it is the contrary of composition. For example, throw a bush into the fire: what will be fire in it will be turned into fire; air will be exhaled; water will be evaporated; but if the wood is green, the air and water will mix and a kind of foam will come out of the pores; the terrestrial will be resolved into ashes. And through this resolution we will judge that this wood was composed of the four elements. In the same way, in the analytic part, we see the whole structure and composition of the syllogism through the resolution of the three pieces of which it is composed – what we call the *subject*, *attribute*, and *intermediate* or *medium*.

Now the Philosopher has subdivided the analytic part into two. In the first he treats of argument and principally syllogism, which is the genus of demonstration, and in the second demonstration itself, for since the genus is more universal it must precede its species.

Let us now return to what we have proposed.

3. Concerning the Two Foreknowledges or Precognitions

Plato, in his dialogue entitled *Meno*, following the opinion of several others of his time, was badly mistaken, thinking that we know or are completely ignorant of everything without allowing for anything in between. For it is certain that only the wise have the true knowledge of things by means of their cause, which is called *science*; nevertheless, the ignorant can have some confused knowledge of it, either through accidents or through some observation. For example, a wise man knows well that the eclipse of the moon occurs through the intervention of Earth between it and the Sun, which causes (as we have said elsewhere) the Moon, which is an opaque and dark body, to be unable to receive the rays of the Sun, and of necessity to be obscured. And an ignorant person will judge this defect or eclipse of the Moon because he will not see it shine in accordance with its custom.

Now, in order to acquire this science, this true, certain, and perfect knowledge, one must previously have two [kinds of] foreknowledge,[2] which the Latins call *precognitions*, of which the first consists in the being of the thing, as the logicians say, *that the thing is*, and the other concerns the essence and is called by them *what the thing is*. I want to speak more clearly. Before we can say that we know something, or that we know it through its cause, we must know that the thing is and that it is not something feigned and, moreover, also what the thing is through its definition. The foreknowledge *that the thing is* is divided into two: in that by which we understand that the thing is simply, such as that man is, that the tree is, and in that by which we understand that the thing is such, such as that man is rational, docile, two-legged, and so on, that the tree is insensible, animated, branched. The foreknowledge *what the thing is* is also dual: the first concerns only the interpretation or etymology of the word, and the other the true essence and definition of the thing – what we will treat in chapter 3 of the next book. Leaving aside here a bunch of useless questions that others discuss, let us pass to the true precept of the art and let us see what science is: that thing

2. Two kinds of precognition or foreknowledge.

whose inquiry by means of demonstration is the argument and the subject of this book.

4. What Is Science?

Science is either universal or singular. The former is called actual, the
latter habitual.[3] Actual is that science which is acquired by a single demonstration. Habitual is that science which is composed of a great number
of actual sciences, tending toward a same subject as well as a habit of
many and frequent actions: such as physics, metaphysics, and mathematics, in each of which there is, as it were, an infinite number of demonstrations, and consequently [of] actual sciences (of which we have spoken about in chapter 10 of book I). Here we do not treat habitual, but
only actual science, which is a certain knowledge of the thing by means
of its cause; in this way, to know that it is day, because the Sun shines
in our hemisphere, is to know; it is an actual and singular science – not
because it is about singular things, but because it is of a single subject,
of a single thing, yet universal, eternal, and necessary. For, since science
is a certain and infallible knowledge, it cannot be of singular things,
which always unfold and flow by means of an uncertain and mutable
vicissitude, both in their being and in their accidents. And to understand
what is meant by necessary, one must review the final chapter of book
II. Now, every universal is eternal, perpetuating and eternalizing itself
in the succession of individual and singular things. For the complete and
perfect understanding of the preceding definition, one must also note
that we have said that science is the knowledge of something by means
of its cause, and not by means of the causes, insofar as there can be
several causes of a single effect, such as efficient, material, formal, and
final, of which we will treat later, in chapter 15 of the next book; but
only one is always the true, proper, and proximate cause of its effect.
For example, one can always give several causes of rain,[4] such as the
efficient, that is, the sun, which attracts several humid and cold vapors
in the middle region of the air; moreover, [one can also give] the material cause, that is, the vapors themselves, in addition to the formal,
which is the proper cause and the one that produces the science of the
following, namely, the overflowing and dissolution of the cloud into
water, which is discharged below and falls to the earth.

3. Definition and division of science.
4. Cause of rain.

5. What Is Demonstration?

After having shown what is science, that which collects itself, concludes, and teaches by means of demonstration, one must also say what is demonstration. The Philosopher says[5] that demonstration is a *scientific* syllogism, that is, [something] making and producing science. Only this kind of syllogism has deserved the name demonstration, because it alone shows not only the being of the thing, but also whence it came and because of what it is – because it shows, I say, the effect by its cause, which is to induce or produce science. It is this difference that distinguishes demonstration from the two other kinds of syllogisms, namely, *probable and captious*, for two reasons.[6] The first [reason] is that demonstration is composed of necessary, eternal, and universal principles, as has been said, and probable syllogism concerns things that are only likely, changing, and often indifferent, and captious [syllogism] results from fraudulent, captious, and ordinarily impossible principles. The second [reason] is that demonstration produces science, which is always certain and infallible, and probable syllogism produces only opinion, which is inconstant and vague; as it appears in that we say we know that which we can in no way call into doubt; and to opine, to have an opinion, to think, to assess, to imagine [is] that which we can doubt. As for the captious syllogism, it produces only falsity, and error, a thing wholly contrary to science. After having roughly understood what is demonstration, let us see analytically and in detail of what pieces it is composed and built.

6. What Must Be the Conditions of the Principles by Which Demonstration Is Composed

In the same way as artisans, when they wish to forge an instrument proper for sawing or cutting hard things, or planing rough wood, or coloring a body, are accustomed to judge the qualities and conditions required of the matter by the former's use – for example, they judge that the matter of a hammer must be hard, because one has to beat the iron and break the stones, and that a paintbrush, on the contrary, must be made of a soft and flexible matter, because one has to paint and stain only the surface of a body – likewise, through the use of demonstration,

5. Aristotle, *Posterior Analytics*, book I, chap. 2.
6. Difference between demonstration and the other kinds of syllogisms.

whose [purpose] is to produce science, one must supply principles[7] (which are the matter of the science) that are *true, proximate and immediate, primary, better known, and causes of the conclusion*, without which conditions and qualities the demonstration will be defective and imperfect. With respect to this, Aristotle has put forth the aforementioned conditions of demonstrative principles in the same terms I have given, following him, terms he has so very subtly laid down; for the first two conditions, namely, that the principles must be *true, proximate or immediate*, relate only to their matter, but the three final ones – which are that these same principles must be *primary, better known, and causes of the conclusion* – relate to the matter as well as to the conclusion. Thus, they are reduced into terms of comparison and relation: to the extent that the first refers to what is posterior to it, better known or less known, and the cause to its effect, so that such principles must be primary, better known, and the cause of what is concluded by the demonstration. Again these conditions must be explained more clearly and particularly.

7. *What Principles Are True, Proximate or Immediate, Primary, Better Known, and Causes of the Conclusion*

By true principles we must understand here that which is truly in nature; for there is no science of what is not. By proximate and immediate, one must understand the things that immediately give being to the effect, of which the effect depends proximately and without any intermediate between the two. I will make this easy by means of a distinction illustrated by one or two examples. There are two kinds of demonstrations, the one called *because the thing is*, insofar as through it we learn that the thing certainly is, even though this is not by means of its proper and proximate cause. The other is called *because of what the thing is*, insofar as by it we not only understand the being of the thing, but also that from which it takes its being. For example, if someone says that trees do not breathe because they have no sensation, he would be truly bringing forth a cause, yet one that is distant and [not] immediate, but if he said that it was because they do not have lungs, that would be to identify the proximate, immediate, and proper cause. Here is another example. If someone said that he knows that man is mortal, insofar as he is an animal, he would truly be bringing forth a cause as such, and one not

7. Conditions of Demonstrative Principles.

too distant; but if he said that it is because he is a mixed body composed of the four elements, he would be demonstrating the true, proper, proximate, and immediate cause, arguing thus:

All mixed bodies are mortal and corruptible.
All men are mixed bodies.
Therefore, all men are mortal and corruptible.

As for the other three conditions, they follow by means of the same interpretation. For whoever would know that the principles of a demonstration are the cause of the conclusion would know in the same way that they are primary and better known, being certain that the cause is always primary and precedes its effect and, in the same way, best known, if not by the external senses, at least by nature and by the intellect, as we must show in what follows; and in the same way we still inquire first whether the things that are best known are universal or singular things.

8. Whether the Things That Are Best Known Are Universals or Singulars, and Cause or Effect

Aristotle's interpreters and commentators have encumbered the proposed question with so many difficulties and covered it with a cloud of so many arguments against one another, that instead of clarifying it, they obscure it further, and instead of allowing us to understand which things are best known, they render them wholly unknown.

Thus, in order to resolve this question briefly and clearly, we must understand that things are said to be better known than one another according to nature or according to us. It is certain that, according to nature, universal and more common things are best known, that is, first in the order of nature, because (as we have said elsewhere) they do not receive any reciprocal conversion with singular things. Thus, all men are animals, but all animals are not men; if it is Alexander, it follows that it is a man, but if it is a man, it does not follow that it is Alexander.

According to us or with respect to us, things are better known either by means of our intellect or by means of our external senses.

The intellect has the universal things and the senses the singular things as object. For when we cannot at first discern the objects of our external senses, our intellect has recourse to a confused knowledge of universal things. For example, if I perceive Alexander from far away without being able to judge what it is [I am perceiving], I would say or imagine to myself first that it is a body, and to the extent that it gets nearer to me, seeing it move, I would judge that it is an animal, and then, getting nearer to it still, that it is a man, and finally, looking at it, that it is Alexander. And this order of knowledge seems to be innate and natural in us. For small children, as they begin to stammer and when they are not yet able to distinguish their fathers from other men, indifferently call all kinds of people *father* by means of a natural and confused knowledge. I speak of their natural or presumptive father, for (as Telemachus says in Homer) it is difficult for anyone to know who is truly his father. Let this be said without blaming women. As for the cause and the effect, there is in this respect almost the same difference as there is between universal and singular things. For ordinarily, the effects are better known to us by means of the external senses, and the causes precede according to the order of nature and by means of the discourse of our understanding. And though they always seem to march together in such a way that it is difficult for the uninformed to discern which of them goes first, still, no doubt, the cause always precedes its effect in the natural order. For example, as soon as the Sun rises in our hemisphere, it is day, and day, which is the presence of the Sun, even seems to come before the Sun to our eyes, but naturally the Sun precedes as its cause. If it happens that we have some brightness a little before sunrise or a little after sunset, it still always comes from the Sun because its splendor comes before the presence of its body. In the same way, when someone brings to us a lighted candle along an incline, or when one removes it, we get some brightness a little before we see the candle itself and after it has been removed. And that is how the principles of demonstration are said to be more known.

9. The Excellence of Demonstration

In the same way that we much appreciate a medicine not only when it is composed of excellent and valuable ingredients, but more principally when it produces good and rare effects for the health of the human body, in that way we can judge the excellence of demonstration not only when it is built upon rare and precious principles, but also in that it cures completely what is the most dangerous and dirty illness of our souls after sin, namely, ignorance. For instead of the other species of syllogisms bringing us only simple opinion and light impression or similitude, leaving us always some doubt and indifference and often even error, demonstration alone producing a certain and infallible knowledge of the thing by its proper cause, that which we call science, renders us entirely content and satisfied by means of a firm belief that we add to it. It is that which leaves a marvelous contentment in the souls of wise men, and distinguishes them from ignorant men and the beasts all together. For ignorant men are in this respect almost like the brutish beasts in that they see well (as the philosopher Iamblichus wisely said) that it is day, that it is cold, that it is hot, that the moon when eclipsed does not illuminate, that in Winter water drawn from deep places is hot, and in Summer fresh, and a thousand other things that are the ordinary objects of our external senses. But they do not know why these things happen thus any more than the beasts, or, at least, most often they do not know the true and proximate causes. Now demonstration being thus the most perfect and excellent species of syllogism or ratiocination because of its matter, one must also try to give it the most perfect form for reasoning.

10. That Affirmative Demonstrations Are More Excellent Than Negative Ones, and in Which Figure One Must Demonstrate

Demonstrations are affirmative or negative. The affirmative are those that teach the thing by means of its proper and true cause; the negative are those that show that a certain cause is not the true and proper cause of some effect. Now, since demonstrations are of universal things, it is easy to see that they must conclude universally and that, consequently, one cannot demonstrate in the third figure because in that figure there isn't a single mode whose conclusion is universal, either by affirmation or by negation.

And although negative demonstration is very useful, because by destroying a false and improper cause it gives us an opening to the knowledge of the one that is true and proper, however, it is not as perfect as affirmative demonstration, which first acquaints us with a certain science and perfect knowledge and, that done, destroys also all the false, improper, or distant causes. In addition, affirmation is more excellent than negation, not only because it expresses the being of something and negation expresses the nonbeing, but also because affirmation can do without negation and negation cannot do without affirmation. For we can conclude affirmatively without there being need for any negative proposition, which, on the contrary, would spoil everything; and we cannot conclude a negation in any figure or mode, whether perfect or imperfect, without the intervention of an affirmative proposition, as anyone can judge by going through all the modes of the three figures.

Thus, therefore, since affirmative propositions are more excellent and more perfect than negative ones, it is certain that the first mode of the first figure, *Barbara*, is the form of the most excellent and perfect demonstrations, because of all the modes it alone concludes a universal affirmative; if I wanted to demonstrate that man is sensible, I would reason thus:

Bar- All animals are sensible.
ba- All men are animals.
ra. Therefore, all men are sensible.

With respect to negative demonstrations, the second perfect mode of the first figure, *Celarent*, is also more proper than *Celantes*, which is imperfect, and more proper than *Cesare* or *Camestres* in the second figure, because, although they conclude universally, they do not do so with such evidence as in the first figure, as I have said in the appropriate place.

Now, to the extent that we have heretofore often mentioned the word *principle*, which is homonymous, we must distinguish its most notable significations.

11. What Is Principle, and in How Many Ways It Can Be Taken

Until now in this book we have often used the word *principle*, taking it for the propositions of which the demonstrative syllogism is composed, with respect to which the five conditions explained previously are required. But we must still discourse more particularly about this. It is in this way, then, that the word *principle* is taken improperly and largely for all certain propositions, but properly only for the proposition that enters into demonstration, and in this sense is called by the Philosopher *immediate proposition:* because it would not be principle (in French, *commencement*) if there were some first cause other than it. Now, some principles are called *axioms*, others *postulates*, which the Greeks call *theses*. Axiom in Greek means *worthiness*, a name attributed to that kind of principle because they are worthy of being believed without any further proof. And they are subdivided into those proper to each discipline and those common to all arts and sciences, as we have said in chapter 6 of book IV.

The theses or postulates are also divided into two, namely, into hypotheses or suppositions, and definitions.

The hypotheses or suppositions (insofar as they are principles of propositions) are referred and granted as being true without absurdity, even though they are not so in effect. They are very frequent and used in mathematics – as when one asks whether a line can be drawn from one point to another, from heaven to earth, from the Arctic to the Antarctic pole – or in logic, indeed in all disciplines, [when one asks] whether of two contradictions one must grant one or the other as true. For in such suppositions, we do not propose or grant anything absurd or irrelevant. As for definitions, we will speak more usefully of them in chapter 3 of the following book; and it will suffice to inquire here briefly whether we can acquire a perfect knowledge and science by means of demonstration.

12. Whether One Can Demonstrate by Means of Definition, and in What Way It Is Different from Demonstration

Given that the Philosopher spent almost his whole second book of the *Posterior Analytics* inquiring into whether the essential definition of the thing can be demonstrated, that is, concluded in demonstration, and whether it is an instrument and means of knowledge, that is, a product of demonstrative science, and whether it differs from demonstration, he has given occasion to his interpreters, who had too much leisure time, to dispute these questions with such almost useless quarrel and contention, that upon reading one would see more noise than fruit – even though all of it has been subtly and elegantly resolved by the same Philosopher in chapter 9 of the aforementioned book. However, because the words there are too obscure for beginners, I prefer giving them an explanation along a different line, keeping the sense, but not the terms. We must therefore note that the definition of substances and that of accidents are completely different. For the definition of substances contains their form, which is nothing other than their proper essence, which is joined to matter by itself and not by any other cause, because it is cause of itself, being by itself. Thus we say that *rational animal* is the definition, and the essence, and the form of man, and its proper cause, and yet, it is the man itself, for he is man because he is rational animal. Hence, to say it in a word, substances are themselves causes of their being, being by themselves and not proceeding from any other cause whatsoever. As for the essences of the accidents, they are not causes of their being, but dependent on various causes, by which the said accidents are applied to some subject. Thus the shadow is not of itself, but [arises] through the intervention of some opaque body that hinders the light. Therefore being certain that science is nothing other than knowledge of the thing by means of its cause – the definitions or essence of accidents, and not the substances, having only a proper cause of their being – it also follows that the definitions or essence of accidents alone, not of substances, can be demonstrated, since they are taken for the intermediate of the principles or propositions of the demonstration. That is what the Philosopher concludes in a word, saying that by the same means we know what is accident and the cause of what it is. Thus we know at the same time what is thunder and its cause, namely, a noise exploding in the clouds. On the other hand, the definition or essence of substances cannot be collected together or concluded by means of demonstration, given that it has no other cause of its being than itself – and neither can substances, but only their accidents and properties, be demonstrated by the same means. Thus I cannot give the cause of man, but [I can give] truly the cause of his redness, his anger, and the like. As for the difference between definition and demonstration, it is dual. The first is that demonstration is accomplished in discourse, for it is a syllogism, and Definition is only simple speech or statement. The second is that demonstration teaches the cause of the thing and definition [teaches] what is the thing.

It seemed to me that this short book was sufficient in order to know what demonstration is and that a longer discourse could have brought more difficulty than utility, since I am certain that anyone who will have the patience to understand all of this small work will have enough of commentaries and will forge enough questions for himself. Therefore we have sufficiently discussed the analytic part.

The Second Book of the Physics, or Natural Science

2. *The Three Principles of Natural Things: Matter, Form, and Privation*

I. What the Principles of Natural Things Must Be

The principles of natural things (says the Philosopher) must be such that *they are not made from external things, nor the one from the other among themselves, and nevertheless all things are made from them.*[8] This definition or rather description and sketch of principles has three components.

II. Why the Principles Cannot Be Made from External Things

The first, *that they cannot be made of anything else,* inasmuch as if they were made of some other thing, they would not truly be principles, and the beginning of all the things that are engendered in the world. For principle in Latin is as much as to say *beginning* in our language.

III. Why They Cannot Be Made of One Another

The second, *that they are also not made out of one another among themselves.* This should be understood as to nature or essence. For the form is indeed produced by and results from the faculty and power of the matter, that is to say, from the natural aptitude that is in matter to receive different forms successively: but yet it does not receive its essence and nature from matter any more than it does from privation – that is to say, from the absence and loss of the preceding form, even though by its means it enters in and joins with matter. For example, when a plant is engendered from a grain of seed, the matter is the grain, which is capable of receiving the form of the plant, and the form of the plant comes from this potency or natural aptitude. Nevertheless, this cannot happen except by the privation of the preceding form of the grain. And all natural things are transformed and engendered in this way, except man alone, whose form is divine, as I shall say later.[9]

IV. That All Things Are Made of These Three Principles

The third main point of the foregoing definition of principles is *that all things must be made and engendered from them.* For all depend on them and could not be produced in nature without them. The first two, which are matter and form, are indeed essential causes of all natural things, as we shall see in what follows.

V. How the Number of These Three Principles Can Be Gathered

Now it is easy to gather even from the generation of natural things that there are only three principles of them. For required here first is the subject that must be transformed and changed, that is, matter, not with

8. Aristotle, *Physics,* book II, chap. 5.
9. In chapter 4 of this book.

the same form as before (for in this way nothing could be engendered), but with the privation of it: which privation, as second principle, brings it about that a new form, which is a third principle, entering into the matter of a thing, results in another thing being made.

VI. Matter and Form Are Essential Causes and Principles, and Privation Only Accidental

However, there is a great difference among these three principles. For the matter and the form that enter into the composition and construction of the thing engendered are essential principles of it; but the privation, which is nothing else but the cessation, the absence, and the displacement of the preceding form in order to introduce another one, is a merely accidental principle, yet also required for generation as well as the other two. For if matter were not deprived of its preceding form, since no other form is able to follow it, the place still being occupied, nothing would be engendered in the world: as if the egg were never deprived of its egg form, that is, if it always remained an egg, a chicken could never hatch out of it. Matter is like an inheritance left by will, which can never be acquired by the heir except by the death of the testator. For similarly it is necessary for the preceding form to be lost, to bring it about that matter be acquired and accommodated to a new form.

VII. In What the Contrariety of Natural Principles Consists

From this, of course, the contrariety of principles can still be noticed. For neither form nor privation are in any way contrary to matter; but only form and privation are contrary to one another, in that form presupposes being, and privation nonbeing. And thus there are only two contrary principles. For if all three were [contrary], and in the same way the matter and the form that remain in the composition of things [were also], how is it that they could be joined and united together: or if they were, how could they subsist, seeing that there would be a continuous fight among them, which would suddenly destroy the subject? This is what must be understood as a whole and in general, concerning the three principles of natural things. But there are still several fine, rare, and difficult remarks on each of them, for which we must pause briefly, and especially about matter, which is by far a longer and more difficult consideration than the others. And inasmuch as this word, *matter*, is equivocal, we must first distinguish its various meanings.

3. Of the Different Meanings of the Word Matter

Of the several distinctions and divisions of matter, I wish to report only the three most notable. The first is that matter can be considered in three ways.

I. Distinction 1. Of Matter in Three Different Senses, in Which, of Which, and in Relation to Which

The first is that it is the subject and seat of form and accidents. Thus the human body is the seat of the rational soul, which is its form, together with several accidents, such as quantities, qualities, and others. In the second place matter can be considered insofar as something is made of it, as a statue is made of stone, wood, or metal. For the third, matter is taken as the subject of the agent: thus wood is the subject of fire, insofar as fire acts on it in burning it. And all these three kinds of matter are called by philosophers in terms quite appropriate and artificial, *matter in which, of which, and in relation to which*:[10] *in which* the form and the accidents are as in their subject, differently, however, as will be said in this same book chapter 6; *of which* something is made; *in relation to which* something acts.

II. Distinction 2. Of Matter into Mediate and Immediate

The second distinction is that matter is remote and mediate or proximate and immediate. Remote and mediate matter is that which cannot be joined to its form except by several removes and alterations. Thus the four elements are the remote matter of all mixed bodies, insofar as mixed bodies are not composed of them taken barely, but only after they have been mixed, crushed, and confused with one another, as we shall say more fully elsewhere.[11] Immediate matter is that which immediately receives a new form. And in this way the seeds of animals and inanimate things are the next and immediate matter of the bodies that are engendered from them.

III. Distinction 3. Of Matter into First and Second

The third distinction is that matter is either prime or secondary. Prime matter is the first principle of natural things, and the first element that

10. "Materia in qua, ex qua, et circa quam."
11. In the ultimate chapter of book 6.

enters into the construction and composition of it, considered, however, without any form or accident whatsoever, in such a way that it is a wholly mental and intellectual thing. For, in fact, matter cannot be found in nature without some form and without accidents. However, in order to consider it better and more simply, it is necessary that through the discourse of reason we separate it from all form and all accidents, thus conceiving it barely and simply. For this reason it is called *prime*, because we must conceive it before form, since it is the subject that receives both the form and the accidents. Secondary matter is in fact the same as we have called prime, but joined to its form, and not considered barely and simply as the other. But when we speak of matter as principle of natural things, we mean simply prime matter; it is therefore of it that we must speak particularly.

4. Of Prime Matter, First Principle of Natural Things

I. Prime Matter Is a Very Abstruse and Difficult Thing to Consider

Prime matter is so abstruse and obscure to consider, that some great philosophers, not being able to conceive it to exist, have said that it was not and could not exist in the nature of things; and the most perspicuous have assured us that it could be known only by an oblique, awkward, and bastard knowledge, as Plato said: or by some analogy, relation, and resemblance, as Aristotle himself confessed. Saint Augustine wrote in this regard *that not knowing prime matter we know it, and recognizing it we do not know it*, because *it is* (as Aegidius well said) *like darkness, which we perceive when seeing nothing, and when we see we do not perceive the darkness*.[12] So it is with prime matter, which has to be considered without any form or accidents, which are like the light, by means of which we see the being of things; and considering it in this way, we do not see it, and would not know how to find such a thing in nature. But still in order that we may give some knowledge of it, we must first establish its being, its qualities and functions, as much by its definition as by comparisons, and then by solid arguments; and afterward we will reply to the arguments of those who try to destroy it and sweep it entirely out of nature.

12. Plato, *Timaeus*; Aristotle, *Physics*, book I, chap. 7; Augustine, *Confessions*, book XII, chap. 5; Aegidius, *Hexameron*, book V, chap. 3.

II. Its Definition

Matter (says the Philosopher) *is the first subject, from which, insofar as it remains, all things arise of themselves, principally and not by means of something else, and it is the last element into which things are resolved and terminated.*[13] This description would seem obscure to novices if I did not explain it word for word. Thus he calls matter *the first subject,* to show that he is speaking of prime matter; *subject,* because it is to it that forms are joined and coupled, and that things are engendered from it as from the first support and the first element. Matter is different from form in this respect, because form is only the second principle and the second element of natural things. By the words, *insofar as it remains,* matter is distinguished from privation, in that privation, although it is a principle, does not remain in the thing transformed, as matter does well with form; and *of themselves, principally and not by means of something else*: to show that it is a true principle, which does not depend in any way on another natural cause. Finally it is said that *it is the last element into which all things are resolved and terminated,* because just as it is the first element that enters into the construction of things, so it must also be that which is the last in the resolution and destruction of them. For (as we have already shown) the form is changed and renewed in each generation, but the matter always remains the same.

III. First Comparison to Express Prime Matter

So much for the definition of matter. Now we have to represent it through some analogies and comparisons derived from artifacts. Thus, just as the artisan cannot make a statue, a chair, or a chest without some matter, in the same way nature could not produce anything without some matter.

IV. Second Comparison

As the potter makes an infinity of different vases from the same clay according to his will, so from the same matter nature produces so and so many different things that we see daily coming to birth and dying in the world.

V. Third Comparison

No more or less than from a single piece of wax we can shape different things, and from the same stuff that has been shaped into a horse one

13. Aristotle, *Physics,* book I, chap. 6.

can fashion a dog and then a bird, a fish, or any other thing whatsoever, in the same way nature transforms differently this matter, which is supple, flexible, and susceptible of various forms, as the wax is of various shapes.

VI. How It Is That the Same Matter Can Be Accommodated to Different Forms

But again it might be doubted whether the first nature can be said to be the same and common subject of all the forms, seeing that it is diversified and changed with the diversity and change of forms: in such a way that the matter of an egg seems to be something quite different from the matter of a chicken, and the matter of the seeds of animals and plants seems to be something quite different from the animals and plants themselves. This doubt is easy to clarify when we learn that quantity is the inseparable companion of matter, and not of form; that this quantity does not change as to its essence, but only as to accidents and dimensions; and this in order to accommodate itself to the forms insofar as they succeed one another in this matter. Thus, according to need, it is extended, increases, and hardens. Or else it is contracted, thinned out, and softened. And thus each form has a portion of this matter, one larger, another smaller, according to what is needed by the order established by God in all natural things. So that if sometimes monsters are produced either by a superabundance and superfluity or by an insufficiency and lack of matter, the error nevertheless does not come from nature, but from some accident, as we shall show later, when we discuss the generation of monsters.[14]

VII. First Argument to Show the Being of Prime Matter, and How It Is That the Form Results from the Potency of That Matter

And it is not sufficient to have represented matter by comparison, which serves rather to teach than to derive a substantial proof. But we still have to look at its being more closely, in imitation of those who, when they have something rare at home, in order to attract people show only its portrait outdoors and in public and then show the thing itself in their dwelling. First then, this matter, being the first subject and principle of natural things, cannot be made or extracted from any other subject, or else we would have to say that this same subject was extracted from

14. At the end of book VIII.

another, and this again from another ad infinitum, which is contrary to nature. Or if the end were found, that would be the same matter of which we are speaking. And thus, since it cannot be made from anything else, it must be the case that it was created by God at the beginning of the world. (For it is to him alone that it belongs to create, that is, to make something out of nothing.) Not, however, that it remains like a chaos or an unformed mass, but surely at the same time that it was created, it was variegated and diversified by as many forms as there are created things. And however much (as we have shown elsewhere)[15] all things were created at the same time and in an instant, yet even if we consider a certain order in the creation of the world, we must necessarily conceive matter before form, as its subject and support, upon which the diversity of forms is produced by a natural vicissitude and sequence. What the physicists say in their terms is *that form is derived from the potency of matter*, that is to say, that form results from the faculty, power, disposition, or natural aptitude in it to receive successively different forms. Thus, the seeds of animals and plants having in themselves the disposition of the form of animals or plants similar to those from which they came, they must engender from them animals and plants of the same species.

It is true that the form of man alone is excepted from this, insofar as it does not result from this material faculty or aptitude, but is created by God at the point at which the matter is disposed in the belly of the mother to receive its form, which is the rational soul: and (as the theologians say), *it is created and infused at the same time*.[16] And even Aristotle understood that this form came from elsewhere than from matter.

VIII. Second Argument

For a second argument, the being of prime matter separated from all form can be proved in this way. Things are said to have being in two ways, either of themselves, or relatively and with respect to some other thing. For example, if a tree is considered in itself, we see plainly that it is truly and in fact a tree. But if we consider that of this same tree we can make a bed or a chest, we can say that it is potentially a bed or a chest. Thus similarly if matter is conceived in itself, it is without doubt actually and in fact, but if it is considered in respect of the different

15. In *Metaphysics*, book III, chap. 3.
16. Marginal note: "Creando infunditur, et infuendo creatur" ("It is infused by being created, and is created by being infused"). This is the Latin version of a sentence from Aristotle, *On the Generation of Animals*, book II, chap. 3.

forms of which it is naturally susceptible, it is not such and such a thing except by faculty, potency, and aptitude.

IX. Third Argument

In the third place, when the fire acting on the water turns it into fire, the matter always remains, in such a way that the very thing, which is changed into fire and no longer water, is what we call prime matter.

X. Fourth Argument

As a fourth argument, we can reason thus: everything made and engendered in nature is made and engendered from something that existed earlier. But this is not some form: for the new form results from matter by privation of the preceding form. Thus it must be the same thing that we call prime matter.

It would not suffice to have established by all these arguments the being of prime matter, if we did not reply to the reasons and arguments that can be alleged to the contrary.

5. Resolution of Arguments That Conclude
That There Can Be No Prime Matter Separate from Forms

There is such a great noise among the Scholastics concerning the establishment of matter, that if I wanted to stop to appease all sides, I would lose too much time, and after all that I would fear to have used my efforts badly. That is why I shall content myself with having reported earlier what considerations there are on this subject and will reply afterward to the principal arguments of those who want to chase out of nature that matter that is the foundation of all natural things, and I will choose only two of their strongest arguments, the ruins of which at once destroy the others.

I. Argument 1: To Destroy the Being of Prime Matter

The first, then, is this: matter cannot be found in nature without some form; but matter joined to its form is no longer simply matter, any more than it is simply form, but a perfect and completed substance and a true composite; hence, there can be no prime matter in nature.

II. Argument 2

The other argument is based on this dilemma: if prime matter is something, it is substance or accident. But it is neither substance nor accident:

substance, because there is no substance (at least material and corporeal) without form; accident, insofar as being accident it could not be principle or part of substance; for substance is the subject and the foundation of accidents, not accident of substances, as I have taught in my *Logic*.[17] Hence, there is no prime matter in any way.

III. Reply to First Argument

That is how the two arguments proceed. The first of them concludes badly, inferring that there is no prime matter from the fact that no matter can be perceived without form. For even though there is no matter without form in the whole of nature, still that does not prevent the essence of matter taken by itself from being different from that of matter joined to a certain form, and it does not prevent me from being able to conceive it in this way without in any way impairing the natural order, just as we ordinarily consider the virtues, the vices, colors, dimensions, and other accidents outside their subjects, even though they are never separated from them, and, similarly, we consider substances without having any regard to their accidents, which cannot be other than in them. That is why the ancient pagans, not recognizing that God had created this matter as well as the forms at the beginning of the world, and nevertheless judging that it would be something separated from forms, imagined a chaos, a confused and unformed mass answering to that prime matter, from which they made all things spring. That is what Ovid wanted us to understand in these verses:

> Before the Heaven was, or Earth, or wave,
> All nature but a single aspect gave,
> Only a face confused and "chaos" called,
> A weighty mass, entangled and emballed,
> Where without order were the enclosed seeds
> Of all the things the Universe now breeds.[18]

And it even seems that Moses, describing the creation of the world, accommodated himself to the natural order, representing that prime matter at the very beginning by the words *darkness, waters, abyss, void*, as the principle of all things that were created.[19]

IV. Reply to Second Argument

To the second argument we must reply with this distinction: that matter is neither accident but substance, not however perfect and complete

17. Book III, chap. 6.
18. Ovid, *Metamorphosis*, book I.
19. *Genesis* I.

substance, as are those in the category of substance, but imperfect, incomplete, and (to put it briefly) a half substance: insofar as it is only an element of the whole substance. It nevertheless deserves the name of substance, because it subsists by itself and is not in any subject.

V. That God Can Make Prime Matter Subsist without Any Form

This reply is founded on the doctrine of the Philosopher;[20] however, it does not satisfy every kind of person, and particularly not Saint Thomas Aquinas and his followers, who maintain that such matter is not at all in nature, and cannot be there in any way – indeed, that it is even so repugnant to nature, that God himself could not make it subsist thus stripped of all form.[21] But this opinion is too bold, badly mistaken, and as such has been refuted by Scotus the Subtle, and by several others who convict Saint Thomas out of his own mouth.[22] For he does indeed grant that God can bring it about that the accident subsists in nature apart from its subject – as indeed all true Christians believe that the accidents of the bread are in the Holy Sacrament of the Eucharist without the bread, and the accidents of the wine without the wine, even though there seems to be more repugnance in this than in making matter subsist without form, insofar as matter has no need of any subject or support, being itself the subject and support of all other natural things, and since an accident cannot naturally subsist without a subject. Let us say then that it is in no way repugnant to nature and still less to the divine power, which is infinite and beyond all nature, and though matter is not found separated from forms, nevertheless it is a distinct thing, separated in essence from form, and even that it precedes form in the consideration of the generation of natural things. Let that be enough about matter; let us go on to the two other principles.

6. Of Form, the Second Principle of Natural Things

I. What Is Form?

Form is an incomplete substance, imperfect, and (as I have already said of matter) a half substance, which, joined to matter, makes an entire substance. But to sketch out a more philosophical distinction, we may say that *form is the second principle, the second element, and the second ingre-*

20. Aristotle, *De anima*, book I, chap. 1.
21. Thomas Aquinas, *Summa theologiae*, book I, part 1, question 66, article 1.
22. John Duns Scotus, *Sentences*, distinction 2, question 2.

dient of natural things, which expresses act and not potency. In that I say it is
the second element of natural things, it is distinguished from privation,
which does not enter into their composition, and in that I also say it
expresses act and not potency, that is to show its difference from matter,
insofar as matter expresses potency, not act.

II. What Must Be Understood by the Words Potency and Act?

But these words *potency* and *act* are artificial and highly significant terms.
For by potency is understood here a gross part and the subject of corruption, and by act a simple thing exempt from corruption as to itself.
For form is corruptible, not in itself, but because of matter, which is
always seeking transformation, that is, renewal and change of form; by
such change it comes to be corrupted and destroyed in matter.

III. The Human Form and the Assistant Forms Are Incorruptible

However, that is not the case for all forms, but only for those that are
elicited from material disposition and potency. That is why the human
form, which is the rational soul, having had its origin in divinity, is
incorruptible and immortal. There are also certain forms that are called
assistant and noninforming, that is to say, forms that rule and govern something without being causes of its being; these forms are equally incorruptible. In this sense the angels and intelligences that rule the movement of the heaven, are called by the Philosopher the forms of the
heavens.[23]

IV. Form, That Is to Say, Beauty

Form in Latin, that is to say, beauty, because it is that which embellishes
matter – of itself wholly gross, unformed, and difform – and even that
which gives being to the thing, and being is beauty itself. That is why
the Philosopher says that *matter calls and desires form as the female desires
the male,*[24] to show the imperfection of matter without the accompani-
ment of form.

V. Form Is in Matter in Another Way Than Accidents

But when we say that form is joined and coupled with matter, that must
not be understood in the manner of accidents in their subject. For form
is united with matter as part of the composite, that is, as one of the two

23. Aristotle, *De caelo,* book II.
24. Aristotle, *Physics,* book I, chap. 9.

elements required for the construction of a natural body, while accidents are not of the essence, nor in any way parts of their subject: although they are sometimes called accidental forms, and never essential.

VI. Why It Is That There Is Not Also a First Form, as There Is a Prime Matter

At this point some noble soul might ask why it is that there is not also a first form common to matter, as there is a prime matter common to all forms. To which question it must be replied that form is not only that which gives being to things, but also which diversifies them and distinguishes them from one another. And it is in this way that nature, which is pleased with diversity and variety, does not permit that there be one and the same form common to all matter, as there is a matter common to all forms. Thus it is that if there were one and the same form as there is one and the same matter, all things would not only be similar, but also uniform and even one. So much for the consideration of the two essential principles that remain in the composite. It remains to discuss privation, which is the third principle, though accidental and transitory.

7. Of Privation, the Third Principle of Natural Things

I. What Privation Is

Privation, as an accidental and transitory principle, is the loss of the form that was formerly in the matter. I call it an accidental and transitory principle in distinction from matter and form, since it is not at all of the essence of the composite thing or part of it, and in no way remains in it, as matter and form do. But ceding and, as it were, leaving its place for the new form, it passes, vanishes, and is lost. However, being the ruin and destruction of a thing, it is the accidental cause of the birth of another. For a thing is never deprived of its form if another does not arise from it at the same time; as also, conversely, a thing cannot originate without another thing's changing its form, that is, without its dying and being corrupted.

II. That Privation Is the Principle of Being, Even Though It Signifies Nonbeing

There are several persons of great learning and good judgment, but ignorant of philosophy, who are so scornful that they distrust all that they cannot understand by themselves; so sick are they with self-love and good opinion of themselves, that they never stop biting and remonstrating with one another about what they have never learned. Such people might here prove carpers and mockers in imitation of M. Montaigne (who was otherwise a man of very noble and subtle spirit), saying that it is folly to establish privation, which means nonbeing, as a principle of what must be. But it is easy to forestall them by teaching them what I have already said, that privation is not an essential principle that gives being or part of being to the thing, but that it is only an accidental principle, which does not remain at all in the thing that is engendered, but which is lost at the same time that the new form succeeds the old one – that it is nevertheless a necessary principle for the generation of things, because nothing can be engendered except by the privation of the preceding form.

III. Privation in Its Quality of Principle Is Something, Since It Is Considered in Matter, Not Barely in Itself

Further, it must be understood that privation, while it is nothing taken barely and simply in itself, is nevertheless something insofar as it is a principle of generation, since in this way it is considered not in itself but in matter. In the same way as when we speak of blindness or deafness outside of any subject, it is nothing, but it is the privation of sight or hearing; but if we consider these in some one, we count them as something. Thus it is with the privation of which we are treating. For insofar as it is simply the loss of a form, it is nothing: but insofar as it comes to matter and is the cause for another form's succeeding in it as a new heir through the decease of the former possessor, it has a good right to be called a principle, not however as permanent, but as transitory, not as essential, but as accidental.

So far we have been discussing the three principles and causes of the generation of natural things. Now we must also speak about other causes that have to do with their changes and properties.

8. *Of the Four Causes, Efficient, Material, Formal, and Final*

I. The Knowledge of Causes Is Very Necessary to All the Sciences and Especially to Physics

After the Philosopher has treated the principles and causes of the generation of natural things, he then treats all kinds of causes, since the understanding of these is emphatically required and necessary for the acquisition of the perfect knowledge of things that is properly called science, which we cannot have except by means of their causes. But again this is more particularly required of the Physicist or Naturalist, insofar as he makes mention of causes at every juncture. However, since I have spoken of this in my *Logic*,[25] and since matter and form, which are the most important, must be well known from what I have said earlier, I shall cut short this discussion of causes.

II. How It Is That the Number of the Four Causes Is Gathered

The ancient philosophers were not in agreement about the causes and their number, as Plutarch notes.[26] But since Aristotle has shown that there can be only four causes, just as there can be only four questions or demands that can be posed concerning the production of their effects, his opinion has always been received and approved. Now, these four questions are: *by whom? of what? how? and for what or why?*, which concern the efficient cause, the material, the formal, and the final. No others can be made; hence there are only four causes. For example, if some one demands, *Who made that statue or that painting?* such a question has to do with the efficient cause, which is the sculptor or the painter. And if some one asks, *What is it made of?* that concerns the material, whether it is wood, marble, metal, or whatever other matter you like. And continuing further, *In what manner is it or how does it come about that it represents a man?* the answer is that it has the form, or rather the shape of a man. For with artificial things we speak more properly of shape than of form. But if someone asked, *How is it that the man is a man?* this is by means of his form, which is the rational soul. And finally, if somebody inquires *why or to what end* something is made, that has to do with the final cause, which is the first in intention and the last in execution. Thus we build a house in order to live in it, but the living follows after all the rest.

III. The End of Generation Is Universal and Particular

I shall say again about the final cause, that the end of the generation of natural things is universal or particular: the universal aspect is the providence of God or nature, which tends to conserve all the species that there are in the universe; the particular has to do with individuals

25. In book VII, chap. 15.
26. Plutarch, *De placi. philos.*, book I, chap. 2.

and singular things. For this reason all animals have in themselves a natural appetite for generation and the conservation of their species; further, each, in the individual and particular case, desires to procreate his like.

IV. That There May Be Several Causes of a Single Effect

After having thus established the number of causes, the Philosopher teaches us that we must notice three things on this subject.

The first is that there can be several causes of the same effect, speaking, however, of different kinds of causes, such as a material, an efficient cause, a formal, a final: for there cannot be several matters or several forms, unless in the case of artificial things.

V. Causes Can Be Reciprocally Causes of One Another

The second is that causes can be reciprocally causes of one another. Thus exercise is the efficient cause of health, and health is the final cause of exercise, that is, the cause for which we exercise.

VI. That the Same Cause Can Cause Contrary Effects

The third point is that a cause can produce contrary effects, but one positively and the other privatively, that is, by its presence and use a certain effect follows, and by its absence and removal another, contrary effect. Thus the Sun by its presence brings us day and light, and by its absence causes for us night and darkness. And in the same way, when it has mounted high in our hemisphere, darting its rays directly and in a straight line on our heads, it brings heat and summer; and withdrawing and moving away from our heads, and darting its rays obliquely, it is the cause of cold and winter.

VII. Proximate and Near Causes or Posterior and Distant Causes

For a clearer understanding of every kind of cause, we must again make some distinctions and divisions. The first is that some causes are preceding and more proximate, and others posterior and more remote. By the preceding and more proximate causes we mean the singular and less universal, and by the posterior and more remote we mean the more universal. Thus Phidias is the preceding and proximate cause of the statue that he has made, and the sculptor is its more remote cause, and the craftsman is a still more distant cause than the sculptor. This is easy to understand through the order that is maintained in questions about the effect. For if some one asks, Who made this statue? the answer is Phidias; and after that, Who is Phidias? he is a sculptor, and after that again, What do you call a sculptor? he is a craftsman.

VIII. Causes in Themselves and by Accident

The second division is that among causes some are in themselves and properly causes, and others are only so by accident. And in this way the sculptor is in himself properly the cause of his work, and Phidias or some other craftsman is the accidental or adventitious cause, since it happens that the sculptor is Phidias.

IX. Simple and Conjoint Causes

The third division is that there are simple and conjoined causes. Simple causes are those that are taken and considered separately, such as causes in themselves, or adventitious and accidental causes, and the two considered together are called conjoint causes. So if I consider that a painter has made a portrait and that this painter is a musician, the cause that is proper and in itself is joined to an accidental cause, since it happens that this painter is a musician.

X. Actual or Merely Potential Causes

The fourth and last division, or rather subdivision, is that all the previously mentioned six causes contained in the three preceding divisions are actually and not merely potentially causes. I call actual causes those that are actually used to produce their effect, and potential causes those that are not used to produce their effect, although they are able to do so. In this sense an architect is actually the cause of a house, while he works at its building, and potential cause while he is not working on it, even though he could.

Any one who wants to see more on this subject should read what I have said in my *Logic*.[27] However, there still remains for us a question about the causes proper to physics, that is, the question as to what kind of causes we should assign fortune, chance case or contingency, and fate, a question that is not without difficulty, insofar as there is not even any agreement about whether there is fortune, chance case or contingency, or fate. However, I hope to give a clear and true understanding of this, refuting the error of paganism, and reporting the Christian doctrine.

27. In book VII, chaps. 15 and 16.

The Eighth Book of the Physics, or Natural Science, Containing Knowledge of the Soul (1604)

23. Concerning the Understanding

I. Various Names of the Intellectual Soul

The intellectual soul is thus named for its most excellent part or faculty, which is the intellect or understanding, and sometimes it is called *rational* from reason, which is nothing other than the discourse of the understanding, and sometimes [it is called] *mind*, insofar as it devotes itself to meditation and contemplation, as Saint Augustine remarks.[28]

II. It Has Three Faculties, Understanding, Will, and Memory

This soul, a product and image of divinity, as I have shown earlier,[29] has three principal faculties, understanding, will, and memory, which we must discuss in the following.

III. Plato's [Doctrine of] Reminiscence Condemned

Plato was in error in that he believed that our souls were filled with sciences before being infused into the mortal prisons of our bodies and that, because of corporeal contagion, they came to forget everything afterward, but that, through instruction and good discipline, they would render themselves capable of reminiscence, that is, of remembering and relearning that which they had forgotten.[30] This opinion is condemned as contrary to our belief, as I will show more amply in the *Metaphysics*.[31]

IV. That the Understanding Is Similar to an Empty Slate

But Aristotle's doctrine on this matter is extremely admissible and probable, received and approved by all men of sound judgment, in that he held that our understanding is similar to a blank slate, that is, a picture that has not as yet been painted upon.[32] For as this picture is open to all colors and paints, similarly, our understanding is open to all intelligible things, that is, [all things] that can fall on the understanding. And

28. Augustine, *De spiritu et anima*.
29. In chap. 2 of this book.
30. Plato, *Phaedo* and *Meno*.
31. In book V, chap. 5.
32. Aristotle, *De anima*, book III, chap. 4.

to the extent that it conceives and understands them, it is more perfected and completed.

V. What Is the Agent Understanding

To understand this better, one must know that the understanding is considered as agent or patient.[33] The agent understanding is that which renders material things intelligible, abstracting them and, as it were, separating the forms from their nature, which because of its crassness cannot fall into the understanding, neither more nor less than the light that uncovers colors renders to us visible the things that were invisible in the darkness. For, to the extent that the agent understanding abstracts the species, ideas, or forms of things material and nonintelligible insofar as they are conjoined to matter, it renders them intelligible to us, that is, it allows us to understand them.

VI. What Is the Passible Understanding

The patient or passible understanding is that which receives these very forms, ideas, or species; and for that reason it is also called understanding in potency because it does not yet understand effectively, but is only capable of receiving intelligible objects, and as such it is properly compared to a blank picture without any paint on it.

VII. How the Understanding Makes the Very Things It Conceives

The Philosopher says that the understanding thus receiving intelligible objects is, in some way, made into the same thing as they. For example, when I have conceived in my understanding the form of heaven, of a man, a plant, [or] a stone, this intelligence, conception, or intellection of mine, as the Scholastics say, entails that the preceding objects are united to my understanding and made into the same thing with it. And thus our understanding, being open to all things, can be made, in some way, into all things.

VIII. That the Understanding Conceives More Properly Spiritual Things Than Corporeal Things

But although the understanding is open to all things, however, some objects are more proper and more familiar than others. For spiritual things, which have no communication with matter, such as God, the

33. Ibid.

angels, and universals, fall directly into the understanding and are in-tellectual without disguise. But corporeal things or things attached to bodies cannot be made intellectual except by being abstracted and sep-arated from matter by the agent understanding.

IX. How the Understanding Conceives the Things Greater Than Itself

And we must not find it strange that the understanding conceives things greater than itself, to the extent that enhances it itself and (so to speak) it extends and inflates itself according to the magnitude of its objects, and there is none it cannot comprehend except God alone, because of his infinity; still it knows him in some way by analogy and by relation from his marvelous works to the marvelous worker, and from the crea-tures to the sovereign Creator.

X. How It Knows Itself

With respect to itself the understanding knows itself, not by means of a direct knowledge (for in this way it can only know the external things outside of it), but by reflection and, as it were, by redoubling itself on itself, as Scaliger says so well.[34] For it knows itself when it understands something else, contemplating itself in its operations, as in a mirror, as I have said before.[35]

XI. What Is the First Operation of the Understanding

Now, all the operations of the understanding – which I have already touched upon in my *Logic*[36] – are three, according to the doctrine of the Philosopher.[37] The first is the one by which we conceive something without disguise and simply, such as a man, a horse, a stone, and so on.

XII. What Is the Second

The second is the one by which we attribute something else to the first, as to man who is capable of science, that he is rational; to the horse, that it is fast, that it neighs; to the stone, that it is hard and solid. And this second operation is called *composing or enunciative faculty*, because it thus composes and conjoins things, attributing the ones to the other by

34. Scaliger, *Exer*. 307, section 2.
35. In chap. 2 of this book.
36. In book II, chap. 7.
37. Aristotle, *De anima*, book II, chap. 7.

enunciation; instead, the preceding faculty is only a bare apprehension and conception of simple things taken separately.

XIII. What Is the Third

The third operation of the understanding is the *ratiocinative or reasoning faculty*. It infers and concludes something from another by some discourse or reasoning. Its precepts are taught by logic, as when, in order to show that man is an animal, I would reason thus: everything having sensation is an animal; man has sensation; therefore man is an animal. And, of course, this third operation of the understanding is like the proof of the preceding [operation]. For, in order to know whether a thing is well connected with another, that is, whether it is well attributed to it – in logical terms, whether it is well enunciated of it – it must be proved through reasoning and discoursing, reason and discourse being the true instruments for discerning true from false.

XIV. What the Understanding Has in Common with the Senses

Nevertheless, the understanding has certain conditions in common with the senses and others that are wholly proper and particular to it. Together they have in common that they conceive the species or images of things abstracted and separated from matter; and moreover they suffer or endure with respect to their objects from a passion that does not lead to corruption, but rather to perfection.

XV. Corrupting Passion and Perfectioning Passion

And in order to understand this better, one must know that there are two kinds of passions.[38] The first [happens] when a certain thing suffers or endures with respect to another because of its contrary qualities, like water with respect to fire or fire with respect to water. Such a passion brings corruption to the passible subject. The other is only a reception of the object, which brings an increase of perfection without any corruption whatsoever.

XVI. That the Passion of the Senses and the Understanding Is Perfectioning, Except for the Extreme and Violent Objects of the Senses

Having noted the foregoing, it is easy to judge that neither the senses nor the understanding suffers or endures from its objects of a passion

38. Aristotle, *De anima*, book II, chap. 5.

that leads either to corruption, but rather to perfection, considering that through the frequent reception of several diverse objects, the senses and the understanding always perfect themselves more. That is why the Greek poet, wishing to represent an accomplished man in the person of Ulysses, said of him:

> That he has known the customs and conditions
> Of men traveling through many countries.[39]

XVII. Why the Extreme Objects Offend the Senses and Not the Understanding

However, what we have just said is certain with respect to the understanding, but it happens sometimes otherwise with the senses, inasmuch as we have previously taught[40] that extreme and violent objects harm the senses, and sometimes even destroy them: a great brightness or an extreme whiteness harms our sight and sometimes blinds us; a noise too piercing harms our hearing and sometimes renders us deaf; an extreme bitterness prevents us from tasting sweets; an extreme heat burns and dries the hand and deprives it of the faculty of touch, as can also happen with an extreme cold. On the other hand, the understanding, through the intelligence of greater, excellent, and sublime things, renders to itself more easily the things of lesser, more vile, and lower importance.

This difference arises from [the fact that] the senses have some commerce with the body because of the corporeal organs through which they receive their objects. The latter organs, instruments, or conduits require a certain temperament from the object; otherwise they would be harmed by it. The understanding, which has nothing in common with matter, but is spiritual and divine, is delighted with spiritual and divine things.

XVIII. Other Differences between the Senses and the Understanding

Therefore, the understanding differs from the senses even in that respect. But here are other differences: the senses perceive only singular things, and the understanding in addition and properly conceives universal things; the senses perceive only corporeal things, or things conjoined to bodies, and the understanding conceives also spiritual things. Moreover, the senses apprehend and receive their objects without dis-

39. Homer, *Odyssey*, book I.
40. Aristotle, *De anima*, book III, chap. 3.

guise and simply, without attributing anything to them and without reasoning with respect to them, and the understanding composes them, enunciates with respect to them, attributes to them various things, and, by reasoning and discoursing, proves its composition, enunciation, or attribution. Thus the understanding has conditions common to the senses, and others that are proper and particular to it. But insofar as there are men who are such enemies of human dignity that they attempt in all ways to disparage it and to render it similar to the condition of the beasts – and in order to construct their atheism and to destroy the immortality of our souls, they dare to sustain doggedly that the beasts have the use of reason – one must refute this error before going further to the other two faculties of the intellectual soul.

The Fifth Book of the Metaphysics, or Supernatural Science (1610)

5. Whether the Soul of Man is Created with Science

I. Adam Was Created with a Singular Science

It is quite certain that our first father Adam was created in so accomplished a state that, among other perfections and embellishments whereby his soul was adorned, he was instilled with a science that was greater than any of his posterity's, one even greater than Solomon's, something on which the theologians remain in agreement and that is confirmed by reason. For since he was the masterpiece of the hand of God, it had to be that he excelled in all perfections above all other creatures of his species. In addition, having been created in the age of perfection, it had to be that he was endowed at least with as much knowledge and science as the strongest and most diligent mind could have acquired until then. And as proof of this, he bestowed upon all the animals their name in accordance with their proper nature. But alas, because of his guilt, he left us the inheritance of his sin and of his misery and resulting weakness, not that of his science and intelligence, and hence we must toil and work with diligent study and labor in order to acquire even a small portion of what God instilled in him.

II. The Error of Plato Who Believed That Science Is Nothing Other Than Remembrance

I believe that Plato, having heard a confused account of this instilled science and perfect knowledge, innate or cocreated with the first man, believed that all souls were created with a similar perfection, which they retained before being plunged into bodies; for he believed that, before this, they animated the stars. But afterward, when, on account of their sins and bad behavior in the previous life, they were confined within the human body, in order to be enclosed there as in a dark prison, this science remained hidden. Just as when, in order to rekindle a covered fire, one needs to give it air and to blow on it, so our soul, being moved by someone's reasons, would wake up and easily discover the rich treasures of its knowledge.

III. Plato's Reason 1

He attempts to confirm this with several reasons, of which I will choose the principal and strongest ones. The first is that, God being the producer (we might more aptly say the creator) of our souls, since he is extremely perfect, he must have created them in all perfection. Now, the most singular perfection of our souls is science. Therefore, God must have created soul with science.

IV. Reason 2

The second is that, since God created from the beginning of the world (as he assumes in his *Timaeus*)[41] a great number of souls, which he infused in the stars in order to animate them, he showed and made manifest to them the nature of the whole universe. From then on, the heavy mass of the human body where they were afterward relegated made them drowsy and dull, so much so that they seem to have forgotten all their science, if it were not for a kind of remembrance or reminiscence by which they would recall it when suitably aroused.

V. Reason 3

The third is that considering that we perceive in this life only accidents and properties [of things] through the senses, and not their proper essence or nature, we cannot know anything of their essence or nature unless we have learned it before this life.

VI. Reason 4

The fourth is based on experience. For he says in his *Meno*[42] that a foolish and unsophisticated man will reply appropriately and in accor-

41. Plato, *Timaeus.*
42. Plato, *Meno.*

dance with the truth to what he will be asked, even though he was never taught about it during this life; thus, it is necessary that he was taught it at some other time, since it is impossible to give an account of that of which one has never had knowledge.

VII. Reply to Plato's Reason 1

Here are the principal reasons upon which Plato has based his error; it will not be very difficult to reply to them. To the first, as I say, it is certain that the first man was created by God with a science and perfect knowledge of all things; however (as I have already said at the beginning of this chapter), this was because he established him in the world at a vigorous and perfect age. For, given that he was alone and not able to have teachers, it would otherwise have been unfitting for the governor of the whole lower world and God's masterpiece, who should have been the most perfect of his species, to have been created with the dirty imperfection of ignorance. God endowed him with a marvelous science. But these causes ceased with his posterity, who were able to learn from him and his descendants from childhood (except that his sin made him unworthy of the infusion of such graces), and the corresponding effects ceased with his posterity.

VIII. Reply to 2

The second reason is based on a fictitious foundation, such that there is no need of any reply other than negation.

IX. Reply to 3

One must also deny the antecedent of the third reason. For in this life we know the essence of things by means of species or notions just as well as by their accidents and properties. But the instrument or manner of acquiring their knowledge is different. For the knowledge of the essence or nature of things is acquired through their definition, and the recognition of their properties and accidents is acquired through demonstration. I have discussed this more amply in my *Logic*.[43]

X. Reply to 4

One must reply to the fourth that since our soul is endowed with reason and understanding, it has a disposition and aptitude not only to learn what it has never known, but also to draw consequences from one thing

43. In book V.

to others about which it has never received any instruction; it does this easily by means of examples and comparison of reasons, and not at all by remembrance or reminiscence. That is what Cicero said so very well when distinguishing man from the beasts.[44] Man (he said), because he is capable of reason, sees the consequences of things and is not ignorant of what is their antecedent; he compares similar things among themselves and adapts the future ones to the present ones.

XI. Aristotle's Contrary Opinion Maintaining That Our Soul Is Similar to a Blank Picture

Having thus demolished these arguments of Plato, we must establish those of his disciple, Aristotle, who wrote that our soul is similar to a blank picture on which nothing has been painted yet, in order to show that it is capable of learning and of science, even though this is not at all innate or cocreated in it.[45] This can easily be confirmed by reason.

XII. Aristotle's Reason 1

First, what is natural and innate to us cannot be lost by any external impediment. Yet if science were innate in us, it could not be forgotten through the union of soul with body. In addition, true science consists in the understanding, the natural perfections of which the contagion of the body cannot harm.

XIII. Reason 2

Second, if science were nothing other than the remembrance of the knowledge that the soul had in previous lives (as says Plato),[46] we would not be so [un]certain about many things, but remembering and recalling to memory what we had truly known at an other time, without swimming in uncertainty, we would soon arrive at a firm and assured science, like the one Plato imagined to himself about the preceding lives of the soul.

XIV. Reason 3

The third reason depends on the preceding, that is, if our science were only remembrance, all those who remembered this science would be of the same opinion – to the extent of making that science uniform and

44. Cicero, *De officiis*, book I.
45. Aristotle, *De anima*, book III, chap. 4.
46. Plato, *Meno*.

the same, no matter how great the number of persons in which it is found, given that science is a perfect and infallible knowledge. Yet, we see most often as many diverse opinions about the same subject as there are heads, most of them false, or rather, all except one: for truth is only of one kind. Plato was aware of this and recognized that it destroyed his opinion; so he toiled hard (but in vain) to reconcile this remembrance of science with false opinions.[47]

XV. Reason 4

The fourth reason is that we would not have so much labor to acquire the sciences, as we do, if they consisted only in scraping and reawakening the slumbering memory. Indeed, the least indication and sign could recall it for us – as we see by experience, when having forgotten someone's name, if we are given only a single syllable, indeed, very often the first letter, it comes back to us all of a sudden in memory.

XVI. Reason 5

The fifth and final reason is that if science consisted only in remembrance, there would be no need to seek after the principles of demonstration so as to derive a sure proof, but simply to recall what we had previously known; and yet we see that every man makes a point of seeking after the best and strongest proofs that he can to confirm his views. And, in this way, since Plato's opinion remains destroyed, its contrary, which is that of Aristotle, must be accepted.

Until now we have spoken of the state of the soul considered in itself, before it is infused into the body, though there is no interval of time between its creation and its infusion into the body, except rationally. Now we must discuss its immortality.

47. Plato, *Theatetus*.

EIGHT

Marin Mersenne, *The Use of Reason, The Impiety of the Deists,* and *The Truth of the Sciences*

[*L'usage de la raison,* 1623; *L'impiété des deistes,* 1624; *La vérité des sciences,* 1625]

Introduction

Marin Mersenne (1588–1648) was a mathematician, musician, and natural philosopher. However, his main contribution to the philosophy and science of his day was his indefatigable promotion of scientific activity. Educated at the Jesuit College of La Flèche (which Descartes also attended), he entered the order of the Minims, and from his cell at their convent near the Place Royale in Paris, he acted as the center of a vast correspondence network, bringing together notable philosophers, mathematicians, and scientists. He championed the new science, publishing translations (or paraphrases) of Galileo's early mechanics and his *Two New Sciences*. Moreover, he served as Descartes' link to the learned world while Descartes lived in the Netherlands, assisting in the publication of Descartes' works, soliciting the *Objections* to the *Meditations* (except for the *First Set of Objections*), and composing the *Second* and *Sixth Set of Objections*. Among his early works were two short religious tracts, *L'usage de la raison* and *L'analyse de la vie sprituelle* (both 1623), a massive commentary on Genesis, *Quaestiones in Genesim* (1623), and two hefty philosophical treatises, *L'impieté des deistes* (1624) and *La vérité des sciences* (1625). The first of the two religious tracts was rediscovered in 1978, but the second remains lost. Mersenne intended the two religious works as contributions to the extremely popular early modern literary genre of devotional exercises, to be placed alongside those of Saint Ignatius of Loyola, Eustachius a Sancto Paulo, and Saint François de Sale. What makes Mersenne's devotional exercises useful as part of the philosophical context of early seventeenth-century France, however, is Mersenne's emphasis in these exercises on the intellect, away from the senses – what has been called the Augustinian tradition of devotional exercises, as opposed to the Jesuit or Ignatian tradition.[1] The Latin treatise, *Quaestiones in Genesim*, takes the form of a commentary on the book of Genesis (through its first six chapters). Interspersed with purely exegetical matters are many discussions of natural philosophy: when God says "let there be light," Mersenne appends a treatise on light; when God creates the stars, Mersenne issues a tract against astrology. Much of Mersenne's commentary in these three volumes is directed against atheism and heresy. When the word "God" first appears in Genesis, Mersenne follows it with attacks against the atheists. The attack is continued, in French, in the other two works. In the course of his defense of the faith against new philosophers, heretics, and atheists, Mersenne makes it clear, however, that traditional Aristotelianism cannot readily withstand their onslaught.

The following selection consists of chapters from *L'usage de la raison*, *L'impiété des deistes*, and *La vérité des sciences*. Those from *L'usage de la raison* detail what Mersenne holds as the relation obtaining between the two faculties of the soul, the understanding and the will – a discussion that throws considerable light on Descartes' later arguments in the Fourth Meditation. The chapters from *L'impiété des deistes* argue for the existence of God (against atheists and libertines).[2] Mersenne gives eleven such arguments (there are thirty-six in the Genesis commentary); interestingly, he reports indifferently those of Aquinas and those of Augustine and Anselm, even though he knew well enough that Aquinas had rejected Anselm's argument (the revival of Anselm's strategy for proving God's existence was, of course, to be a notable feature of Descartes' own reasoning in the Fifth Meditation). The chapters from *La vérité des sciences* give the core of an argument among three characters, a

---

1. See G. Hatfield, "The Senses and the Fleshless Eye: The Meditations as Cognitive Exercises," and B. Rubidge, "Descartes's Meditations and Devotional Meditations."
2. The terms "atheist" and "libertine" had a broader meaning in the seventeenth century – witness Mersenne's statement that there are 50,000 atheists in Paris (*Quaestiones in genesim*, col. 671); 50,000 would have been a large proportion of the population of early seventeenth century Paris, estimated to have been 300,000. For a discussion of such issues, see Robert Lenoble, *Mersenne ou la naissance du mécanisme*, chap. 5. On seventeenth-century libertinism, see R. Pintard, *Le libertinage érudit dans la première moitié du XVIIe siècle*.

Christian Philosopher, a Skeptic, and an Alchemist. Needless to say, the Christian Philosopher wins the argument.[3] The extracts canvass many of the arguments for the unreliability of the senses that were later to preoccupy Descartes, as well as (in the closing section) giving a strong sense of the authority claimed by the church in restricting the scope of philosophical inquiry.

[RA]

THE USE OF REASON

Preface

My dear reader, this small publication has no other purpose than to prepare your soul for its entry into the heavenly Jerusalem, so that it may eternally praise its creator, with the angels and all the blessed, who fully enjoy the admirable beauty and ineffable goodness of the living God. . . . Now the paths I wish to trace for you, my dear reader, are not borrowed from the stars and planets, and not even from sublunary things. They will not be far from your mind. It will not be necessary to roam and sail to the Indies, or to the Canary Islands, in order to see their beginning, middle, progress, or end. And I do not want to seek them in the Rabbinate Sephiroth,[4] with its deific tree, even though conforming to the divine attributes and emanations would be a rich manner of perfecting oneself. This has been taught very excellently by the great bishop of Geneva in his Theotime.[5] But I will take the paths I trace for heaven from inside yourself, so that at any moment you wish, in the midst of royal greatness, during banquets, dances, pastimes, day and night, in prosperity and adversity, whether poor or rich, caressed or abandoned, healthy or sick, you will be able to practice that which will be your salvation. I will take, therefore, the motions of the soul, insofar as it is rational and capable of accruing merit or giving offense, and I will set aside that which concerns the brutal passions, common to men

3. For more on Mersenne in relation to late Scholastic thought, see P. Dear, *Mersenne and the Learning of the Schools.*
4. In the philosophy of the Cabala, the Sephiroth consists of the ten attributes or emanations by means of which the Infinite enters into relation with the finite.
5. That is, Saint François de Sale, in his *Treatise on the Love of God* (1616).

and beasts. . . . I therefore want us to suppose that the only path leading to heaven for those who have the use of reason and who remain within the order established by God is to train and perfect the spiritual actions and motions of the understanding and will. I will now describe these spiritual actions and motions, in order subsequently to show how we must govern, practice, and understand them. . . . Now, in order that we do not say anything not well founded on truth and reason, we will first relate what belongs to doctrine, so as to give a firm foundation to the whole edifice; thus, having persuaded and convinced the understanding, the will may direct itself to that which is its salvation with more ardor and greater effectiveness. That is why the first book will be more speculative than the second, which will be like the fruit of the first. In the same way that the great light of the Sun reflected and collected into a point engenders a fire and living flame, when it is reflected by a parabolic glass or broken by an anaclastic medium, so also the light of the first book, being reflected on the will, renders it wholly ardent and burning for what serves God; and being, as it were, broken by the senses, as by a medium for refraction, it comes to fill the whole body, so that not just the mind but our whole fleshly being may become filled with jubilation in serving God, even as the Psalmist was when he declared "My heart and flesh rejoice in the living God." . . .

2. The Understanding and the Will

The understanding and the will are the two pivots about which all spiritual and rational life revolves. They are the two powers or regal faculties in the mind, serving God and adoring him. They are the two principles on which depends everything that art and ingenuity bring forth. In brief, there is nothing produced in the world that does not proceed from these lively and fruitful sources.

The understanding is that which sees and discovers everything and which we use as a kind of spyglass to give order to what can creep up on us and oppose our designs. It is the torch that lights the midst of the darkness, the lighthouse that guides the will and shows it the goal to which it must aim. This has caused philosophers to say that the understanding is the *primum mobile* that carries the will to what it contemplates, not by constraining it, but by persuading it very gently, not with respect to its exercise or actual resolution to act, or the act itself, but only with respect to the kind of action that they call "action considered as form, specification" or "designated act," as opposed to "action considered as exercise," or "performed act."[6] And, of course, it is necessary that this intellectual light precedes the action of the will, given that will has no light of its own.

But the will is not illuminated in the manner of a blind person, for whom the light is nothing other than the hand, the cord, the stick, or the shoulder lent to him so that he may walk – if we are speaking of external light, which serves to guide his actions [*démarches*] – for he is not deprived of internal light (whether sensitive or mental), but on the contrary, he sees more clearly internally than those who have clear-seeing eyes, divine goodness supplying internally what he lacks externally. This light that the will receives is thus not similar to the one we receive from the Sun, despite the fact that we can call the intellect the Sun of the soul. For the will is not capable of light in the manner of a diaphanous body transmitting the splendor of the Sun, or an opaque body reverberating and reflecting it, but in a wholly admirable manner, similar to the one by which the imagination illuminates the sensitive appetite. This is accomplished so subtly that we need to have recourse to the identity of the one and same support and to the source of a single essence to acknowledge or explain this marvelous irradiation and spiritual motion by which the understanding transports the will to hate or love the object presented to it; the will can still turn away from this object and not come to love or hate it, given that this action of the intellect cannot prevent the voluntary exercise of the will. This is so much in its power that there is nothing that can constrain it to will or not to will; otherwise the action would be both voluntary, since it is accomplished by the will [*volonté*], and not voluntary, since it would be constrained – which is completely contradictory.

I know well that the will can be necessitated, as philosophy teaches, such that it cannot avoid willing the thing when it encounters an object so good that it contains no imperfection. The good considered in general is such an example: if the will wants to act, it cannot hate this goodness, but will love it necessarily. This is what we call hypothetical or suppositional necessity. For the will loves this goodness necessarily only if first we suppose that it determines itself to will, given that it is always free to will or not to will. Theology proposes another way in

---

6. "Quoad speciem, specificationem" or "in actu signato," and "quoad exercitium" or "in actu exercito."

THE USE OF REASON

which the will acts necessarily (not just "with respect to its exercise" but also "with respect to the form of the act"),[7] which is when it sees God clearly in Paradise. For, in that case, it no longer has any freedom toward this infinite object, which it loves with all its power and does so necessarily, to such an extent that it cannot resist this love even for a moment. Thus, I conclude that, in this encounter, necessity is better than freedom; and I confirm it in that God himself is not free in his essential and notional actions (called *ad intra*), given that God loves himself necessarily and the Father produces the Son and the Holy Spirit necessarily. Yet all three have created the world with a most complete freedom, a world they could have not created and can still, at this moment, or whenever it pleases them, annihilate by the mere subtraction of their most free concourse and conservation, by which they maintain it. And yet, if we come to consider the excellence of these actions to our way of thinking and conceiving, we would confess that the action by which God created the world and makes or conserves everything here below is less excellent than the action by which he loves it, if we consider only the former action, insofar as the world is produced by it, given that we judge the action by the effect or by the termination, which is produced by virtue of it. For otherwise, the action by which God produces the world is nothing other than the one by which he loves himself, given that everything in God is God himself. That is why some theologians do not admit of action in the creation, for fear that we would think that this action is received in the effect, and thus cannot be called divine, and for fear that we would admit something between God and creatures. Creatures depend immediately on him; he acts on them as he wishes, without any medium, as he did when he formed them out of nothing and drew them from nothingness.

I do not wish to push deeper into these profound considerations, so that I may have the opportunity to say something about the other part of man and reason – that is, the will – which is compared to fire, as it is ardent in its designs and desires. It is, accordingly, a power of the rational soul, which brings us to will or not to will whatever the understanding presents to us, without which reason would seem to be lacking and imperfect. It is like the spiritual hand that receives what is offered by the intellect. It is so tightly conjoined with it that some have thought that it is only one thing signified by different words, and that the understanding and the will are

7. As much "quoad exercitium " as "quoad specium actus."

only the essence of the soul, insofar as the soul is rational. Others have thought that they are two faculties really distinct both among themselves and from the being of the soul. According to them, through a miracle, the soul could be without understanding and will, if God wished to deny his concourse to the emanation of these powers, which could also remain separate from one another by divine virtue, regardless of whether they could act separately or remained idle. I do not wish to discuss this further, being satisfied with having said a few words about the powers of the soul, in order that we can understand their actions and train them for the glory of God. I will only add that the will is the mistress and queen of reason, for it commands with a stick and gives the intellect the motion we call exercise, applying it at one time to the consideration of one object and, at another time, to the contemplation of another, constraining it to consider the object as long as it pleases. For reason is not free, as will is, even though one calls it the root of freedom, insofar as it discovers various reasons in each object according to which the object can be hated and loved – so well that the will does its bidding. But, properly speaking, only the will has this freedom: it depends only on God and is not just the external root of freedom, as is the understanding, but is its subject, in which it resides as a form. Or rather we prefer to say that freedom is the same as will, insofar as it operates, or ceases to operate, hates, or loves, as it wishes. And it is this freedom by which we cooperate in our salvation. That is the foundation of this small spiritual edifice; the rest will be clear and easy to understand.

THE IMPIETY OF THE DEISTS, ATHEISTS, AND LIBERTINES OF THIS TIME FOUGHT AGAINST AND DEFEATED POINT BY POINT USING REASONS DERIVED FROM PHILOSOPHY AND FROM THEOLOGY[8]

In Which the Theologian Proves That God Exists, against the Atheists and the Libertines

THEOLOGIAN: I am very glad that you have put me on this subject; for I greatly desire atheism to die out and the whole world to recognize the great motive force of the universe as the creator of all things. I assure

8. The extracts below come from chapters 5 and 6.

you that I have very often been astonished on being told that there are atheists, given that there is no creature, no matter how paltry, who does not teach that God exists and that he is unique and supreme. I believe that one must have a marvelously stupefied soul to go so far as to think that there is no God. Certainly I am truly bothered by where I would begin in order to show you that it is necessary to admit that God exists, for there is nothing at all in the world that does not prove it; and I am no less bothered by discovering what may be the cause for some to fall into that abyss of impiety, even though I have related eighteen reasons for this in article 3 of the question which I published last year against the atheists. I will now content myself with extracting some proofs from it, in order to arm you against the atheists.

Reason 1 for the existence of God. There is no one who does not grant me that if there is a supremely good being, it deserves the name of God, since we do not understand anything else by this name, except that which has all sorts of perfections and which lacks nothing. Now I demonstrate the existence of this supreme good as follows. If it does not exist, it must therefore be that its privation, which would be supreme evil, exists, and consequently supreme nonbeing exists, since evil and nonbeing are one and the same thing; but it is not likely that the privation would exist rather than its actuality, which must necessarily precede it. It must therefore be admitted that a supreme goodness exists, since a supreme malice cannot. We therefore have a supreme being, since we reject a supreme nonbeing. Given that it is necessary that one or the other exists, it must therefore no longer be doubted that there is a God, the latter being so necessary that it is impossible for it not to exist; for otherwise the existence of anything at all of what exists would be impossible, since there would be nothing other than an eternal nonbeing, with which any kind of being is incompatible.

Reason 2. In addition, it is necessary that there be an independent being that has no bounds or limits of perfections, otherwise it would be impossible that there would be anything in the world; for it would have to be that everything in the world would be dependent. Now, this dependence cannot go back to infinity, which would mean that everything in it would have received its being and there would be no being that did not receive its own being from anybody. And then, if there were no God, or independent being, it would be impossible that there have been any, and in this way we would have a greater imagination than all the beings of the world, and the being of our thoughts and of our phantasms would surpass infinitely all the real beings, and what is imaginary would

surpass what is actual – that cannot be. It is clear that our imaginations
and thoughts would be greater, because we conceive an infinite being
when we wish; and can it really be said that these thoughts will have no
object? How is it then possible that the understanding, or the will, bear
on it so greatly, so powerfully, and with such fervor? Let good minds
retreat from the accursed thought of those who are so dizzy that they
believe that there is no God.

Reason 3. Tell me, I beg of you, is it possible to persuade oneself that
there is no God? Can it be that this handsome celestial canopy, these
four elements, and everything that we see were not made by anybody?
Would it be easier to believe that an oration of Cicero, that the *Aeneid*
of Virgil, that a house, or a town, cannot exist of itself, than the stars
or the elements? But, I beg of you, why is it that heaven is not larger,
why is it that it is not square, or six-sided, instead of round, if it does
not depend on anyone? It is a most evident contradiction to say that
what is not infinite has not been made, for if it is finite, it is necessary
that someone has set boundaries to it and limited it. Now, everything
we see is finite; it follows that it has received its bounds from someone,
which is an infinite being and the true God, and the latter, being im-
mense, bounds all things according to his good wishes.

Reason 4. Here is yet another reason from among a hundred that one
could bring to this subject. Everything in the world is resolved into
principles from which it is composed. For you will not find any body
which does not resolve itself into these three principles, salt, sulfur, and
mercury, or, as some say, into body, mind, and soul, or into earth, fire,
and water. Now, everything that resolves itself and dissolves has been
conjoined and composed, given that the same order that is kept at dissolution exists again at composition. It must therefore be that someone
has made this composition; and it has not been composed, but is most
simple. Moreover, since all things, whether stones, plants, animals, or
minerals, which are part of the four or five families and stages of this
world, have terminations and are made with time, it is certain that they
also have begun with time, as the first historian of the world so aptly
noted when he said that God created heaven and earth at the beginning
of time. But it is impossible that God has been created, since he is before
all time and before everything that we see. He was, as he still is and will
be eternally and immutably, this very profound Ensoph of the Cabalists,[9]

9. "Ensoph" is a cabalistic word, from the Hebrew *ein soph* or "no end, infinity";
   it thus refers to the Infinite or Supermundane Being from which all the others
   spring.

blessed by himself, who has made men only for his glory and in order to contemplate supreme goodness, so that they may serve it and adore it forever. Therefore that is what we should aspire to, and we should have no other end or aspiration than to revel in this infinite good, not bothering with and not using anything except to the extent that it will serve as a step toward uniting us to God, who has made us and maintains us with nourishment, life, clothing, and everything necessary for us, so that we may praise him eternally and love him above all things.

DEIST: Blessed be the Eternal who has given me today such an encounter; never have I heard a discourse that has pleased me more. Good God, can there be someone so stupefied, so blind, who thinks that there is no God? As for me, I believe that this can only come from a lack of mind and judgment, for everything in the world preaches this truth to us.

THEOLOGIAN: Truly, when one contemplates the beautiful order in the world and sees that each thing maintains its rank and place, in spite of all disorders that seem to arise, one must conclude that there is someone who governs the whole world and maintains all things in good order; for the world could not keep the inviolable oscillation and regular cadence that we perceive in it, if it were not for the divine Orpheus who touches the cords of the great lute of the universe and who takes care of all the activity and motions that appear in the heavens and in the elements. Could it happen that a ship without a pilot or rudder would avoid shipwreck? Not at all. What would then happen to this great ark, to this great ship of the world, if God did not rule it and govern it in all its proceedings? . . . [10]

Even though the reasons I have deduced for you so far are only too sufficient to make atheism disappear, nevertheless, since you take pleasure in this discourse and it seems that you wish to make use of it in order to disabuse some of your acquaintances, I will add some more reasons that I will take from among those I more amply deduced in the question against the atheists.

Reason 6. It is impossible that there would be the number of planets and stars that there is, and that the heavens could keep the distance between them, if there were not someone who gave them these proportions and who made them in this number, rather than in another.

---

10. There follows a lengthy cosmological poem concluding the existence of God from various features of the universe.

For, I beg of you, why is it that the Moon is distant from us by 56 radii of the Earth, when it is at its average distance? Why is it that the Sun gets farther from us by 1,182 radii when it is at its apogee, the latter being found this year 1624 in the tenth degree of Cancer? And why is it only distant by 1,101 radii when it is at its perigee, which is found at the sign of T[aurus]? What makes it take this path, descending from one sign to the other by 81 radii?

I could ask you the same for Saturn, Jupiter, and Mars, and wonder why they are at times higher and at times lower, but this would be too lengthy; it is enough that you see clearly that it must necessarily be admitted that there is a divine being ruling everything, and who is not ruled by anybody.

For the Sun would not be any less the Sun, if it were closer or farther from the Earth, and the stars could still be stars if they got farther from us than 14,000 terrestrial radii. The proportion found among all the bodies of the world also entails that there is a God who has made the whole universe in weight, number, and measure.[11] For the Earth would not have a similar ratio with the Sun as 1 to 140 and with the Moon as 40 to 1, and would not have a comparison with the whole spherical solidity of the visible world as 1 to 2,744,000,000,000 (i.e., that it would not have the proportion that holds between unity and two trillion, seven hundred forty-four billion, taking each billion for ten hundred millions); the earth, I say, would not have this ratio with the planets and with the whole world, if there were not a supreme architect who gave them these quantities, these measures, these distances, and these proportions.

DEIST: You would give me a singular pleasure if you would take the trouble to tell me all the proportions that the five other planets and all the stars have with the earth and all together.

THEOLOGIAN: It seems to me more appropriate to go on to other considerations, as much because you can see all this in the . . . reasons that I brought forth in the aforementioned question against the atheists, as because Tycho Brahe, Kepler, Blancanus . . . and several others have deduced these matters most amply. That is why I put an end to this discourse; it is enough that you consider attentively from what the reason drawn from these distances and proportions derives its force – which is that neither the Sun nor any other planet was able to determine itself, to get somewhat farther or somewhat nearer, or to make it be that its

11. Marginal note: Proportion of the earth with the whole solidity of the world.

magnitude were other than it is. Nor indeed did the Earth have 7,200 leagues in its circumference because it did not want to have any more, but because the one who made it wanted to give it only that.[12] There is no means of finding another cause; seek as you wish for why the circumference of the firmament is 100,800,000 leagues and consequently its diameter is 32,074,000 leagues, you will not be able to give another reason, except that God has wished it thus for many reasons that we will know only in Paradise.

We also find the same reason inside celestial motions, that is, motions that have no cause except for divine will: why the sea moves in 25 hours rather than in 100, or in some other number; why the moon crosses the whole zodiac in 27 days and 8 hours and catches up with the Sun in 29 days and 13 hours;[13] why the Sun takes 365 days, 5 and 5/6 hours, to complete its annual path and why its apogee takes 28,800 years – which is the time of the proper motion of the stars – before completing the whole zodiac. For we cannot say that the Sun or other stars need these motions for their conservation, given that rest is not contrary to them; and even though someone thought that this motion would be necessary to prevent the corruption of the star or of the individuals he imagined there, like new worlds, still, we must establish the reason why these individuals would need this motion, and always have recourse to a first motive force, so that, whatever side we turn to, we must admit that God exists.

DEIST: I see clearly that all these reasons are irrefutable. For whether one wills it or not, it is necessary that everything limited in magnitude, shape, number, weight, and motion has been limited by someone; the latter has no limits and is infinite, given that it is impossible not to arrive at a first cause that imparts being, difference, and all properties to all things, and which has also well determined the number of genus and species, as well as that of individuals. Now before we leave these motions, I beg of you to tell me whether one can show how many leagues each star of the firmament accomplishes in an hour.

THEOLOGIAN: . . . [14] Does it not seem that man has marvelous prerogatives above the animals, since he subjects the heavens and the Earth to himself by the force of his understanding? In this way he finds that these

12. Marginal note: Circumference of the earth and the firmament in number of leagues.
13. Marginal note: Motion of the moon and of the stars.
14. There follows a lengthy digression on the issue.

stars accomplish no more than 23 paces in a minute, almost 2 feet in a second, 5 lines in a tierce, and a thousand other things that seem to surpass our capacity, if we did not have some seeds of immortality.

DEIST: There is no way to deny this; that is why I firmly believe that the soul is immortal and that God will grant us all our desires to know and to enjoy all things in this world; otherwise we would have to say that our wishes were useless and that nature would be an unkind stepmother who makes us desire so ardently what it would be impossible for us to acquire if God did not give it to us.

THEOLOGIAN: We do not lack other reasons to convince the atheists, such as those taken from this axiom: *everything that moves is moved by another; or everything that exists has being from another, which does not receive its being from elsewhere, except God, who has his being from himself.* But I content myself with having deduced them in question 1 on Genesis, from which I bring to you two more, the first taking off from truth and the second from goodness and the supreme being.

Reason 7. Think, if you can, of when it was not true that something was future, or past. If you were unable to imagine either one or the other, and nevertheless neither one nor the other can be true without truth, then it is impossible to imagine that the truth has an end or a beginning. Therefore, it is eternal and consequently necessary; it is God. For if truth began or if it must end, it was true that the truth existed before it existed, and after it will no longer exist, it will be true that it no longer exists. Now, the true cannot be without truth. Therefore, after there will no longer be truth, there will be truth; for truth will make it be that the truth will no longer be. Therefore truth will be and will not be, which is too manifest an absurdity. For the latter to stop, we must admit that there is an eternal truth that does not depend on anything else and is God himself.

Saint Augustine also uses a reason derived from truth when he says:[15]

> If there is no truth, since it follows that it is true that there is no truth, even if you should say that "there is no truth" is not true simply speaking, at least this will turn out to be true partially and in a certain respect.

15. The paragraph is in Latin. Marginal note: Augustine, *Soliloquies.* But the actual paragraph is not there. What Mersenne quotes is a paraphrase of Augustine's argument in *Soliloquies*, book I, 15, 27–29, and II, 15, 28–18, 32; cf. also the argument for the eternality of truth in II, 2, 2. The previous argument, not attributed to Augustine, is closer to what Augustine actually says and looks like a faithful reporting of Anselm's *Monologion*, chap. 18.

THE IMPIETY OF THE DEISTS 149

But everything is in a certain respect and is said to be by a comparison having been made and by a relation obtaining to some other, which is without qualification, insofar as that which is in a certain respect exists as such by participation. If, therefore, there is something true in a partial way, in a certain respect, and by participation, there must necessarily be something true without qualification and by its essence. And from this, other things derive their own truth; and they bear their own truth as something received from that truth, which truth is God himself.

Reason 8 taken from Saint Anselm.[16] Let us complete this discourse with another reason derived from supreme goodness, addressing ourselves to it with Saint Anselm in his *Proslogion*. Lord, we believe that you are so great that one cannot think of any greater, nor of any better; must we say that such a nature does not exist because the fool has said in his heart that there is no God? Surely when he hears what I am saying, when he hears me state and assert that there is a being so good that a better cannot be conceived, he understands something so great that there can be no greater; now what he conceives is in his understanding, even though he does not understand that it actually exists in fact. For it is one thing to have something in the intellect and another for it to exist. Thus the painter, thinking what he must do, knows how to differentiate between what has to be done and what he has already done, and recognizes that what has to be done is not yet done.

The fool is thus convinced that at least he has in his understanding a thing so great that there can be no greater; for he hears me and understands me, and everything he understands is in his understanding. Now the being, which is the greatest of all those that can be conceived, cannot be in the understanding alone; for if it is in the intellect alone, one can conceive that it exists really and effectively – which is greater than if it existed in the understanding alone. From this it follows that if this being, above which a greater cannot be conceived, is in the understanding alone, this same being which is the best and the greatest of all that we can conceive will be the being, above which we could conceive a greater – that which cannot be said and cannot be. Therefore, there must necessarily be something not only in the intellect, but really, and in fact, that is so good, so excellent, that we cannot conceive a better, and that truly there cannot be a more excellent. The latter will be this

16. This is a paraphrase of Anselm's argument from *Proslogion*, chap. 2, except that Mersenne's version equates "the being which is the greatest of all that can be conceived" with "the being than which none greater can be conceived."

great God who has made us and formed us in his image, in order for us to serve, love, and adore him, and in order to enjoy his divine essence in the glory of the blessed.

Reason 9. You can derive similar reasons from everything we see here below. For there are no properties that do not depend on God and are not an actual participation of his perfections, such as when we say that heaven is great, it must be that God is greater, but of a more heightened and more eminent greatness, which has no imperfection. If the Earth exists, if the sky, if the Sun has being, it must be concluded that there is a being incomparably more excellent, according to the maxim of all the philosophers, "because there is one thing, there is something of such a kind, and that is greater."[17]

Reason 10. In addition, if you thought about eternity, omnipotence, supreme goodness, justice, wisdom, understanding, will – in brief, about everything we can talk about – you will find that there can be no time, no goodness, no justice, no wisdom, no understanding, no will, within finite beings, if you did not admit first that there is an eternal, omnipotent, supremely good, and infinitely just, wise, and knowing being, on whom time and everything here below depends. For time cannot be made by itself, and our powers, our goodness, our justice, and all our other faculties do not derive their being of themselves. Therefore it must be that they have received them from something, which did not receive its own from another; otherwise, we would be falling back into the same absurdity.

Reason 11. And then, if there were no eternal, independent, supremely knowledgeable, just, and good being, our thoughts would be better than this supreme being, to the extent that it would not be in existence and could not be there and, nevertheless, would be in our understanding. He would not be in existence, as we assume, and he could not be there; for what would make him and what would give him existence? And in this way, this supreme being would be better, being only imaginary, and produced by our thought alone, which does not put anything into the existence of things, unless it were really in itself, and which cannot be conceived, and is completely impossible. In this way you see that it is so necessary that God exists, that it is infinitely necessary, that it is impossible that God does not exist.

If you grasp these arguments and you are able to understand them and deduce them validly when you find yourself among these sorry

17. "Propter quod unum-quodque tale, et illud magis."

groups of atheists and libertines, I am sure that you will bring them back along the good path and will compel them to say and to admit in all frankness that it is impossible that God does not exist, and to acknowledge that it is necessary that there is a being that is supreme in all perfections, upon which everything in the whole universe depends.

THE TRUTH OF THE SCIENCES AGAINST THE SKEPTICS OR PYRRHONISTS

1. In Which the Skeptic Disputes against the Alchemist, Trying to Prove That Alchemy Is a Certain Science

ALCHEMIST: We can be proud that there is no science as certain as ours, for it proves everything it teaches by experience, the mother, the source, and the universal cause of all the sciences. Lacking it, Aristotle and the other philosophers have spectacularly failed in their philosophy, as much because they assumed and received false stories as true, as because they did not bother to see whether what they said about the nature of things was in conformity with the truth. I am sorry that the worthy Stagirite did not avail himself of this path. Given his excellent mind, he would have accomplished marvels, since, with only his strength of mind and without any experience, he penetrated so far that most men up to the present have accepted his doctrine, as if he were an oracle from whom one was not allowed to stray in any way. Nevertheless, we who are the other offspring of learning and are disciples of the great Hermes, knowing *that everything below is the same as what is above*[18] discover the errors of the Peripatetic and marvel at how it is possible that no one has refuted and torn down the pretended doctrine of this man, who is recognized as Master in the ordinary schools, and whose opinions are espoused even though they are erroneous, as if he were not capable of failing like other men. Were God to allow some worthy minds to help me, I would quite soon establish a new philosophy, or rather restore the ancient one into its splendor, so that we would from now on no longer be abused by the diversity of opinions that arise from the caprice of so many strange and fantastical teachers.

SKEPTIC: To hear you speak, one would say that your alchemy would be capable of restoring the whole world and make the shadows of ignorance

18. Marginal note: Maxims of the alchemists.

disappear by some extraordinary burst of light. But I do not consider it
as more certain or true than the other sciences; on the contrary, I believe
that if errors have slipped into some art, that it is particularly in that of
chemistry.[19] For if there were something certain in that science, we
would not see so many blowers who, after having amalgamated, calcin-
ated, burned, and reduced into cinders all their means, become so poor
and needy that they are constrained to beg for their bread, if they do
not meet up with some dupe whom they persuade that in a short time
they will show some marvels – and all in order to retrieve their losses
at his expense.

If I wanted to make a catalog of all those who brag of having discovered the stone and powder of projection, I would need a larger book
than the library of Gesnerus, though they have never found anything
more than some smoke, some powder that is useless for anything, some
confusion, and some need. I know very well that it will be objected that
Arnauld de Ville-Neuve, Raymond Lull, Trevisan, and many others have
discovered the secret, but it would be just as easy for me to deny it, as
it will be for them to assert it. And then one sees well enough when one
considers their reveries and their ridiculous propositions whether they
have minds that are lost and full of vain subtleties – as appears well
enough in their words, which they make use of, but whose sound is all
one understands.

As for Aristotle, even though you despise him so, I would much prefer to follow his philosophy than yours, for if there were nothing or few
true things in it, as you claim, at least it is not the cause of the loss of
means and honor, as is your alchemy, with its athenors, alembics, re-
torts, and other utensils for blowing and emptying the purse of all those
who engage in this exercise, which is as vain and misleading as it is la-
borious.

ALCHEMIST: This is good to say to these cheats and braggarts who prowl
around the towns and chateaux, lest they be recognized, and who do not
have the means by which to live, if they do not grab a coin under the
pretext of having found the stone. But I am, thank God, well removed
from that condition, for I have enough means to work for hundreds of
years without my household being inconvenienced; what I do is only for
my pleasure. I know that most of those who bother with this art are
grossly mistaken because they are ignorant and have in mind only some

19. Marginal note: Errors of alchemy.

universal dyes that they wish to turn into white or red with some minerals, or some metals, looking for magnesia where it is not;[20] but they will never find it, for they do not know how to reduce the Moon, the Sun, or Mercury, into prime matter any more than any other thing. And this causes their hopes to become frustrated.

Try as much as they want to change the Moon into the Sun with their fixed spirits of salt and minerals, they will never do anything worthwhile with their sophistical solutions or with their acid and corrosive spirits; that is why one must hold them for sophists and impostors.

Are they not ridiculous with their empty and fantastic dreams, to want us to believe that the matter of the stone is found in man and in animals? Some throw themselves into honey and the butter extracted from it; others prefer eggs, urine, germs, blood, and other excrements and foods. In the end, everything they do and say is nothing more than a waste of time and money, fraud, lies, folly, and errors. But I do not wish to relate for now all the abuses of these alchemists who seek the stone, without recognizing the magnesia of the wise. I will give them only one word of advice, that is, that if they wished to do something good, they should not pay attention to the mercury, gold, or silver of the vulgar, nor to the philosophical homunculus to which they have recourse, when, having blown everything and despairing to be able to arrive at the powder, they no longer know which stone to turn.

If they had a little judgment, they would not undertake this labor unless they knew the true matter on which one must work and how one must prepare it:[21] that to purify it one must dissolve it and burn it – that it is necessary to purify it with the arms of Neptune and of Vulcan; how much weight it should have; that it must rot, which is necessary for it to multiply; what is its fermentation, as is specified by the universal stone; and, finally, when and how is its projection achieved. This is what they should know from the theory, before coming to actual practice, and then they would have the great elixir, the foundation of the universal medicine and of the burning and incombustible water; in brief, they would be in possession of the true stone of the philosophers and their drinkable gold.

Now, I advise you not to speak further against the true alchemy, for if you knew it as it ought to be known, you would not blame it; but if you have something else to say, I am ready to listen.

20. Marginal note: Ignorance of the alchemists.
21. Marginal note: Difficulty in alchemy.

2. In Which the Pyrrhonist Proves That We Know Nothing with Certainty, Together with the Replies of the Philosopher

SKEPTIC: Sir, your discourse did not so satisfy me that I regard your alchemy as true. I believe that no one knows anything with certainty in this world; for who knows anything such as it is in itself? We cannot know whether there aren't other stars and other systems than the ones we see. Who can boast that he knows what is in the sea: what is the nature of the fish and shells there? Or who knows what is its origin and all its properties, since no one till now has been able to understand its motion and the reason for its ebb and flow? We also do not know what the earth is, for we see only a part of it, like a flea seeing a part of the head and an ant seeing a part of a mountain or an oak; we can no more know the whole earth, not having seen it all, than know what a man is, having seen only the nose. It is not enough to say that we know it from accounts, for that would not be knowledge, any more than eating from the mouth of another is nourishing oneself. In the end, all things past are outside our science, the future things are not present to us, and the present things are entirely unknown to us, for that which we see is but a point with respect to the whole earth on which we live as poor little worms.

As for what comes from our sensations, we are deceived in all respects, for the Sun appears to us no larger than a foot and we do not know whether it moves or whether it remains at the same place.[22] If the Sun, the most manifest thing in all the world, remains unknown to us, what of the rest? Let your eyes fall anywhere you wish, we see only the surface and the color of things. We only sample their flavor; as for what is inside, we don't make it out at all. We are like those who are satisfied with touching the cloak, and sensing the smoke and the shadow; we know nothing of the substance and of the body. That is why this dreamer whom we call the master of the Peripatetics wrongly says that the understanding knows the essence of things, since there is nothing that enters into the understanding that doesn't pass through the senses. And even if we could get inside of things, we would not know them any better, for we could perceive nothing other than some external accidents.

Moreover, we do not know the effect perfectly when we are ignorant of the cause, which we see, however, only by means of the effect. And

22. Marginal note: Reasons why we cannot know anything.

in order to arrive at the knowledge of all the causes, we would have to pass to infinity. Now, the infinite cannot be grasped within the limits of our mind. But, I beg of you, consider the madness of Aristotle who wanted us to believe that, by some means or other that all men and things have together, we will come to know everything, even though we do not know the essence of a single thing.[23] We are not any wiser when we know that Peter is a man and that Paris is a city. We would have to know what are its walls, its palaces, its lodgings, and its government, and be able to specify everything that is in Peter to be able to know him. That is why I am of the opinion that the Peripatetics guard their universals as asylums for their ignorance; their universals are extremely ill-founded, since they assume a particular knowledge of individuals that we cannot know, insofar as they are innumerable and, what is more, subject to corruption; that is why they cannot serve as foundation for any science.

It is the madness of the Platonists to have recourse to their Ideas, since they are even more unknown to us than any other thing;[24] and even should we one day know them, they would not be the science of what is here below, for they are spiritual and the things here below are corporeal. I let you consider whether the doctor heals his patient with an Idea.

I know that Aristotle would reply that the knowledge of a certain number of individuals is enough to form a universal, true, and permanent thought; but aside from several opposite reasons that I could put forward, I deny that one knows any individual. For although the paper on which we are writing seems to be well known, nevertheless, we do not have knowledge of it through all its causes.[25] For if we were asked what is its matter, form, its craftsman, the place, pestle, water, and all the instruments that have been used to make it, we cannot respond. What would we do if we were seeking to know all its atoms and how its parts have been stuck and conjoined together?

It is not enough to know that it has been made in Venice and from pieces of linen, for we would have to know where the flax has been produced and from what seed; under what stars; in what longitude and latitude, during what time; and why this earth was meant to bear flax instead of other herbs; to what extent the matter of this flax has received

23. Marginal note: Against Aristotle.
24. Marginal note: Against Plato.
25. Marginal note: Things required for the knowledge of the paper.

forms from the beginning of the world; where the form of the paper came from; according to what idea it was made, going up to the divine idea and to all causes; what God, nature, and art contributed to it. We would also have to know why it was made at such a moment, and what times and motions of the stars preceded this generation; what proportion, disposition, and relation obtain between all the parts of heaven, Earth, and sea (and each part of all these things), and the water in which the paper has been made.

What is the craftsman called?[26] What are all his homogeneous and heterogeneous parts? What is his soul? When has it been infused? Why, how, and from where did it receive its name? What are its anagrams, that is, everything that can be said of it by means of Cabbala and onomancy. Who are his father and other relations, that is, what has brought him to want to become a papermaker? Why has God given him this will? Why has God determined that this man made paper rather than some other thing? Why did he not make the world sooner? If he has created us in order to show his glory, why do we not show ours to the ants? Why are there so many ills, given that he is so good? Why is he God rather than some other thing?

That is everything one must know in order to understand an individual, for an individual is a portion of the world such that, if one does not know everything that belongs to the world, he does not have the science of this paper or of anything else whatever, any more than a person who has seen only a single leaf knows the tree. What would the answer be if I asked you why the paper is white? What is whiteness? From what degree of light and heat does it arise? What is light? And in how many ways can it be reflected? It is a pleasure to see Aristotle occupied with his proximate causes and his principles, in order to establish and defend science. For he does not know the proximate elements any more than the remote ones, since he disputes about them with Pythagoras, Plato, Democritus, and others. From this I conclude that we know nothing or as little as nothing.

CHRISTIAN PHILOSOPHER: Sir, you have taken great pains in fighting against the truth, but it seems to me that your reasons are truly weak; if you do not put forth others, I fear that your adversary will carry off the palm, for one can reply briefly that all your reasons prove nothing, except that we know very few things. The proverb, "The greatest part

26. Marginal note: The craftsman's knowledge.

of what we know is the tiniest fraction of what we do not know,"[27] is derived from this.[28] But that does not imply that we do not know something. What you produce against Aristotle shows only that we do not know the ultimate differences of individuals and species, and that the understanding penetrates the substance only through the accidents, which is true, for we make use of the effects in order to elevate ourselves to God and other invisible substances, as if the effects were crystals through which we perceive what is inside. Now this small amount of knowledge [science] suffices in order to serve as a guide in our actions.

I leave to the side what you said about the Sun, which is judged to be a foot in magnitude, for reason corrects the defect of the eye, both with respect to the magnitude of the Sun and all other things which are distant, since when we see that the shadow of the Earth terminates into a pyramid, we conclude assuredly that the Sun is larger than the Earth. As for what concerns ideas, whether Plato was mistaken or not, it is certain that the craftsman must have an idea in order to effectuate his work; otherwise it would never come to an end. But to say that in order to know something, for example, what is paper, one needs to know everything you have related, that is what I deny, even though it would be necessary in order to know it perfectly, as God knows it. It is therefore sufficient in order to have knowledge [science] of something to know its effects, its operations, and its usage, by which we distinguish it from every other individual, or from the other species. We do not wish to attribute to ourselves a greater knowledge [science] or a more particular one than that.

I was expecting a stronger argument taken from all our sensations, which know nothing certain,[29] for taste is often mistaken, given that what we find pleasant and sweet, we call unpleasant at another time, and someone else finds it tart or bitter; and that which appears bitter, tart, and bad is found extremely pleasant by many animals. The same can be said for smell, since the odor that a child likes is unpleasant to an old man. And insofar as there are different temperaments, to that extent odors themselves appear variable and dissimilar; consequently, opposite species would not be opposite with respect to various individuals. What will happen if what some take for a tree, others take for a human being, if the ignorant is recognized as learned, the wealthy is thought to be

27. "Maxima pars eorum, quae scimus, minima est eorum, quae nescimus."
28. Marginal note: Refutation of skepticism.
29. Marginal note: Reasons for skepticism.

poor, and if the wise among the savages is thought to be foolish among us; and what if those who are thought saintly are held by us to be profane, and vice versa?[30]

The same thing must be said about touch, since the sick person finds cold what is hot, and since what seems hot, hard, heavy, thick, and so on to us, seems to many others, men as well as animals, to be cold, soft, light, and thin – so that everything that falls under our senses seems to be nothing other than cases of imagination, or perspective, or habit.

If we consult the ears, we will not find them any less problematic, since we do not hear a thousand kinds of sound that are in the air and even in ourselves, and since the sounds that are pleasant to young people are very unpleasant to old ones and to animals, and since each finds beautiful what is in conformity with his temperament and his humor.

Certainly, we do not even know whether the octave and the fifth, which are sounds that are conjoined most pleasantly and the principal harmonies of music, are pleasant to every type of nation. It can happen that donkeys and snakes do not find these pleasant, and perhaps our harmonies seem dissonant to them. For we see that different temperaments require different kinds of music. The musicians of this century are largely ignorant of this. They do not know how to vary their music and rhythmic motion to match the distinct temperaments and varying national tastes of all the different people they meet. They will never do anything worthwhile unless they put this into practice. Sight, which is the most subtle, most universal, and most penetrating sense, is often deceived. We do not even know what are color and light. What is a saffron color in the sun is green under a candle; the sea appears variously colored in deep water but white outside it; what seems to be a mountain to an ant is not similarly perceived by an elephant; what you see as large seems smaller to me; and we do not know what distance one must take in order to see the object best, since, seen from various places, it seems to have various forms, various magnitudes, and different colors. We do not know from what place it is seen best and who sees it best, men or animals, or those who have round organs of sight, or oval ones, and what constitution one must have in order to perceive the object with the most certainty.

Finally, if we contemplate all the senses, their modes of operation and the great variation which is found in all their operations, we shall see clearly that we do not know anything. And we would have grounds for

30. Marginal note: Uncertainty of all the senses.

wondering whether it would not be surer to follow the sensation of animals, rather than ours, in order to establish a new philosophy, since the latter is more subtle, as it appears with respect to the sight of eagles, spiders, and cats, who see at night, and of all the little animals who perceive a thousand things we cannot see. Their sense of smell is also much more penetrating, as we can see with dogs and wolves, and other beasts. Do we know whether the braying of a donkey is not more pleasant than our music according to nature, given that it is more pleasant to that animal? As for taste, we see that there is no need of salt or sauces with the meat that dogs and wolves devour, and perhaps they judge flavor better than we. As for touch, we must not doubt that thousands and thousands of animals surpass us. And if these animals follow the nature of things, and what seems to us of a certain color and light, agreeable to smell, to taste, to the ear, and to the touch is of another color to them, and dark, smelly, and disagreeable, we cannot value our knowledge (*science*), since the understanding receives nothing except through the senses.

ALCHEMIST: Sir, I did not expect that you would aid the skeptic in violation of the proverb which says, "not even Hercules [can succeed] against two."[31] I had only undertaken to reply to his arguments. That is why, although I am indebted to you for having replied to his first objections, you have so removed the debt by supporting his side so powerfully, that I am ready to quit the game if you do not stop helping him.

SKEPTIC: I am quite comfortable with the fact that you have become worried; with courage I need only one or two more reasons to convince you completely. I would have complained as much as you, if the gentleman had not said something on my behalf, as he has done for you.

PHILOSOPHER: I would be sorry if one of you were unhappy; that is why I will reply to what I have said in order to bring you into agreement, and then you may dispute to your hearts' content. What I said does not prevent one from having some knowledge [*science*], for at least one knows that the objects of the senses appear variously according to the various dispositions of the organs. As a consequence we inquire into why a taste is pleasant to someone and unpleasant to someone else: for example, why goats find gorse sweet and man finds it bitter. We know that we cannot hear all sounds, or see all kinds of light and colors, or discern every kind of odor, or taste all flavors, or discern every kind of cold and

31. "Ne quidem Hercules contra duos."

hot, for the objects must surpass what is similar to them inside the organ. We do not doubt that several degrees of every kind of quality and operation are too subtle for our sensations; given that light, which allowed us to see a white thing, being a little more opaque, renders it yellow, then purple, green, and so forth, we must not doubt that by passing from one color to another, a thousand other colors are engendered that we do not perceive at all, because of their weakness or because of the speed of the change

Now we are certainly acquainted with all this variety. That is why the understanding does not follow the simple apprehension of a sensation, but collates all things before it forms a conception and a judgment that it wishes to retain as scientific and resolved. It does not matter that the eye is mistaken, for man corrects himself by the other senses until he attains the certainty necessary for a true knowledge. And although the animals perceive objects differently from us, we must not worry about that, for we do not understand their speech and they do not know what we are saying, and because it is enough to know things according to how they are proportioned to us. As for morality, that is, as for human civil or canonical law, it is enough that it fits with our manner of living, and with what concerns the law and service to God – which does not ask anything more from us. If we are thought crazy by the savages, it matters little to us, for apart from the fact that we are ready to defend our ways of living, we have natural and divine law that guides us to everything that pertains to our salvation, a consideration that surpasses everything that can be said on this matter. But it is time to let you speak and debate your opinions. . . .

5. In Which the Christian Philosopher Replies to the Arguments of the Skeptic

I now approve of the division some make of the sciences. Among others, there are some who treat of their object according to how it is apprehended by our senses – such are medicine, rhetoric, poetry, music, perspective, astrology, grammar, and others; and there are some who speak of their subject according to its true nature and its essence, without respect to our senses – such are physics and metaphysics. That is why we must not expect that all persons reply in the same way, when they are asked about the same thing, for people who have no other knowledge than the one by which they know that such and such an individual is useful to us and suitable, would not judge these individuals absolutely.

For example,[32] the medical doctor would say that lettuce is cold and that water has no odor because we are not aware of its odor. But the physicist would say that, absolutely speaking, lettuce is warm, since it is nourished and engendered by heat, and that water can have an odor, even though we do not sense it, any more than we perceive the odor left behind by the buck, the wolf, the fox, or the hare in the path it has crossed – that which the dog notices very well. And who knows whether birds of prey do not sense the odor of the bird that they are pursuing in the air?

The astrologer says that the Moon is cold and that Saturn has bad effects.[33] However, the philosopher will say that these stellar objects are rather warm and have good effects, or at least that they are neither cold nor warm. The musician will reply that the things we do not hear do not make any sound and that there are only three or four agreeable harmonies. But he who knows all things such as they are in truth, without regard to our disposition, will certify that the motion or fraction of air and water makes a sound, even though it is not heard, and that there are many other harmonies, since many sounds are agreeable to animals, even though they displease us. Perspective discusses colors of magnitudes and shapes according to how they appear to us.[34] Finally most of the world speaks of what it sees, to the extent that it falls under the senses, and following its affection, its inclination; that is why the rhetoricians praise the speeches of Cicero and Virgil so highly, and reproach those of the philosophers and theologians, though inappropriately, for the latter apply themselves to finding the most meaningful and clearest words.[35]

Now, physics and metaphysics speak of each thing absolutely, without regard to this one or that one, such that when they touch the naked truth and teach us the thing as it is in itself, they can be called wisdom, because we savor and taste things as they are. Now, in order for me to do what I promised, I will begin with metaphysics, and then I will speak about logic, since it is the first cousin of metaphysics – for the former involves general principles of the being and essence of creatures, and the latter involves propositions and discourses that are relevant to all things.

Metaphysics teaches that there are beings and natures, and that every-

32. Marginal note: Sentiment of the medical doctor.
33. Marginal note: Opinion of the astrologer and the musician.
34. Marginal note: Perspective.
35. Marginal note: Comparison of logic and metaphysics.

thing that is and has an essence is one, true, and good. It holds as principle *that it is impossible for the same thing to be and not to be.* This is so true that it cannot be doubted, if one has ever so little power of mind and judgment; I do not believe that any person ever had wished or could have contradicted this principle, unless he were ignorant of what it signified.[36] It happens that some malicious or stupid people have thought that the principle was false, because what seemed to be green to one, seemed gray or red to another, and what I find sweet perhaps will seem bitter to you, and in this way they have concluded that the same thing was sweet and bitter, or that it was and was not green, and this seems to entail a manifest contradiction. But before speaking thus, they should have taught themselves how to interpret the axiom of metaphysics, namely that *it is impossible for the same thing to be and not to be, with respect to the same time, in the same sense, in the same judgment and in the same consideration, according to which we discourse about the thing proposed;* otherwise it would not be surprising to find one and the same thing which appeared round and square, or large and small, when seen by two diversely disposed persons, or even by the same person looking at it from two different places, or when a new circumstance is added, for then the truth of the axiom will not be understood to apply to such a case, because the axiom does not allow any circumstance to be changed, diminished, or added.

Logic similarly has very certain principles, for it is certain that the discourse about the disposition of figures that is taught initially (called syllogisms of the first figure) is extremely good and very certain.[37] But its main principle is similar to the principle of metaphysics, namely that *what is said of one thing referred to is true or false, and it cannot be together, according to a same consideration, both true and false.* For while something is, it cannot be that it is not, or that it is a nothing while it is something. I am certain that there is no skeptic who doubts so much that he does not grant me that there is something in the world and that what we touch, what we taste, or what we see is something, even though we judge it differently according to the various dispositions of our sensations.

Physics, which seems to be most doubtful, has its known objects, for who can deny that there are bodies and motions? Are there not light, quantities, causes, and a thousand other things that fall under the senses, of which physics treats? It does not matter that there are so many diverse opinions

36. Marginal note: Concerning the first principle of metaphysics.
37. Marginal note: Principle of logic based on the principle of metaphysics.

with respect to the principles of nature, for everyone has known something true, even though they have mixed in some errors with it, given that they have not considered all causes, circumstances, and effects. . . . [38]

9. In Which the Christian Philosopher . . . Shows When and How One Can Set Aside Aristotle's Doctrine and Opinions. . . . [39]

Even if Euclid was the most evil man in the world, the whole would still be greater than its parts and right angles would still be equal, for the truth of sciences is independent from our customs and our ways of living. And since all kinds of truths proceed from God, who is the essential, uncreated, and independent truth, we must receive the truth of the sciences and hold it in great esteem, whether it comes to us from heaven by means of a trough of lead or by means of a tube of gold. For God is its master and author, and he gives it to us as it pleases him. He has wished that we learn philosophy by means of Aristotle's books, mathematics by means of the books by Euclid, Apollonius Pergeus, Archimedes, and Ptolemy; he has imparted his sciences to them in order for them to give these sciences to the public. For it is quite certain that God conducts all our works as it pleases him, whatever we have intended, and he has wanted and willed that we make use of the works of Aristotle and of others, even before these authors were in the world. That is why we ought to give thanks to the divine majesty for all the truths given to us or explained by ancient or modern authors. . . . [40]

It is not that I want to say that there cannot be a more excellent and better arranged philosophy than Aristotle's, for I know that God is all powerful and that he can arouse some mind who will penetrate a thousand times deeper into the nature of things than have all the Peripatetics, all the Platonists, all the alchemists, and all the Cabalists. We have not seen such minds as of yet, but when it will please God to send us these

38. Marginal notes: Various opinions concerning the principles of nature; principles of nature according to the alchemists; morality and its principles; praise and usefulness of morality; replies to the Skeptic's observations concerning morality; various sayings of the ancients; how the true religion is known.
39. Marginal notes: Alchemical terms; skeptical terms; two reasons why the alchemists work in secret; why an academy of alchemists is necessary; enigmatic terms of alchemy; praise for the doctors' procedure; science and mores are different.
40. Marginal note: Authors who have written against Aristotle.

rare minds, we will receive them, with acts of grace. However, I am of the opinion that we should use Aristotle's doctrine, particularly in those places and parts that all the learned accept and follow with a common consent; as for the other places that are controversial, each person can follow what he deems most true and what is based on better reasons.

As for the books of Aristotle's *Metaphysics* that Rigord says have been condemned in Paris, we would have to see whether the council held in that city mentions the said books and if they were not by some other author. I have not read this account elsewhere than in Rigord's; that is why I have reference to its contents. Although, if it is true, I would be surprised that Saint Thomas did not recall it in his commentaries on the *Metaphysics*. Be that as it may, the prelates and doctors could have prohibited the reading of these books for a time,[41] having perceived that they were badly used and that this doctrine, which was not yet well understood, was being used to destroy the Catholic faith, which does not depend on Aristotle's doctrine or on any other philosophy, but only on the first truth on which it is founded and by which it is communicated to us.

That is why the church, the bishops and doctors, can suppress, prohibit, or condemn all the books that the heretics use in order to attack the faith, as they judge necessary, for a time or for always, for they have the right to do everything required for the preservation of the church and of the souls that God has put into its hands for their welfare.

This allows me to conclude that, as the king can justly prohibit card, dice, and chess games, tennis, deer and hare hunting, the hunting of other creatures, and the like, if he deems that these prohibitions are necessary in order to maintain his kingdom, and to prevent debaucheries and the abuses committed at these games and at the hunt, even though the game would not be bad in itself, and neither would the hunt; and as he can prohibit alchemy and the reading of books about alchemy in his kingdom (as, it is said, the king of England has done in his own kingdom) when he perceives that his subjects are wasting their time and consuming their wealth seeking the stone, even though these books did not teach anything false, then, in the same way, the prelates and pastors of the church can prohibit the reading of books that heretics and the other enemies of the church use to upset our belief, even though these books do not contain anything false. For example, if some new heresy based on Euclid's *Elements* or Aristotle's *Physics* or *Logic* arose to fight

41. Marginal note: Aristotle's metaphysics can be [justly] prohibited.

the Catholic faith, and the supreme pontiff and other prelates judged that it would be appropriate to remove these books from the hands of Christians, for fear that they would be dissuaded from their faith by the subtleness of the heretics' sophisms and paralogisms, they could prohibit the reading of these books until they saw the danger passed and the poison of the heresy destroyed.[42] For it is sometimes necessary to abstain from things that are good or indifferent, according to the various occurrences of people, times, and places. This should impose a perpetual silence on the heretics and libertines who attempt everyday to slander the prelates of the church and the general councils for their prohibition of the reading of censured books and of the Bible in the vernacular, for fear that those who do not have well-formed minds or firm enough judgment, such as the ignorant and women, may run the risk of losing their faith after having read things they did not understand, and will explain in a way other than they should. I set aside many other reasons for which one could prohibit this or that book according to various circumstances, in order to exhibit some of Aristotle's errors. I do so in order to show you very clearly that we do not embrace the doctrine of this man universally, nor with stubbornness, but only insofar as we deem it to be the most true and the best ordered of all those we have received until now.

42. Marginal note: The reading of Euclid's elements can be justly prohibited.

NINE

Pierre Gassendi, *Unorthodox Essays against the Aristotelians*

[*Exercitationes paradoxicae adversus Aristoteleos*, 1624]

Introduction

Pierre Gassendi (1592–1655), one of the major figures of the seventeenth century, was a philosopher, theologian, classicist, experimental physicist, and astronomer. Initially he was a priest at Digne and college professor at Aix (both in southern France), but his teaching was interrupted when the Jesuits took over his college. His philosophical career continued under the patronage of Fabri de Peiresc, who introduced him to the intellectual community in Paris; after Fabri's death, Cardinal Richelieu's brother, the archbishop of Lyon, procured for him a professorship of mathematics in the Collège Royal. In Paris, Gassendi was associated with the circle around Mersenne, which provided him with the opportunity to set his Neo-Epicurean views in contrast with those of Descartes, who was in correspondence with Mersenne's circle. The occasion resulted in Gassendi's best-known works, the *Fifth Set of Objections* to Descartes' *Meditations* and the subsequent *Disquisitio metaphysica*. Paris also provided for Gassendi a close association with a group of *libertins érudits*, and even closer friendship in the Tetrade, the subset of *libertins* that included Gabriel Naudé, Elie Diodati, and François de la Mothe le Vayer. Though most of his life (from about 1626 on) was devoted to his Christian rehabilitation of Epicurus' philosophy, his first published work, *Exercitationes paradoxicae adversus Aristoteleos* (1624) was a skeptical attack on Aristotelianism. In the preface to the first book, Gassendi sketches a multivolume project to provide an antidote to dogmatism by attacking the most seemingly secure Aristotelian doctrines taught in the schools. After an initial book, the project was to take on the collegiate curriculum: logic, natural philosophy (in

three parts), metaphysics, and ethics. Gassendi wrote the first two
books but published only the first one. The selection here contains
most of the general preface to book I of the *Exercitationes* and some
articles from book II on whether God should be excluded from the
category of substance, on quantity as external extension, and on the
question whether the "eternal" truths are eternal.[1]

[RA]

UNORTHODOX ESSAYS AGAINST THE ARISTOTELIANS

Book I: Preface

A few preliminary explanations are necessary regarding the kind of philosophy I have adopted and the order and divisions of the work, as if all
of it were to follow here. On the first point, when in my youth I was
steeped in peripatetic philosophy, I remember clearly that it did not at
all appeal to me. I had resolved to devote myself to philosophy because,
when I left my study of humanities, I had fixed in my mind this oration
of Cicero's: "Philosophy can never be sufficiently praised: he who follows its precepts can live a whole life without being troubled." It seemed
sufficiently clear to me that this could not be expected from the philosophy taught in the schools; once I became independent and began to
study the whole thing more deeply, I soon was able to see how vain and
useless it was for attaining happiness. Yet, that deadly arrow – the general prejudice in favor of Aristotle I saw in all the orders – remained
embedded. Reading Vives and my dear Charron gave me courage and
dispelled all my timidity; as a result, I saw that there was no harm in
supposing that one should not entirely approve of this sect, just because
most people approved of it. My strength increased, especially as I read
Ramus and Mirandola. I mention them because I have always professed
to name those from whom I have profited. Thus, from then on, I began
to seek the opinions of other sects, in order to see whether by chance
they offered anything sounder. I found difficulties everywhere, but I
frankly confess that I found none of these opinions as pleasing as the
suspension of judgment [*akatalêpsia*] recommended by the Academics

1. For more on Gassendi's philosophy in relation to Descartes', see L. S. Joy,
Gassendi the Atomist; T. Lennon, *The Battle of the Gods and Giants;* and M. J.
Osler, *Divine Will and the Mechanical Philosophy.*

and Pyrrhonists. In fact, after I had penetrated the great distance divid-
ing the Spirit of Nature from the human mind, what else could I think
except that the inner causes of natural effects escape completely human
observation? I began to pity and be ashamed of the vanity and arrogance
of dogmatic philosophers who proudly boast and so seriously declare
that they have acquired the science of natural things. Yet, would they
not have to remain rigid and silent like the rocks of Marpesia if someone
pressed them to explain seriously by what skill and with which instruments were constituted the limbs and organs of a single mite, one of
the smallest of Mother Nature's works? Much wiser are those philosophers cited earlier who, in order to demonstrate the vanity and uncertainty of human science, make themselves able to fight for and against
any position equally well.

That is why, having been charged afterward with teaching philosophy, and particularly Aristotle's, for six full years at the Academy of Aix,
I always made it a point to have my listeners be able to defend Aristotle
well; but, as an addition, I also presented opinions that would utterly
undermine Aristotelian dogmas. There was certainly a necessity for proceeding in the first way, given the place, the people, and the time; but
an honest mind could not omit the second portion, which gave one a
legitimate reason for holding back assent. Thus, my listeners were
warned not to make pronouncements casually; for they saw that no
proposition or opinion is so thoroughly accepted or so attractive that its
opposite cannot be shown equally probable, or even, in most cases, more
probable. . . .

But, in any case, whether I defend something dogmatically, or I put
another to the test in the manner of the skeptics, or if I present something as true, or if I say something else is probable (as for the false, it
is far from my thought ever to maintain it), I always submit myself and
all that is mine to the judgment of the One, Holy, Catholic, Apostolic,
and Roman Church, whose foster child I am, and for whose faith I am
ready to give my life with my blood. I think this entire work should be
submitted to its censorship, such that if, contrary to my hopes, it should
find something to disapprove of, then I would truly wish to be considered as the first to have reproved it. . . .

To continue, philosophy is commonly treated under four parts and,
among these, physics is subdivided into three sections; this constitutes
the well-known six parts of philosophy, to which one adds at the start
some introductory chapters commonly called prolegomena. Thus, I have

divided the philosophical exercises that follow into seven books corresponding to the totality of Aristotelian philosophy.

Book I is entitled "Against the Set of Doctrines of the Aristotelians"
because it contains some general exercises. In it I discuss and argue
against the manner of philosophizing commonly admitted by them and,
above all, I reclaim the philosophical freedom they have rejected. And I
demonstrate by many arguments that the Aristotelian sect or what it
teaches does not need to be preferred – especially because of the
omissions, superfluities, errors, and contradictions in the text commonly
attributed to Aristotle.

Book II is directed against Aristotle's Dialectics. In it I state first that
Dialectics itself is neither necessary nor even useful. Then, after discussing and arguing against Aristotelian universals, categories, and propositions, I put into question and debate Aristotle's conception of science
and demonstration. It is there, above all, that I argue that human science
and knowledge are weak and uncertain. The principal foundations of
Pyrrhonism are confirmed in it, and above all the maxim, nothing is
known [nihil sciri], is established.

Book III is devoted to an exposition of physics. A number of the
Aristotelian principles are attacked in it; among other things, it is proved
that forms are accidental. It is shown that natural motion is not what is
commonly believed to be. The space of the ancients is recalled from
exile and is substituted for Aristotelian place. Void is introduced, or
rather reestablished, in nature. Time is recognized as other than what
Aristotle defined it to be, and in this way a great many other things are
introduced in relation to this subject.

Book IV takes in the books on simple corporeal substance. In it, after
attributing rest to the fixed stars and the Sun, I recognize the Earth as
having motion – as if it were one of the planets. Then the multiplicity,
or rather the immensity, of the world is shown as probable. In addition,
a great many theses are presented in the form of paradoxes on the causes
of motion, light, phenomena, generation, and corruption in celestial
bodies. To this is added a discussion against Aristotle's elements, their
number, their qualities in regard to both movement and alteration, their
reciprocal transmutations, and their role in the composition of mixtures.

Book V attacks the treatises that are commonly devoted to mixed
bodies. In this part, I trace the motion of comets through ethereal space,
and show that their paths are not less continuous than those of the
planets always in view. Further, I disclose a new and different channel

from the Mesaraic veins for the passage of chyle from the stomach to the liver. I distinguish between more than three distinct kinds of living animals; I argue that semen is informed by an animating principle; I restore reason to animals; I find no difference between the understanding and the imagination. Finally, I attempt to persuade people not to believe in what is not.

Book VI is directed against the *Metaphysics*. After rejecting the greater part of the eulogies given to metaphysics, I attack as strongly as I can its well-known principles and those famous properties of Being: the One, the True, and the Good. Then I attribute solely to orthodox faith whatever knowledge we have about intelligent beings and the almighty Three-in-One God, for I amply show how vain are the arguments concerning separate substances, about which people usually philosophize by means of natural light.

Finally, book VII concerns moral philosophy. It does not at all require a lengthy recapitulation. In one word, it teaches Epicurus' doctrine of pleasure; it shows how the greatest good consists of pleasure and how the reward of human actions and virtues depends on this principle.

These are the principal subjects I undertake to discuss in the following books. No doubt, I omitted many things, but I did not believe I needed to examine every single opinion of the Aristotelians. For they are almost infinite and growing daily. It seemed preferable to imitate those who capture prey in abundance with nets and stakes, rather than those who follow the tracks of a single beast, who fish with a rod, or who hunt with an arrow. Thus, I thought it best to select those opinions which were, so to speak, the foundations of Aristotelian doctrine; when they cave in, the complete collapse of the others will ensue. In this I appear to be imitating those who dig underneath the foundations of a town under siege; when these fall in, the whole mass of walls and towers collapses at the same time.

Concerning the specific order of these exercises, I have more or less followed the one that gave me the Aristotelian philosophers' most common arrangement of subjects. Of course, if I wanted to create a philosophy of my own from whole cloth, I could have, indeed, I would have needed to introduce a new order; for today if we are considering the very nature of things studied in philosophy, everything has been turned topsy-turvy. But since I am not philosophizing here absolutely, but in relation to others, by attacking a doctrine that has an already established order, it is fitting to preserve the prescribed order. . . .

Book II, Exercise 3:
That It Is Foolishness to Distinguish Ten
Categories as Divisions of Reality[2]

Article 6: It Is Wrong to Exclude God from the Category of Substance

... Let us touch upon this difficulty concerning substance and consider whether God is rightly excluded from the category of substance, as is commonly done. First, if God does not have a place in this category, I do not see how he can be placed among the causes in the *Topics*, in the class of accidents by grammarians, in the series of movers by the physicists, and so forth for the rest. Where is there a better argument? If God is truly a cause and consequently deserves to be counted among the causes (and is even the prime cause), then he is truly a substance and must be counted among the substances (and in fact even as the prime substance; for there are obviously better reasons for calling God a prime substance than Socrates, Bucephalus, or this stone). Therefore what is a substance? Is it not commonly defined as a being existing through itself [*per se*]? This definition is sufficient, unless you deny that the opposite of substance, the accident, is defined adequately as a being that exists in another [*in alio*]. In truth, whenever we hear the word substance, we think of nothing other than a being that subsists or exists through itself. Likewise, does not the triply maximal God truly and properly subsist? Does he not truly exist through himself? What am I saying? Is it not God alone who truly subsists through himself, since he alone is independent, absolute, and persists immutably from all eternity? Indeed, all other things subsist only to the extent that everything is ruled by him – "with a powerful hand and a raised arm," as the Scriptures say – so that they could not subsist for even a moment, but would return to nothing or to the chaos of the ancients, if he withdrew his hand in the slightest. And who would not rightly be astonished that that which deserves the first and principal place in the category of substance, or of entities existing through themselves, would be rejected from such a class?

2. As we have said, Gassendi wrote, but did not publish book II of the *Exercises*; thus, the small sections translated here are not displayed as influential texts, but as fairly typical anti-Aristotelian arguments from the skeptical point of view, a perspective Gassendi will abandon, in any case, to pursue the reestablishment of Epicureanism.

You will say that substance in general and insofar as it is opposed to accident may be defined adequately as a being existing through itself but that the category of substance is defined by adding one more word: a finite being existing through itself. This is the consequence of the condition that whatever is to be ordered under a category is finite. Be that as it may, everything goes well if the definition of substance in general can be applied to God, for it constitutes the true category of substances, while what you fabricate is not the category but a part or fragment of it. For, when you say that substance is finite, you are merely taking away one of the species of substance. What reason requires you to attribute to the category of substance the condition of finitude, unless it is in particular to be able then to exclude God from the category of substance? But renounce the imposition of that condition, and immediately you include God in this category without any problem. Why do you prescribe such narrow limits to category? You should allow it instead to take the greatest possible amplitude. If not, you will be forced to leave a great many things outside the category, or someone else might with equal right impose conditions that, once accepted, would allow him to reject something or another. In the end such a category thus stripped bare would become an object of ridicule for most people. . . .

Article 10: The Essence of Quantity Is External Extension

To continue, let us now turn our attention to the celebrated difficulty concerning the essence of quantity. Our philosophers explain it in such a fashion that, although quantity is the most evident thing, nothing could be more obscure. Moreover, I must say that the mystery of the Eucharist, such as it is established by our faith, may add some difficulty in this matter. But if we are able to preserve perfectly this ineffable mystery and yet retain the clarity of the notion of quantity, why should we not adopt such a view? First then, since it is recognized that the essence of quantity consists in extension (the difficulty arises with respect to continuous and corporeal quantity), it seems to me that this extension is nothing other than the extension of things, which our eyes behold, which is usually measured, divided, and considered in terms of length, width, and depth, and which, conversely, has such a nature as to make extended things commensurate with place, such that each part corresponds with a part of place. I have said a lot; but if you wish let us abbreviate it: I say that the essence of quantity is nothing other than what is called external extension. In fact, I ask you, do we conceive anything other than this sort of extension when we hear the word quantity? Others commonly distinguish it from another extension, called internal, which constitutes the essence of quantity and of which our sort of extension is no more than a property of theirs. But still I ask, in the name of immortal God, of what kind is this internal extension? They say that it is the position of the parts outside of and in relation to one another; in this way, for example, in a person, the head is outside the neck, the neck outside the chest, the chest outside the arms, and so on. From these relative positions is thus derived as property the position of the parts outside one another in an order relative to place, which is what we call extension. But when these parts outside of one another are posited, either they are or they are not commensurate with the parts of place. In the first case, the two views are one, and that is our opinion. In the second case, there is really no extension or consequently any quantity. Here our opponents are not being evasive, but admit simply that the separation of these two extensions can be admitted in such a way that external extension is rejected and internal extension remains.

You might ask, Is it not possible for a body as large as a mountain, for example, to be stripped of its external magnitude such that the whole mountain is concentrated in a point, yet retains its internal extension and consequently its quantity? This is what they profess and defend as they would their gods and their hearths. In truth I ask whether, in good faith, you can conceive of some extension in a point – of some magnitude in something with no parts? You will say that there still remains the extension of the parts in an order relative to one another, but how can there be an order of parts where there is no up or down, nor absolutely any other difference of position? The parts, you will say, are ordered in relation to one another, but how are they not just jumbled together since they have been merged into such a narrow space? You will say that the top of the mountain is still outside the middle, and the middle outside the base, but how can this be when the top, middle, and base and absolutely all the other parts are together, and in an atom, and it is not possible to explain how you can say that the top is here rather than the base, the middle rather than the top? You can always have recourse to the thought that this comes from the fact that the mountain has no position of its parts in an order relative to place. But believe me, there cannot be an extension of parts in an order relative to one another, without the parts being so arranged that one of them occupies this part of place and another occupies that part, such that, if you removed that situational extension which is ordered relative to place, the parts could no longer retain any order among themselves, but necessarily would be thrown into complete confusion. You may seek other recourses as you wish – I will grant you the victory in this – but whatever prattle you may find, you will not, in my opinion, convince anyone who examines the question seriously that it is possible to find any magnitude, extension, or quantity in a point.

Book II, Exercise 4:
That Many Futile Things Have Been Propounded about Propositions

Article 4: The Propositions Called Eternal Truths

Now, then, they teach that this proposition, "Man is animal," for example, is endowed with eternal truth because the verb or copula "is" joins man to animal with such necessity that the bond cannot be broken even by divine power. As a consequence they also teach that this proposition "Man is an animal" has been true not only from the several thousand years before humans inhabited the world, but even from eternity itself. No doubt we can grant that Aristotle can be forgiven in this, since he believed the world was eternal and believed also that humans had existed from eternity; but, however, what legitimate excuse can there be for us, since we believe that the world and humans have existed for only about six thousand years and we profess that outside of God there is nothing at all that can exist from eternity? When no man existed, how could it truly be said that man is an animal? For, if no man existed, then there was no animal either, since for man to be an animal, there would have to be a man in the first place. Thus, if it were false to say "man is" and therefore false to say "he is an animal," it would not have been possible to speak truly by joining the two into "man is an animal." . . . In fact, you cannot say that man is something unless you assume that there is a man; and every time you use the verb "is" to proclaim that an attribute is suitable for a subject, it is not possible at the same time not to indicate a present suitability, and hence an existence. And, of course, if you do not suppose and conceive the subject to exist, what can you say that is to be attributed to it in reality? You say that the attribute is connected to it and is suitable for it, but how can something that is nothing be connected to or suitable for a subject? I grant that "is" is the copula, but how can it connect the terms [*extrema*] if they do

not exist? But as long as there is nothing other than the sign or mark
of the copula – when in virtue of its own meaning it is the sign of the
presence of something – how could it signify the nonpresence or non-
existence of something? . . .

TEN

Jean de Silhon, *The Two Truths* and *The Immortality of the Soul*

[*Les deux vérités*, 1626; *L'immortalité de l'âme*, 1634]

Introduction

Jean de Silhon (1596–1667), a French statesman and moralist, was a friend of Descartes and of Guez de Balzac (an essayist and another of Descartes' friends). There are several references to de Silhon in Descartes' letters, Descartes asking for news of him, and there is evidence of actual correspondence between the two, although their letters do not seem to have survived, except perhaps the letter to an unknown correspondent surmised to have been de Silhon.[1] Along with their friendship, Descartes and de Silhon shared an antiskeptical apologetic program. In his treatise, *The Two Truths* (1626), de Silhon combats skepticism by attempting to establish that God exists and that our souls are immortal. He revisits some of these themes in his *Immortality of the Soul* (1634). There he maintains that Christianity is in conformity with the natural light of our understanding. He also maintains, three years before Descartes' *Discourse*, that each person possesses a certain knowledge of which it is impossible that a person capable of reflection and reason can doubt and not be certain: every person can know his or her existence and being.[2]

[RA]

Roger Ariew gratefully acknowledges the invaluable work of Marjorie Grene, who cotranslated the extracts from de Silhon.

1. AT I 352–353.
2. For more on de Silhon and his apologetic program, see R. Popkin, *The History of Scepticism from Erasmus to Spinoza*, chap. 8.

THE TWO TRUTHS, ONE OF GOD AND HIS PROVIDENCE, THE OTHER OF THE IMMORTALITY OF THE SOUL

First Treatise

Introduction to the Subject

... Since we are in a century where there are such wretched minds, whom the truth frightens, and who, to protect themselves from the alarms of conscience, try to destroy the belief in the immortality of the soul – so natural, so universally received, so solidly demonstrated – and then the belief in providence, and consequently in the existence of a divinity, it is important that I make you grasp vividly its foundations and the weakness of the contrary opinion.

First Discourse

That, in Order to Prove the Immortality of the Soul,
It Is Necessary to Prove That God Exists, and the
Demonstrations of This Truth

In order to establish the belief in the immortality of the human soul, I climb, Agathon, right up to its source, and the cause of its duration. For either the human soul takes its being from itself, and without dependence on any cause that has communicated its being to it, so that there is nothing that could rob it of its being – which we shall show in what follows to be false – or else its being depends on the generosity and benevolence of some principle, which, since it has granted its being out of pure kindness and goodwill, can also conserve its being for it for as long as it likes, in other words, without end. (Note that a more powerful force is not required to conserve something in its being than to communicate being to it; we shall explain this later and show it to be very true.) But this source, this cause, and this free and unfettered principle of the being and of the duration of the human soul is what we call God. Hence we must see if by the light of nature we can penetrate this plan of his, and if in the order and disposition of the universe and its parts, he has left sufficient impressions and marks to persuade us of it. But since there are minds so far advanced in impiety that, in order not to acknowledge a providence responsible for this order, they altogether deny a Divinity to which it is attached, let us see if we have something to content them with, something to demonstrate the contrary to them.

First, if they want to take refuge in an opinion received even by some Christians, *that there is knowledge of nothing, and that it is permitted to doubt everything*, and consequently that they can exempt themselves without temerity from the belief that God exists, I beg them to consider that this question is no trifle; that one cannot maintain the negative without evidence and without arguments that demonstrate it; and that without this evidence, those who maintain it make themselves guilty of divine lèse majesté against the great lord, if God indeed exists. So much the more so, since by this freedom of opinion they deprive him of the esteem, the love, and the honor that are owed him. It is just as if a stranger who, without being properly informed about it, should announce in a state that there was no king, and that the yoke of obedience and the title of sovereignty were imaginary things, would be punished as guilty of lèse majesté and as a disturber of the public peace, if there were a king. So – to remain with the subject we are treating in terms of doubt, according to the maxim *that there is knowledge of nothing* – since the truth can occur as well in the affirmative as in the negative, as a maxim of prudence we should embrace the affirmative and adhere to its consequences. That is to say, we should serve and honor that divinity we know only by conjectures and probable arguments just as religiously, and observe the laws that we assume it has established for us just as faithfully, as if we had an indubitable insight into it. Here indifference is altogether ruinous. So the first defense is removed.

And to say a word in passing of that maxim, *that there is knowledge of nothing*, I say that among Christians it is full of temerity and among philosophers, of ignorance and contradiction. As to the former, the Holy Scripture teaches us, even on our subject, that visible things can guide us to the knowledge of invisibles, even of God himself and his eternal power, and woe to the pagans for the fact that, knowing God, they did not glorify him as God. As to the latter, one can argue against them that there are propositions and maxims clothed in so much clarity and carrying in themselves so much evidence, that as soon as they are conceived of, they carry conviction. It is impossible for there to be an understanding capable of rejecting them; that is what experience shows us. These are *that everything is or is not, that everything there is takes its being from itself or another, that the whole is greater than its parts, and so on.* And if we want to take the word "knowledge" [*science*] strictly, experience shows us as well, if we judge of it without emotion, that we can draw evident and certain conclusions from naturally known premises, or from their consequences. But to vanquish our adversaries with their own weapons: if they know that there is no knowledge, they entangle themselves and furnish us a proof of what we claim, namely, this knowledge that there is no knowledge; if they do not know it, why do they affirm it? For in order to construct Montaigne's chain and linkage of doubts, one has to accomplish the contrary of his intention; wishing to prove that there is no knowledge in order to beat down the vanity it often inspires in us, he makes our understandings capable of an infinite progression of acts.

Second, to go directly forward, I say that our belief is so well suited to the natural light of our understandings, that without any repugnance and without any proof at all, if they are not in a disturbed state, they consent to it. But nature would not have imprinted in them this great inclination and this very lively disposition, if it were not genuine. For since truth is their object, after the search they labor at unceasingly, and on the possession of which they feed as on their proper nourishment, they have no purely natural movements toward the false. This can be confirmed by the example of other faculties that nature trains and pushes toward their fitting objects, while giving them an aversion to the contrary of those objects. This is confirmed once more by a perfectly ordinary experience, that is, that when we find ourselves surrounded by a certain danger, without discourse or previous deliberation, but only through a momentum and instinct of nature, we have recourse to God and implore his assistance.

In the third place, there has never been a time, or any nation whatsoever, however barbarous and uncivilized it was, where men have not recognized some divinity, and which has not had temples, altars, priests, sacrifices, prayers and invocations, and other marks of religion. Let them say, if they like, that the assent of all the peoples and all the nations of the world is not a strong presumption of the truth of our belief, that the number of fools is infinite, that there is nothing so easy to dupe as the common people, that the principal motive for belief in religion is that it is not understood. On what illusions have we not in fact fed in the past in the name of religion? How many Gods have we not forged for it? How many absurdities and extravagances have we not cultivated about their nature? Let us reply, Agathon, that the consent of all the ages, and of all the nations, entails the conclusion that this belief in general, namely, *that there is a divinity*, is, as it were, born with the light of nature, and consequently genuine, that the errors that have been in

fashion in the world concern particular subjects to whom divinity has
falsely been attributed, that people did correctly believe in general that
there is divinity; also if religions had not been universally received and
embraced through all the ages, it would be possible to notice more or
less both their birth and the occasions that gave rise to them.

Add to that, that neither the ambition nor the vanity of men, nor the
artifices of the devil, could have spread them with such speed and ease
throughout the world, if they had not been a result of the general, natural, and true belief in a divinity. For you would say that idolatry was a
deluge that, in almost no time, nearly flooded the whole earth; but since
Jesus Christ by his coming has dried the waters, the devil has changed
his weapons, and instead of an infinity of Gods that he had introduced
into the world in a short time, in sixteen centuries he has not been able
to make half the world, not a kingdom, not a city, not a family, entirely
susceptible to the other extreme, *that there is no God*. And this proceeds
from the contradiction and repugnance to that belief we have naturally
imprinted in us, which is an indubitable sign that the belief is false. He
has met only some desperate minds, who, having attained within themselves as many tormentors and furies as sins, have found no other means
for giving some relief to their pain than to imagine that he whose justice
they so vividly dreaded was only a phantom and a pure figment of imagination.

In the fourth place, the most famous persons who have ever existed
in the world have held this belief. Would it be possible that so many
philosophers, so many legislators, so many magistrates, whose knowledge, wisdom, and virtue were admitted by many, should be mistaken
in such an important matter, and that only some particular persons who
were known only by their vices and by the novelty of their opinion
should alone have penetrated to the truth? Certainly the authority of
those great men is a reproach to the temerity of those persons and must
cast into their souls the mistrust of their opinion.

I go further and say that if there were no God it would be impossible
that there should be one, inasmuch as, since all that is in God is necessary, whatever is not there is impossible. For if a God who is not should
be brought into being, it would have to be by the power of what is
already. But since nothing can communicate any perfection that it does
not possess, and since nothing that is is God, what already is would also
be unable to produce a God. Again, would it be still possible that not
only all the nations but again the wisest, the most virtuous, and the most
learned men in the world should have believed in and worshiped some-

thing impossible? That they would have ordered such atrocious torments and sufferings against acts of sacrilege and blasphemy? That they
would have held for the most abominable of men those who offended
the majesty of what cannot be? That so profound an error was the cause
of all the virtues that adorn the world, the pivot on which the happiness
and repose of all human society turns? All that is unimaginable.

In the fifth place, this law that nature has etched in our soul, which
dictates the good that we must follow and the evil that we must avoid –
these Gehennas and secret torments, these pleasures and agreeable sat-
isfactions that it gives us by their transgression or observation – makes
us presume with reason that there is outside ourselves some legislator
and author of our being who has in his hand the punishment and the
recompense for our actions, whom we call God. Thus till now, Agathon,
we have great advantages in favor of our belief, and more than reasonable conjectures and probabilities to oblige us to consent to it. Let us
pass to decisive proofs that come to an evident conclusion.

In the sixth place, since there are things that are, which have being,
it follows necessarily that there always had been some, inasmuch as if
there had ever been an instant when there was nothing, then nothing
of what is would be; and it would be impossible that there ever was
anything, for where would that which is have come, when there was
nothing – nothing is produced of itself and there was nothing to produce
it. Thus, since there is something, there is an evident necessity that there
has always been something. But to build an infinite ladder of effects and
causes, and to climb from one to the other, without ever finding the
end: that is to allow the progression to the infinite that all philosophy
rejects, and to feed on an imagination that no mind could digest. How
much more appropriate is it to recognize an eternal, necessary, original,
and fundamental cause of all the other causes, which we call God.

In the seventh place, here is an argument clearer than the Sun. If
there are things in nature that are the effects of some cause (philosophers
call them contingent), there must be something that is of itself, and
consequently necessary, independent, and eternal. But there are a number of these contingent things: first, those that have been and are no
more. For if these had their being from themselves, how would they
have lost it? Who would have robbed them of it? Of those that are, we
know clearly, and we will show in the following discourses, that there
are several whose being does not depend upon themselves. Let us
therefore take in general all contingent things, dependent on another,
and put them in a group, without excepting any (for, indeed, he who

says all excepts none). It must be that beyond all these there is some one thing that is their principle, root, and cause. These correlatives entail one another; and since the latter does not belong to the group of those which are contingent, dependent, and effects, it is in consequence necessary, independent, and only cause, and this is what we call God. I am distressed, Agathon, that I do not have in hand more delicate terms in which to present to you these two arguments, for they have a marvelous force, and a powerful clarity to convince the atheists. I have only tried to make myself intelligible.

It may happen, Agathon, that you will encounter sick and doddering minds that will assault your ears with this chimera: that we must be content with the order under which we see the world turning, that Pierre was begotten by Guillaume, Guillaume by Gautier, Gautier by Garguille, and so on without end, always ascending, and that to search for anything else beyond that order is to produce mental convolutions at will. Answer them that this is the subject of the dispute, that it is not everything to advance a proposition. It is necessary to have something to prove it if it is not known in itself, as that one is not. Answer that they should show you on what basis and by what argument they are building that ladder without end, and that order without goal. Their whole argument is that it may be so. We must respond to them that the contrary is also possible, and that there could have been a first man, a first horse, a first lion, and so on – indeed, that this opinion is sweeter and more acceptable, that our minds find a footing there to rest on. On the contrary, they languish, falter, and lose their way in following their retreating order without end. The consent of the philosophers, the tradition of nations, the authority of history, everything favors our opinion. Thus they are very much mistaken in wanting to make their vision prevail, if they do not have some clear and powerful argument to convince us.

Further, how will they save this order without end for the heavens and for the elements? Can they say that the heavens were engendered by other heavens, and those by others, and so on to infinity, and the same for the elements? If they want to say that these are eternal and necessary bodies, independent in their being of every principle, we will show the contrary with conclusive evidence in the following discourses. And thus if there were only the heavens and the elements that did not receive their being from themselves, it must necessarily be the case that beyond them there is some principle that has communicated it to them, which, being of itself, is consequently necessary, eternal, independent, and indefeasible – what we call God. Further, how will they exempt from dependence on the principle of the heavens and the elements the things that achieve success either through the mixture of the latter or the influence of the former?

I have seen people so deeply hampered and entangled by this thought of an eternal succession, that they wanted without consideration of anything else to find God in it; and not finding him there, to persist in believing that he could not be demonstrated: a delusion similar to that of someone who would take the road to Saint Denis in order to get from Paris to Orleans, and who would not want to follow any other route; and, when he could not get there by that route, would maintain that there is no road that leads from Paris to Orleans. So let these people not tire their minds with that endless chain; but let them turn aside to this other consideration, that whatever has been and is no more, of whatever number, and however long it lasts did not take its being from itself, but had received it. This proposition has no exception. For if there were something that had its being of itself, it would still have it and could never have lost it. Hence, since it has lost it, it had received it. It must necessarily be the case that beyond everything that has received, there is the principle that has given; the one cannot be without the other. And that principle, not being among all those things that have received their being, consequently has it of itself. The more so since it is a thing naturally known, that all that has being either has it from itself or has received it from another. We call that being that is of itself God.

Again, it will be objected, as has happened to me, that in truth all individuals may be corruptible, but the species are incorruptible, eternal, and necessary. Answer them, first, that they do not know what they want to say. In the second place, tell them that it does not prevent the preceding demonstration from retaining its force and its clarity (otherwise it would not be a demonstration), inasmuch as, all individuals being corruptible and there being no one that has not received its being, it remains that beyond them is the principle that has communicated it, which principle we call God.

Moreover, in fact, the species is nothing but individuals, and there are and can be in nature only particular things outside the operation of the intellect; and thus, there being no individual that has incorruptible, of itself, and necessary being, how can one attribute this perfection to the species? If all the captains and soldiers of a regiment came to be massacred, without excepting a single one of them, could one not say, strictly speaking, that the whole regiment had been massacred? And if

somebody said that in truth all the captains and soldiers had been massacred, but that the regiment was still standing, would he not deserve
being hissed at? For suppose the word "species" is taken for a universal
nature that our intellect abstracts from several individuals through a
recognition and comparison that it makes of the first and radical perfections in accordance with which they are similar to one another and
different from others. There is nothing in the world so frail and so
perishable as that nature, which in fact does not exist and subsists only
through the operation of the intellect, and which ceases to be when the
intellect stops operating. Finally, I want to warn you, if you enter into
dispute with these desperate people and seekers of authority who are
making so much noise at the court, do not accept any proposition from
them on credit and without proof and require them, as it is quite reasonable to do, to reply categorically to your propositions, assuring yourself that in this way you will put them straight, however far astray they
may be.

In addition, this sovereign principle has appeared in the course of the
past centuries through prodigious effects, surpassing nature, and has
shown its power, and the empire that it had over all other things. But
that has to do with faith, and, God willing, we will write a separate
treatise on that.

Ninth Discourse

Creation, Conservation, and Concurrence

We are all (Agathon) naturally taken with the desire to know, just as we
all naturally aspire to our perfection. Truth is the perfection of our
understanding, and not only its own proper perfection, which consists
in the conformity of its knowledge to the object it embraces, but also
that of the object itself: its perfection is a living light and an animated
image, in a manner of speaking, which formally embellishes it and fills
it with beauty; and in such a way that knowledge of ugliness is beautiful
in it, like a well-drawn portrait of a Moor. The truth of the object, which
is inseparable from its essence, heightens that of the intellect, and transmits to it some of its perfection. That is why in the human intellect,
whose power is limited, there must be order and moderation in the
search for objects that it desires to know. This passion was reprehensible
in Empedocles and in the elder Pliny; it caused their death and sacrificed
them to the flames of the volcano (*Montgibel*), both victims of curiosity.

It was pardonable in Anaxander, who was so ravished by the beauty of the Sun, that he said he would not have been in the least concerned about being burned by its heat, if only he could contemplate its face for some time and at will. It cannot be too highly praised in Saint Augustine, who said there was no torment that would not be desirable, in order to see the divine essence clearly for one hour. That object should be the everyday support of our minds and we should burn unceasingly with a holy curiosity to know its perfections. Besides the fact that there is nothing comparable with that knowledge, it would make grow in us the love and recognition that we owe it. That is why I have desired to explain to you, beyond what has been touched on so far, three further marks of the aforesaid perfections, and three great subjects of obligation to men (the knowledge of which is also necessary for my plan), to wit, creation, conservation, and concurrence in the operation of secondary causes.

Creation can be taken either actively or passively (the same judgment is to be made about conservation and concurrence). Actively, it is simply a cause or power insofar as by its force something is brought into being from nothing for the first time, that is, without the concurrence of any matter or subject from whose power it is extracted. Passively, it is simply the effect, insofar as it is brought into being from nothing in virtue of its cause. To seek any other dependence or cement that binds the effect to its cause, and the conclusion to its premise, would be unnecessary, since they hold together sufficiently and are fastened together, the one by the exercise of its power, and the other by the being that it receives from it. This kind of action is so strange that it astonishes our intellects, and we could not imagine for ourselves a more explicit mark of an infinite and all-powerful force. In fact (Agathon), it is marvelous that there is an intelligence accompanied by such fecundity that it can bring to light all that it understands to be possible, and that in God power has no measure other than his idea and his conception. In this the excellence of the divine conception surpasses all other thought. For the angels and we can well conceive of the being of several things, but it is not the case that this knowledge has the power to give them being. . . .

Now that we have explained the nature of creation, it is easy to recognize that of conservation, since they are measured by the same criterion, and there is no difference, either for the cause, or for the effect, except insofar as creation concerns the first moment in which something has being – I am referring to the time that it receives it, for one and the same thing could be created several times – and conservation supposes this first moment; in such a way that it is only the consequence and continuation of creation, which occurs by the same force and with the same effect. These considerations make up the whole difference. Saint Paul expressed this simply in the first chapter of the Epistle to the Hebrews, when in speaking of the son of God he said that he carries all things by the word of his power. One can only carry what is already in nature.

Reason persuades us that God is also indeed the author of the conservation of all other things, as well as of their creation; for since their being is not necessary, and depends only on the divine will and power, it must be the case that the same will supports it, in order that it subsist and persevere, and that to the extent that will stopped sustaining it, it would be necessary that it lapse into its original nothingness: no less and no more than if you held a stone in your hand, as soon as you let go it would fall to earth. Since, then, conservation is the continuation of creation, it must be judged in the same way, and what God draws purely out of nothing, and without the concurrence of any subject, he also conserves, without the concurrence of any subject. He first created the angels and prime matter; he creates rational souls in matter; he has created the hypostatic union of human nature to the divine word, without there being in the said nature any disposition that could invite him to this. He creates the union of the human soul with the body, provided that the required tendencies are already there. A number of people, considering the excellence of the state of grace, believe that it cannot originate through the power of the soul, but is created there. There are accidents in the holy sacrament that God conserves without a subject, and creates there, in order to veil this great mystery: all accidents and material forms are drawn from the power of the subject, and cannot properly be called "created."

Creatures do not only take their being solely from divine generosity, but he has also provided them with powers and faculties proper for action, either in themselves or outside, which faculties would remain paralyzed and without motion, if God did not fortify them by his concurrence, something he never denies when it is needed by secondary causes. Of secondary causes, some are *natural*, that is, they act without knowledge and without freedom, tending by necessity to what they are born to, provided the necessary conditions for action are not lacking, those of subject, reasonable distance, and other circumstances. The others are free, and operate by choice, although not always; for divine providence – seeing natural causes ready and on the point of acting, and foreseeing, by an incomprehensible subtlety on what side the choice of free beings will fall – provides that the one and the other be accompanied by its help, joins and allies itself to them, to form the complete principle of action.

In proof of this truth, the light of nature furnishes us this argument: between several effects of the same kind that proceed successively from the same cause, [why] is one pushed rather than the other? What is there in the effect or what is there in the cause to establish this order? Why, for example, when the same fire kindles the same matter three or four times in a row, had the form that was extracted the second time not departed the first time? When the fire acted, was it not just as able to make the second form emerge? And was not the matter just as rightly disposed to receive it? One can say the same for its dispositions: why when being alike in species and imprinted by the same agent, have not the second gained first rank? Is there something in the first form that determines it and nails it down to the first dispositions, and the second to the second? It seems not, insofar as the dispositions of the first can serve as introduction to the second, as when one extinguishes a torch and lights it again now and then. And so it is for natural causes.

For free causes, we know that one and the same will is going to form a hundred similar desires, one after the other, toward the same object that is represented to it, with the same qualities and the same circumstances, without any variation. Certainly there is nothing in itself or in the object that determines it rather to the first act than to the second, and to the third, or to others. Suppose one says it has the freedom to determine itself. I reply that its freedom does not consist at all in the choice of the order it takes to produce several similar acts, one rather than the other; but rather in the power it has to act or not to act toward one and the same object, or to approach it through two different acts, such as loving or hating. But the choice of several similar acts belongs to the first and sovereign cause, which never lacks for want of secondary causes. But this determination is made by his concurrence. Again, they will say that since causes are born to act, and since action tends to something singular, they need no other determination but that which follows the nature of action.

It is true that the end of action is something particular, but among several similar particulars, it is always necessary that one passes before another; as a man will set the price of some merchandise, of a horse, for example, and the seller will present him with several to choose from, so that the price is set for one only, and yet it is not decided which one, but that depends on the will of the buyer. So in the same way the order that creatures' actions follow belongs to God.

But suppose it is objected once again that this doctrine is true for what concerns natural causes, but for free causes it is entirely appropriate that they be the complete principle of their actions; otherwise it would be necessary to make God guilty of all the evils of men and angels, since he contributes more than they to the actions from which mischief issues. It must be said in reply that it is all very well to say that the mischief of sin springs from the determination of the creature, as I have depicted it already, to the extent that it does what it should not do, violating both the promptings of reason and the commandments of God. But this disorder cannot take place by the divine determination, since God as first and general cause, assisting the force of secondary causes, does nothing he should not do. Indeed, he evinces the traits of an infinite providence and goodness. The saying of Saint John speaking of the Word accords very well with this: *all has been done by him and without him nothing has been done.*

SECOND TRUTH: THE IMMORTALITY OF THE HUMAN SOUL

First Discourse

In Which Is Shown the True Foundation by Which We Know That the Soul of Beasts Is Mortal and That of Men Immortal

It is with opinions as with buildings: they could not subsist if we did not give them a solid footing and foundation. And as water takes on the quality of the surface mines through which it passes, conclusions always retain the conditions of the principles of which they are woven, and the least stain spreads in time over them, so that it is relevant to know their nature perfectly, and not to assume them well established, and to build on them with proportion and dexterity. Otherwise they who imagine they know something are deluding themselves. So let us probe a little, Agathon, into the foundations of the belief in the immortality of the human soul, and let us see if they are complete and massive, or if this is indeed an artifact of policy to keep the peoples in check through fear of the pains of an afterlife and through the hope of recompense.

The principal argument commonly alleged is that the human soul is immortal insofar as it is immaterial and spiritual. This argument, thus bluntly stated, will not satisfy every one. For in the first place there are few who understand the difference there is between what is *material and immaterial,* or indeed *between being extracted from matter or being spread out in it by the path of creation.*

In the second place, it has not become manifest that what is immaterial is incorruptible and that what is material is corruptible. Indeed, taken in general and without any other determination the two propositions are false and the two considerations of *materiality* and *immateriality,* taken universally, are not the root of corruption and of immortality: for prime matter by the consent of all philosophers is incorruptible, and of the forms that have emerged from its potentiality, some are liable to perish, like those of mixtures, while others are joined to it by an indissoluble bond, like those of the heavens, and of the elements according to their totality, even though one can always remove some part of them. As to immaterial forms, it is an act of faith among true Christians that the state of grace is often extinguished in the soul of sinners, and in others, at least the principal state remains eternally, as in the blessed, and the natural conditions of our soul are often effaced and lost either through a long cessation of the acts that supported them or by contrary impressions.

In the third place, there are several doctors who hold that it is not a determination of faith that angels are not corporeal substances, and nevertheless it is a determination of faith that they are immortal substances. Thus it is false generally speaking that *materiality* is the root of corruption, and immateriality of immortality, and consequently (Agathon) you see that one needs to go further before asserting that proposition and to give it other supports.

Now the fundamental reason why the human soul is immortal is that since God has given it being out of his pure generosity, he also wants to conserve it eternally. This argument is in itself so acceptable and enchants with such clarity all intellects that the most savage and stupid are constrained to assent to it, provided it is demonstrated to them that it is so. For since God has an infinite and necessary being that can receive neither increase nor diminution of its power, it is no more trouble to him to conserve something a hundred years, a thousand years, indeed according to the whole extent of his duration, which is eternal, than to draw the being it has out of nothing. Conservation is nothing but continued creation, as has been said in the preceding treatise. And it is evident that the same cause provided at all points with the same force and power of action, and without any hindrance, is capable of always producing the same effect. Indeed, all things persist in such a way in their being, by the conservative concurrence of God, that they could not fall from it except by the removal of that concurrence. And although he allows several causes auxiliary to his power in the production of various effects, and the influence of the same causes always accompanies his own in the conservation of some of them, as with light and the so-called intentional species, since it costs him no more to supplement the deficiency of the secondary cause than it cost him to communicate to it the power of producing and conserving (I except vital operations, which essentially include the principle of life, since God is not able to supplement this, given that he cannot make a thing be without its essence, and he cannot enter into the constitution of any other essence), he could well make this principle of life apply always to the production of his act.

Thus, it is clear that nothing can have being without the will of God, and without his will nothing can lose it. This is what he himself has taught us, when, to rally the courage of his apostles and of all the faithful, and to show them how many times the effort of all created powers was vain and useless, he said that all the hairs on their heads were counted and that not a single one falls without the will of his Father who is in heaven.

To this it may be replied that it is undeniable that God has the power to conserve human souls eternally, but on what ground does it appear to us that he has this intention? I say, by the light of nature, since he does nothing beyond himself except with freedom. Here, Agathon, is the keystone of the vault, and the cornerstone of the edifice. We must show that he has left marks so clear, and traces so visible of his intent in nature, that they are more than sufficient to oblige us to live in conformity with that belief. To do this, we must first demand of those with the contrary opinion that they show us by the light of nature that human souls are mortal. For, strictly speaking, it is not up to us to produce the warrants of our belief. We are always in possession of it. It began with the birth of the human race; if not, let them show us the beginning and the occasion of this usurpation. All the sects of philosophers except that of Epicurus conspire with us; all organizations are maintained on it; all the nations of the earth have embraced it, and feel all the better for it. In short, it is a fountain of happiness that irrigates the whole human race. Why do they come and trouble us? Why do they come and meddle with our rights? Let them show us why.

If it is that their opinion smooths for them the path of pleasure to which they are totally devoted, if it fills up the precipices, if it tears off the thorns, if it edges the path with carnations and strews it with roses, if it makes of it a paradise and a felicity, so be it, let them follow it, and let it make them happy, so long as they leave us the enjoyment of what belongs to us. But no (Agathon), it is our opinion that opens those precipices, that makes those thorns grow, that plucks those carnations and those roses, through the pangs of conscience, through inner disturbances, through the dread and apprehension of the other life. That is why they want to extinguish it entirely, miserable in that they do not know that it is virtue alone, legitimate daughter of our belief, that dispenses pure and genuine delights, that its comforts have no alloy or consequence of repentance like those of the body, that they are tempered of a constant and indefeasible satisfaction and consequently are in accordance with nature. And this is a sign that the opinion that flows from them is so also, and therefore true; as, on the contrary, nature testifies through the repentance and the disavowal that it forms of them, that the others are its enemies, and hence the belief that gives rise to them is false.

Let us ask them, therefore, since it is up to them to chase us away, that they show by the clear and indubitable light of nature, that God has the purpose of relinquishing his influence in conserving human souls as soon as they are separated from the body. Do they want to say that it is clear enough that human souls are of the same condition as those of beasts, which are mortal, and that the Bible itself, which we hold for the infallible rule of our belief, assures it by these words: who knows whether the death of man and beast is not similar. If we accepted their denial that the souls of beasts are mortal, perhaps we would be rendering them foolish and putting them in the position of demanding some courtesy from us; in fact, the same difficulty arises again, for since God could conserve the soul of beasts eternally, let them make us see by the light of nature that he does not wish to do so.

Nevertheless (Agathon) let us do them the remaining courtesy, as we have a perfect right to do, and teach them the reason by which we recognize by the light of nature, that the separation of the souls of beasts from their bodies is their annihilation, and in imitation of the good king of the Spartans who pierced his enemies with the same arrows that he

pulled from his own body, let us draw from the same foundation that
God conserves human souls after this separation. Here it is. God does
not want anything in nature to be useless. But since this is the effect of
an excellent wisdom, he has prescribed ends to all things, for which they
are, such that when they become quite incompetent and unable to arrive
at those ends, he casts them out of nature and stops conserving them.
And, on the contrary, the sweetness of his providence is such that as
long as they are in a condition to attain the end for which they have
received their being, he permits them to enjoy it, and he maintains his
conservative concurrence. This is a truth that experience makes so well
known to us that it cannot be called into doubt.

The total and complete immediate aim of the soul of beasts consists
in vegetative as well as sensitive operations, including movement (the
ultimate end cannot be attained if the immediate end is destroyed). It is
only for that and can do nothing but that. To realize these operations,
it is necessarily dependent on the assistance of organs. As long as these
organs are complete and as long as their constitution is sustained, God
conserves it, and it continues to inform its subject, as long as it is in
condition to perform that for which it has received its being, which is
to be nourished, to grow, to see, to hear, to walk, and so on. As soon
as the organs come to be totally ruined or so markedly damaged that
they can no longer serve for those operations, God stops conserving this
soul, and it is annihilated. For to what purpose should one maintain a
useless thing in nature? By the same argument, as soon as a soul soils
itself with mortal sin, the state of supernatural charity withers away
(since according to the order God has laid down, it cannot reside in the
same subject as mortal sin). For what would be the use of conserving it
separately, since it would be of no use, being unable to serve for the
production of supernatural acts of life, which must proceed essentially
and with all necessity from the principle of life that is the soul. Thus, if
the forms of the heavens could be separated from the matter that they
inform, they would doubtless be annihilated. And, on the contrary, as
long as there is nothing that can dissolve the harmony and destroy the
dispositions that bring them to their substrate for ends that God knows,
we assume that God will conserve them eternally.

It is true that the qualities of the elements and of mixtures could act
in separation from their subject, as the experience of the holy sacrament
of the altar shows us. But they do not exist strictly for the sake of acting,
and to produce similar qualities, but rather to produce them in the service of the form that is to follow, and to prepare matter and render it

capable of receiving form, so that this disorder would [not] result: in driving out the dispositions of the form already in the matter, which maintain it there, in order to substitute new forms, this first form would be lost, and would have no agent to imprint on it the one for whose reception the matter was being prepared, which would consequently remain deprived of all form. Thus, it is more fitting that accidents be extinguished when they are separated from their subject, since they cannot serve the purpose for which they exist, that is, the introduction and conservation of the forms for which they are appropriate.

Let us now return to the human soul. If it exists only to perform functions that it cannot carry out without the assistance of the body and its organs, such as seeing, smelling, imagining, moving, and the like, and if the purpose of its being consists in the use of corporeal faculties, truly it must be admitted that once the constitution of the body and its organs is destroyed in such a way that the aforesaid operations cannot be carried out at all, then in abandoning the body it is annihilated just the same as that of beasts. For what use would it be in nature? But if it has in itself and without any dependence a power and force of acting, and much more nobly and excellently than it operates with the organs, it must then also be admitted that, since God conserves it in the body as long as it can produce lower operations similar in a way to those of beasts, he will conserve it eternally outside the body, if it can produce operations that are higher and more worthy of its condition. The following considerations will give rise to clear and violent presumptions that it has this force of acting in itself and in its simple substance and without the interference of organs – indeed, that its simple essence is the principle of several fine and excellent operations.

Second Discourse

In Which It Is Shown That the Human Soul Can Dispense with the Assistance of Organs for Its More Elevated Operations

I do not want in the least, Agathon, to combat here the error of those who believe that the soul in general is nothing but an excellent equilibrium and a perfect harmony of the qualities of a composite. For as to what concerns the human soul, experience shows us in several cases that when some great illness has sullied the good condition of the body and when its constitution is so corrupted that the soul is ready to abandon it, like a building all in ruins, never has that soul shed such bright beams of wisdom, or conceived of more solid discourse, or evidenced so clear a knowledge of present things, or so much foresight about things to come as on that occasion; this is a sign that it does not consist in that equilibrium, and a clear enough proof that its noblest operations do not depend in any way on the organs of the body.

In the second place, we have shown already, that there are substances that act and live in separation from the body, and pure of its admixture. It is also plain that there are purely organic forms drowned in the mass whose operation is limited by purely corporeal objects, and are stimulated only by what is pleasant or disagreeable to the senses. According to the order of the universe there had to be a medium to bring together these two extremes, and an essence that would share the conditions of the one and the other to tie them together. As the Lateran Council says, that essence is man, who resembles the angels according to the substance of the soul and according to his higher faculties, but according to the body and the lowly operations of the soul is similar to beasts. In accord with all of them together, one can rightly call him, as the Platonists do, the prayer [*Orison*] of the universe and the epitome of its perfections.

Further, the alliance is much more natural and much closer between men and angels than between men and beasts. Men converse with angels, both good and bad, and demand their help, counsel, and assistance; a man would be very stupid if he related his affairs to his horse or his dog.

Add to that, that the capacity to know that is in human souls is not more limited than that of angels, and both extend generally to every sort of object. But angels have in themselves and in their proper substance the principle of their operations, and therefore we can justifiably presume the same of our souls in what concerns their superior portion. Aristotle also recognized that the great capacity for understanding every sort of truth that is in intelligences, as he calls them, proceeds from the fact that they are simple forms, elevated above matter, and independent of it. By the same argument, since the force of our souls is equal as to the extent of its objects, even though it is unequal in the perfection of its acts, we can judge them to be independent of matter for similar operations.

In the fourth place, the finest operations of our minds are directed to purely spiritual objects, which are beyond what belongs to the senses, and from which neither the body nor its organs reap any advantage or any displeasure. How then do we want them to contribute to those operations, and claim that souls are not their only principle? For every power that acts on some object is necessarily altered by that operation, whether that alteration tends to its perfection or to its harm. Thus our vision is pleased and becomes lively at the sight of bright and greening colors and is offended by those that are too brilliant. Thus the excellence of a piece of music charms our ear and bathes it in pleasure, and on the contrary the harshness of a voice or the discordance of several voices grates on it. Thus the polish and soft evenness of a body tickles our touch and in contrast its unevenness and sharpness wounds it.

But I ask what is gained for the senses and the organs from the investigation that our soul conducts into spiritual substances, their nature and perfections, or the nature of other things, causes, effects, signs, comparisons, correspondences, proportions, and conclusions and consequences that it draws from them: in short, from all discourse and reasoning? What good or what evil results for the body from an error embraced or a truth discovered? It is only the soul alone that is stained by error and that is beautified by the knowledge of truth; it alone feels its attractions and is impassioned by it, and consequently it alone is the principle of the aforesaid operations. Indeed, far from its being the case that the senses and the organs are of some use here, on the contrary they often trouble its pursuits and throw clouds before it.

I go further and say that not only are the finest operations of our souls performed without the presence of the organs and the senses; they are contrary to them. An object will present itself to our imagination full of charms and sensuous appeals, the imagination judges it to be the good of the body, the appetite is stimulated by it and burns to possess it. The intellect, on the contrary, reproves and sets aside this judgment of the imagination, and the will abundantly rejects those bodily delights as enemies of its good. Similarly, it encounters objects all surrounded by difficulties and bristling with spines for the body; the imagination is astonished, the sensitive appetite passes them by; and nevertheless the intellect discovers in them a certain spiritual beauty, which so gently entices the will that it resolves to obtain possession of them across the sufferings and discomforts of the body. Would it not then be an unbearable blindness to say that the organs and the senses contribute to the rich and divine operations of the soul, and hence it has their principle in itself? From this contradiction and repugnance of reason and the senses spring the precious fruits of the virtues, of which our religion furnishes us with admirable examples.

To give more clarity to the foregoing, you will notice, Agathon, that while a bodily faculty can be extended only to purely corporeal objects, it does not follow from that, as some people think, that the object of an immaterial power must not include anything but the immaterial in the whole of its extension, but it is enough that it can attach itself by its operations as much to the immaterial as to the material. Indeed, it is necessary according to the order of the universe that the perfections that are in the lowest subjects be comprised par excellence in the most elevated, which have some other perfections besides that. Thus the moving force of earth and fire is united in the mobile faculty of animals, which being but one and simple, also inclines to other movements. Thus the faculties of the vegetative soul are allied in the sensitive, and both in the rational soul, which possesses yet other perfections. In the same way the powers of the external senses are gathered in the imagination, and that of the imagination in the intellect, which besides that is gifted with a more outstanding power that embraces not only corporeal objects, such as the senses, but also immaterial objects. For otherwise nature would have imprinted in it in vain the desire and the yearning to know them.

Here is a fuller proof. God whom they know to be an utterly pure and utterly simple spirit penetrates distinctly and in themselves all material and corporeal things. For how could he have applied his will and his power to produce them without knowledge? How would he conserve these heavens, elements, stones, men? How would he join with the secondary cause for the generation of this plant, of this metal, if his sight did not reach it? And the angels who roll the heavens, according to Aristotle, how would they apply their power to moving, without knowing what? Consider that saying of Aristotle so often chanted in school: *that he who would understand something must envisage and contemplate its phantasm or species in the imagination.* Is not this species material, being the effect of a material power, and residing in a material substrate according to the opinion of many? But the *active* intellect, they say, divests it of its material conditions; so the intellect must know in advance that the species is clothed again in those conditions, and would not know how to deprive it of them without acting on it. But the intellect is an immaterial power, and this species is material until just after its action – hence, an immaterial power can have for its object a material thing.

In the sixth place, we know by certain experience, attested to by reliable witnesses – unless there are no reliable witnesses in the world – that God raises certain souls with such great favors that in their ecstasies and ravishments they have visions and illuminations that there are no words to express, nor consequently any imagination to grasp them. Of this kind was the transport of Saint Paul, when he was snatched up to the third heaven, where he saw marvels and secrets of God that it is not possible for a man to represent, and that made him say, *that no eye had seen, nor ear heard, nor had there entered into the mind of any man, what God has prepared for those who loved him.* From this it follows that since the senses contribute nothing to this knowledge, the soul has what it takes to dispense with them for its finest operations.

Some libertines and courtiers laugh at these experiences and distort them either into fable or into sickness of mind. But we need not be moved at all by them; the light of the Sun does not stop being agreeable to men, even though it frightens owls. Let us consider only that those experiences have witnesses who cannot be reproached either with simplicity or with imposture. That is why we must scorn their railleries with as much courage as they have impudence in spreading them. For it would be folly to argue with people whose reputation is injured by good opinions and who would be thought uncivil if they did not profess to be impious. They remind me of the accursed George Vicoujch, despot of Serbia, fatal instrument of the destruction of the Christians in Hungary. That impious man mocked every sort of religion, and made use of it only for the benefit of his own concerns, sometimes following the party of the Ottomans, sometimes that of the Christians. When a Franciscan called Capestran, a famous and zealous preacher, represented to him that his impiety was the cause of his unhappiness (he had been persecuted to the utmost by Mohammed the second), and that he ought to renounce the profession that he had always made of despising sacred things, he replied that he did not know, and that he preferred to be considered an unhappy prince than an old dreamer – a reply corresponding to the humor of a number of courtiers. I am not writing this without some grounds.

In the seventh place our soul disentangles and abstracts from a number of individuals a species and common nature, strips it of its circumstances of time, place, and the like, purifies it of sensible conditions, contemplates it and penetrates it all alone, and by an admirable Alchemy draws from a number of species a more universal principle [*raison*] that they share in and that is common to them. These abstractions, I say, and these separations exceed more than probably the capacity of any bodily power, and must proceed from a spiritual principle. Thus the soul is the only principle of such operations.

We can say the same of its reflective acts. To be able to conceive of something, to contemplate that conception, and judge of its truth or its weight, to consider, again, if that judgment is well formed, and so on up to a certain number of acts formed one on the other, more or less according to the force of different intellects: these acts seem to be too subtle and too delicate for an organic faculty; hence, the soul is the only principle of such operations. Although this argument has a very plausible appearance, there are nevertheless some who believe that the inner sense that judges of the operation of the external senses is in some way capable of this reflection. We see some traces of it in the imagination of little children, in whom the intellectual faculty is still dormant and, as it were, immobile beneath the weakness of the senses. We can answer that it is not the imagination, but indeed the intellect that is beginning to awaken and to shoot forth the first rays of its force.

Finally, we no sooner have the use of reason, than we have a desire to be happy, and the first traces of our knowledge are inevitably followed by that appetite. It is a law that no legislator has prescribed, that no occasion has established, that no age has seen commence except the age that saw the birth of the human race, but that Nature has graven in our souls with her own hands. On this point all the sects of philosophy agree both among themselves and with the sentiment of the common people: the flight from evil and the pursuit of good, which are the two aims of all our actions, what is this but the search for happiness, since it consists in the elimination of the one and in the enjoyment of the other? And although the vulgar do not know the terms, they never stop laboring unceasingly for the thing. The philosophers, who knew that God did nothing in vain, and that he had not imprinted inclinations and appetites in the lowest and vilest creatures without having prepared outside them something to satisfy them – those philosophers have judged that it was not at all likely that he put this desire for happiness into so excellent a nature as the human soul, without there being something to assuage it. The earth moves, but it has a center to quiet this movement and give it rest. The needle rubbed by a magnet is in perpetual agitation until it is turned toward the polar star, but then it quiets down and becomes immobile. We have an appetite to drink and to eat, but there is something to satisfy it. Thus it is a point without controversy that this appetite of our soul can arrive at some repose and be contented. It cannot do so in this life; hence, let us conclude that it will be afterward. But if it is to be happy without the body, it must be able to act without the body, and consequently its separation from it will not be its annihilation.

THE IMMORTALITY OF THE SOUL

Second Discourse

*That It Is Necessary to Show That God Exists before Proving the
Immortality of the Soul*

*Refutation of Pyrrhonism and of the Arguments That Montaigne Brings
Forth to Establish It*

Various Kinds of Demonstrations

... But in order to satisfy entirely the most difficult minds, and to convince the most opinionated; in order to force those wills most determined to believe nothing at all and to place everything in doubt; and so
that there may be no ground for answering in vain, or any for making
a bad objection in favor of Pyrrhonism: here is a piece of certain knowledge – in whatever direction you turn it and in whatever light you regard
it – of which it is impossible that a man capable of reflection and of
discourse could doubt and not be assured. Every man, I say, who has
the use of judgment and of reason can know *that he is*, that is, that he
has a being, and this knowledge is so infallible, that, even though all the
operations of the external senses might be in themselves deceptive, or
even though we cannot distinguish between them and those of an im-
paired imagination, nor wholly assure ourselves whether we are awake
or asleep, or whether what we are seeing is the truth or illusion and
pretense, it is impossible that a man who has the power, as some have,
to enter into himself, and to make the judgment *that he is*, should be
deceived in this judgment, and *should not be*. This truth is as perceptible
to reason as that of the Sun is to healthy eyes – that action presupposes
being, that it is necessary that a cause exists in order for it to act, and
that it is impossible that nothing should make something. God himself
can elicit being from nothing and existence from what is not; he needs
neither subject nor matter in order to act, and all created things have
issued immediately from his power. But to bring it about that what is
not should act before it is: this is what entails contradiction – it is what
the nature of things cannot suffer, it is what is entirely impossible.

Now this judgment that a man makes, *that he is*, is not a frivolous
piece of knowledge, or an impertinent reflection. He can rise from there
to the first and original source of his being, and to the knowledge of
God himself. He can draw from it the demonstration of the existence

of a divinity, as I shall show in the first division of the following book. He can draw from it the first movements toward religion and the seed of this virtue that inclines us to submit ourselves to God, as to the first cause, and to the supreme principle of our being. It can expand from there to the inquiry into and discovery of everything that has principally and voluntarily contributed in giving us being, or which helps in maintaining it, and extract from that the sentiments of love and piety that we should have for our parents and for our country. In brief, the most holy and inviolable duties of man, in accordance with his purely natural condition, grow from this root and flow from this principle.

ELEVEN

François de la Mothe le Vayer, *Dialogue on the Diversity of Religions* and *Little Skeptical Treatise*

[*Dialogue de la diversité des religions*, 1630; *Petit traité sceptique*, 1646]

Introduction

François de la Mothe le Vayer (1588–1672) trained and practiced as a lawyer in Paris, and belonged to the circle of writers called *libertins* – freethinkers, known for their insistence on relativism and their hostility to the use of any power, religious or secular, for controlling conscience. Gassendi and Hobbes were both well acquainted with la Mothe le Vayer.

The *Dialogue on the Diversity of Religions* is one of the essays la Mothe le Vayer published under the pseudonym Tubero Orasius in 1630 and reissued with additions in 1631. The *Dialogues faits à l'imitation des anciens*, as the whole series was called, contains much material that, for its time, is shocking, either because it is blasphemous or because it is sexually risqué. It is sometimes thought that the *Dialogues* was the "wicked book" that Mersenne and Descartes corresponded about when Descartes, relatively newly arrived in Holland, first began to write about metaphysics in 1630. The dialogue excerpted here is relatively tame. Its theme is that, of the main schools of philosophy, Skepticism is the most compatible with Christianity, despite its method of displaying the uncertainty of received opinion. What is more, Skepticism is best placed to accommodate the diversity of religious belief and observance that is revealed when ancient (i.e., ancient Greek) and modern (i.e., seventeenth-century) Europeans are compared, or when modern Europeans are considered together with their heathen contemporaries in New France. The excerpts have a clear bearing on Descartes' preoccupations both in 1630 and at the time of the *Meditations*. Orasius considers whether divinity is a demonstrative science.

He considers arguments for God's existence and doubts their effectiveness against atheists; he comments on the connection between
divine and celestial things in ancient writers and the relation of celestial things to physics; he comments in passing on the relation of
the soul to the body. He even reports the opinion that belief in
divinities starts in people's dreams. Descartes' conviction from his
early days in Holland that he had found how to prove the truths of
metaphysics more conclusively than those of geometry might make
sense in the face of the doctrine that proof was out of its element
in relation to divinity, and that the mysteries of Catholicism had to
be matters of faith.

The second set of extracts is from the *Little Skeptical Treatise*, a pamphlet that was first published in 1646. The dedicatory letter that precedes it in the 1669 edition of le Vayer's *Oeuvres* says that it is "one of
the games of my first years," which suggests that its contents date from
well before the time it went into print,[1] perhaps around 1630. Le Vayer
considers different things that might be meant by saying that other
people lack common sense. What is usually meant, he suggests, is that
the person who supposedly lacks common sense is out of step with others, has opinions different from those of the majority, or different from
the opinions of the one who charges him with a lack of common sense.
Should the one accused of lacking common sense feel slighted? Not at
all, says le Vayer: to lack common sense by having unusual opinions is
to be in good company – it is to be in the company of, among others,
many of the finest minds of antiquity, whose thoughts ran so far apart
from those of most of their contemporaries that they were often considered mad in their lifetimes. To fall in with widely shared opinion is
often to submit to erroneous opinion. And one may go wrong also in
deferring to prevailing expert opinions – le Vayer has different
branches of scholastic science or philosophy in mind. It is better, in

---

1. R. Pintard, whose two-volume *Le libertinage érudit* (Paris, 1943) is the most
authoritative text on the group of thinkers to which la Mothe le Vayer belongs,
doubts that le Vayer actually drafted a separate work on common sense long
before 1646 (vol. 1, p. 524; vol. 2, p. 651). He thinks that certain parts of this
pamphlet recycled clandestine material, specifically from writings published in
1630 by le Vayer under the pseudonym "Oratius Tubero." The writings in
question form *Les dialogues faits à l'imitation des anciens*. Whether recycled or
not, the claims of the pamphlet on common sense seem to belong to the period
from 1630 onward, when Descartes produced both the *Discourse* and the *Meditations*.

view of the diversity of opinion and practice in the world, and in view of the limitations of the human cognitive faculties, to be open-minded and tentative – or, in other words, to be susceptible to uncommon sense, and so not think of the lack of common sense as a defect.

In considering le Vayer's deflation of the rhetoric of common sense, it is hard not to feel the contrast with the opening of Descartes' *Discourse*. There Descartes endorses the good opinion that each person tends to have of his or her own powers of telling the true from the false. There is nothing wrong with common sense, Descartes implies. People are naturally endowed with good powers of judgment, and if they go wrong, it is for lack of method rather than from some innate intellectual failing. If Descartes is a critic of common sense at all, it is common sense in the form of received and unquestioned opinion. This is open to doubt, and the beginning of wisdom is to become conscious of its dubitability – the effect of applying the first rule of Descartes' so-called method. How is the dubitability of common opinion established? Not, as in le Vayer, by a sort of anecdotal anthropology in which reports about the huge variety of human belief are used to weaken our confidence in the truth of the beliefs of any one nation or group, but by the failure of any proposition to present itself to an attentive mind so as to force its assent. In the *Meditations* the detachment from common opinion is more thoroughgoing, because the first rule of Descartes' method is transformed by exercises in hyperbolical doubt. The hyperbolical doubt acts against whole classes of belief – even beliefs that Descartes will eventually endorse, such as belief in the truths of mathematics. But in the *Meditations*, the ground for detaching oneself from common sense is not considered sufficient for an attitude of open-mindedness toward all propositions whatever; certain truths are such that we cannot detach ourselves from them or withhold our assent from them; and these make others evident, so that a whole system of science – not a traditional science but still a science – becomes possible for us.

[TS]

DIALOGUE ON THE DIVERSITY OF RELIGIONS

ORASIUS: I admit readily, Orontes, that few listen as willingly as I do to unusual opinions. Perhaps I am naturally disposed to them. In any case, my skepticism has been helpful in giving me this peculiar inclination toward paradoxical views, being the philosophy best able to turn them to its advantage. It is not my body that is the enemy of the crowd, even though the crowd greatly inconveniences it; it is really my mind that abhors the violent constraint of the multitude; I do not fear the contamination of intellectual contact any less than that of physical, in the manner of those who think that intellectual disease is much worse than any other. Most of the great Roman names charm my ear by the memory of the virtues of their bearers, but I can't hear that of a Publicola without feeling indignation against the first that deserved it, and I believe that in a republic such as theirs I could never have been accused of the crime of corruption they call *ambitus*, for having identified myself too closely with the good graces of the people. I have such a hostility against anything popular (you know how far we stretch the meaning of this word) that I couldn't condemn the blinding of Democritus – that he actually punctured his eyes so that he would no longer see the impertinences of the foolish multitude – and think that this story must be taken literally. It must also be interpreted morally to represent the eyes of the mind, so that we might make use of this great character altogether differently from how it is vulgarly used: seeing and considering nothing as the vulgar do. But it isn't for this reason that I side with what is contrary to the popular opinion: my way of philosophizing is too independent to allow for unbreakable attachments; rather, it is because nothing is so opposed to the happy suspension of the mind as the opinionated tyranny of the popular outlook. I have always thought that it is against the torrent of the multitude that we have to concentrate our energies and that, having subdued this monster, we would deal easily with the others.

ORONTES: This liberty, Orasius, of being allowed to follow the movements of your inner life obliges me to reveal with the same candor my fears for you since you started to admit so openly this capricious disposition of yours; I call it so, since it takes you, as it does goats, to remote and lonely places away from the herd. Indeed, I broach the subject all the more willingly, seeing it is what I think I owe to the friendship that has united us. I am going to explain to you in the same way the reasons that keep me from deferring to those of your skeptical indifference, and from joining you in the charming procedures of your Pyrrhonism. Already many are astonished that of all the different systems of philosophy you have applied yourself to the one that has the least followers, and must be the most hated of them all, since it is so suspicious of the others, and does not agree with any of them, in short, making all of the others its adversaries, like that Ismaelite whose hand was turned against all others, and all others turned against him. . . . For after all, what can you expect but a general assault against you by all the savants, and a public condemnation by all of the other schools?

But what seems more important, and what causes me more concern, given my interest in your fortunes, is that I can't see how, establishing uncertainty as your sect does, and making fun of everything the others have wanted dogmatically to establish, you can also defend Christianity against all the objections that will be directed against you. For if it is true that nothing at all is certain, and that all of the sciences are vain and chimerical [as you hold], it follows that our sacred theology, which is the science of divine things, will be as fantastic and illusory as the others – which is an impiety I take you to be far from, but that I fear you may not escape the suspicion of.

ORASIUS: To take the first of the two points you have just touched on, regarding the envy or hate of those you call savants, I consider that they aren't taken aback as much as you suppose, for just as I don't take up any of their maxims, I don't condemn or pronounce on any, contenting myself with gentle and quiet suspension of judgment in regard to them, which would in my opinion dispose these learned men to be more moderate toward me than they are toward one another. . . . As for the second point, concerning what can be imputed to the skeptical philosophy as far as incompatibility with Christianity goes, it is necessary that I deflect something of the appearance of this slander. I am proud to have turned my mind and my reasoning to something that could best prepare it for our true religion and that couldn't have suited it better for the mysteries of our faith. You can be sure that when we deny the truth or certainty that anyone wants to establish in the science he is professing, and when we raise suspicions about the vanity and error of such a person, we nevertheless say nothing to the detriment of Christian theology, which although it is still, though improperly, and in some way at times called a science, if the sacred doctors would have it so, it is not really a science at all, since such a thing requires principles that are clear and evident to the understanding, whereas theology takes practically all of its principles from the mysteries of our faith, which are a true gift of God and completely surpass the human mind. That is why, rather than acquiescing easily in the certainty of principles known by the intellect, as in the sciences, in our theology we consent to its divine principles by the sole command of the will, which makes itself obedient to God in matters it does not see, in which resides the value of Christian faith. "Faith does not give its consent by means of the senses, but from an order of the will," says Saint Thomas.[2] That is why all our complaints about the other sciences have no bearing at all on Christian theology, whose dignity and eminence are not diminished by our refusing it the title of science, as the excellence and greatness of its object, as well as the certainty of its revealed truths, put it far above all other human knowledge. But I go further, and want you to see that our religion has never suffered more persecution than from those who pass for great savants – whence it comes about that the heretics were the foremost and most disciplined men of their times. Thus no other way of philosophizing so lends itself to Christian faith or gives so much peace to the Christian soul, as our dear Skepticism. . . .

If . . . we consider the different opinions of all the other philosophical schools up to now, we won't be able to find any that hasn't axioms and principles directly opposed to the articles of our faith. The Pythagoreans are full of magical superstitions, Plato's academy supposes in the creation of the world a matter coeternal with God. Democritus and all of the Epicureans thought the same about their atoms, to say nothing about their voluptuous end. The Stoics made their wise man equal or at times superior to God, whom they subjected to their famous destiny or fate. The Cynics publicly made virtue out of vice. And as for the Peripatetics, with their eternity of the world (from which Aristotle never departed, according to Alexander Aphrodisias), isn't it a wonder that, having smothered all other sects, in the style of the Turks who left none of their brothers alive, they were able, notwithstanding the impiety of their doctrines, to establish themselves so masterfully in all of the Christian schools. . . .

It is thus (dear Orontes) that I imagined that, in professing skeptical ignorance, I would give the dogmatic pedants no purchase on me that they could formulate, but that, on the contrary, like the Greek musician who found nothing more difficult than to teach his art to those who had bad starts, so it is also true that there is no mind on which the divine graces work with more resistance and in whom the mysteries of Christianity imprint themselves less readily than in those who presume to know demonstratively the causes and purposes of all things. But when by a reasonable discourse we have skeptically examined the trifles of human knowledge, it is then that the recognition of our own ignorance

2. "Fides non consentit per evidentiam objecti, sed ex imperio voluntatis."

can make us worthy of the graces infused by heaven, which will fall on a soil happily cultivated, and from which we will have pulled out all the weeds that prevent it from flourishing. You can rest assured that, so far as I am concerned, nothing has made me hold our sacred religion in such veneration as the consideration of other religions to which I have been brought by following the rules of our own sect, which so differs from all the other religions found throughout the world. Nothing apart from God has so attached me to the true way of worshiping him [son vrai culte] as contemplating all the countless and grotesque varieties of religion that obtain wherever the true rite is unknown. . . .

ORONTES: . . . I no longer see anything to prevent my sentiments falling in with yours and adopting your neutrality with its constant suspension of judgment. Since, in closing, you said that you had often reflected on the many religions of the world and the methods of worship that they prescribe, always to the advantage of the true religion, I hope I can ask your memory to call up your observations on this subject. . . .

ORASIUS: Of all of the thoughts of which human beings are capable, none is as elevated as those which concern divinity. As Aristotle said to Alexander the Great, a proud heart and high courage are not only permitted to those who command here on earth, but also to those who have true and appropriate thoughts about the gods. On the other hand, there is perhaps nothing that better reveals the weakness of our nature, because there being no proportion of the finite to the infinite, of the creature to the creator, the immensity of this divine object, as Simonides and Melissus experienced, altogether defeats our intellect as the excessive light of the Sun dazzles us, "as vision stands to the highest object of vision, namely the Sun, so the intellect stands to the supreme object of the intellect, namely God,"[3] which is what Plato strongly concluded in the course of the seventh book of the *Republic*. This is also what makes some people say that the French word for heaven, *ciel*, is not derived from the fact that heaven is engraved and etched, *caelatam est insculptum* in Latin, but from the fact that it disguises and hides [*celer* in French] what it contains. For although the divine is considered to extend throughout nature, "all things are full of Jove,"[4] all of those who have imagined God have always assigned him heaven in particular for his

3. "Ut se habet visius visus ad visibilium summum nempe solem, sic intellectus ad intelligibilium nempe Deum."
4. "Jovis-omnia plena."
5. "Pater noster qui es in coelis."

principal home, "Our Father, which art in Heaven,"⁵ just as our soul,
which is diffused throughout the body, seems to be more attached to
the heart or brain, because that is where it exercises its most noble
functions. This is how Aristotle explains the matter in book I, chapter
3 of *De caelo:* "All who believe in the existence of gods at all, whether
Greek or barbarian, agree in allotting the highest place to the deity,
surely because they suppose that immortal is linked with immortal."⁶
That is also where he put his prime mover, on the periphery or convex
circumference of the first mobile, and even in the most rapid part, given
that it is equidistant from the poles. However, celestial objects, and in
particular the divinity that animates them, have so little in common with
our understanding that the great disparity keeps them from coming
within our knowledge. . . . However, many have held entirely to the contrary that no object is more suitable and proportional to the human mind
than the divinity of which it is like a particle, and that there is not so
little relation between man and God that one would not find at least
that of cause and effect. In addition, the creation does not seem to have
had any other purpose on the part of the creator than to make man
contemplate the goodness, power, and wisdom in all his works. In this
way, tracing the things produced to their producer, which are the links
of that chain of Homer, we are easily brought to him and made capable,
if not of understanding his essence, then at least of admiring the excellence of his works, which is called a posteriori knowledge. There we
have the different opinions one finds concerning the application of our
mind to the discovery of a divinity. And one finds the understanding
divided by two opinions: one that holds that man is naturally brought
to the knowledge of God by physical principles, which are born with
him, and the other that absolutely denies all of that. . . .

I now turn to those who believe that they can demonstrate by good
reasoning that the existence of God is true, and that it is spiritual blindness, or malice and stubbornness that makes one deny it; in this they
are contradicted by the Mezenses, Cyclops, and a whole host of other
atheists that past centuries have produced and that the present is renew-
ing. . . . [T]hese people . . . make use of the same artifice that has been
employed in our civil wars, where even those who take up arms against
the party of the king protest that they are his faithful servants. They
follow Saint Thomas in establishing a divinity by five principal means,

6. "Universi qui Deos esse putant, tam Graeci, tam Barbari, supremum locum
   Diis tribuerunt, propterea quod immortale ad immortale est accommodatum."

of which the first is from motion, which was mainly made use of by Plato and Aristotle to arrive at a first mover: "whatever is moved is moved by another."[7] The second is by the consideration of an efficient cause, which takes us necessarily to a first cause if an infinite regress is to be avoided. The third is based on the possible and the necessary, which makes us recognize that "there is something necessary in itself causing in others their necessity,"[8] which is God. The fourth considers the different degrees of good, truth, and other essential perfections that allow us to rise up to that *ens summum* or supreme being in which all the others participate. The fifth depends on the government of everything, which allows us to admire a supreme intelligence by which all things are brought gently to their ends. Our great master Sextus puts forward four other ways, of which the second and third include the five of Saint Thomas; his first is founded on universal assent, of which we spoke earlier, the second on the order of the world, the third on the absurdities that result from holding the contrary opinion, the fourth and last on the response made to contrary arguments. In the light of these one can well conclude that it is one of the greatest derangements of the human mind to deny one's God, "the fool hath said in his heart, there is no God."[9]

Atheists nevertheless put themselves beyond all of these arguments, none of which they think is conclusive. They are helped by the rules of an exact logic, to such an extent that, giving themselves a free rein with this subject, some, such as Petronius, consider how the marvels of nature, the eclipses of stars, earthquakes, thunderclaps, and such things gave people the first inkling of a divinity,

> First God made fear on Earth, when from the heavens
> high bolts of lightning fell.[10]

Others such as Sextus are more or less of the opinion of Epicurus, who relates this first consciousness of a God to those notable visions which our imagination supplies during sleep (though without admitting that it supplies us with images of God) and about which we often feel extraordinarily moved when we wake up. But everyone agrees that the greatest legislators have only made use of the common opinion on this subject, which they haven't just stirred up but have magnified as much as pos-

7. "Quicquid movetur ab alio movetur."
8. "Est aliquid per se necessarium caeteris causa necessitatis."
9. "Dixit insipiens in corde suo, non est Deus."
10. "Primus in orbe Deus fecit timor, ardua coelo / Fulmina dum caederent."

sible, taking control of the stupid multitude so that it might be later led by its fantasy. This is how Joseph Acosta represents the Mandarins who govern China and use the religion of the country to contain the people, not believing, as far as they are concerned, in any other God but nature, any other life but this one, any other hell than prison, any other paradise than the office of a Mandarin.

. . . I find myself in perplexity over two other opinions disputed by those who agree that gods exist. Some attribute to the gods not only the general direction of the universe and the orderly movement of all its machines, and its orbs, but also a particular concern with everything that takes place down here, from which flows the reward of virtuous actions and the punishment of those which appear to them vicious. The others submit that it would make more sense to deny altogether the existence of the gods than to attribute to them cares so lowly or to kit them out like humans with passions so shameful, that is, so incompatible with divinity. . . . Those who are of the former opinion say that we must revere and serve religiously the gods who know everything, down to the movements of our hearts, having in their hands rewards and punishments. The others who like Epicurus mock divine providence . . . laugh as a consequence at any sort of cult or worship as something vain, as a way of trampling people under foot so long as there are religions.

. . . Let us consider the reasons of the former, which seem the more pious, and then come to the latter. In the first place they point to all the nations that have from ancient times addressed their prayers to the gods, which shows that the prayers have been heard and granted; otherwise there would be no appearance of their wishing to continue with them. . . . Again, apart from the innumerable examples from past times, we have every day so many testimonies to the gods' visible anger or assistance that it would be churlish not to recognize them. The funeral pyre of Croesus was extinguished by a downpour sent from the heavens . . . in return for his piety, and the blow of the sword with which Cambises wounded the god Apis or Ephanus in the thigh is known to have been avenged a little time afterward by a self-inflicted blow to the thigh by this king, of which he died. . . . It is not without reason, therefore, that Aristotle, appearing more religious in this connection than many have been willing to admit, shows that virtue consists in a certain mean (between extremes), which is unsettled as much by excess as deficiency, and gives the example of courage, that if someone is so undaunted, and so intrepid that he has no fear even of the gods, that is no longer strength and courage but foolishness and madness. For if you do not want to set yourself against all of antiquity or even our century with your knowledge and sensibility, you must admit that the gods don't leave human matters to chance. . . .

PAMPHLET OR LITTLE SKEPTICAL TREATISE ON THE PHRASE "TO LACK COMMON SENSE"

Nowadays there is nothing more commonplace than to hear people who are not very bright being told that they lack common sense. It is hard to think of a way of putting things that is more misunderstood by the people who use it and more ill taken by the infinity of persons who feel injured by it. . . . [L]et us examine only what importance these words *To lack common sense* can have, and then we will judge how great the injury is, if there is one, and as a consequence the resentment we should feel, supposing even that we should have to respond to this kind of insult.

To understand properly what common sense is, one has to know the faculties of the soul, since it is one of them, and how by means of them the soul manages its various operations. However, because here as elsewhere the opinions of the philosophers differ, let us take the one most widely accepted in the schools as the most likely, as this will serve our purpose.

The most common doctrine teaches, in accordance with the text of Aristotle, that after the external senses have received the species of objects, they transmit their sensation to the common sense, which is internal. This in turn transmits it to the fantasy, which presents it to the understanding, under the name of phantasm, to make a judgment. It is following these different functions that the understanding, whose job is to pronounce on the true or the false, finally moves the will, which is in charge of all action, fleeing or following, according as the appearances of good or bad are presented to it. In this respect it is compared to a blind master, who, even though guided by a sighted servant, does not cease to be in command. There in a few words is what the colleges say about the matter. . . .

But it is quite clear that when we impute to someone a lack of common sense, we do not mean in the least to call in question the participation of the internal sense, which is connected to the five external ones, which are attributed by philosophers to the whole range of animals. . . . If we take account of the usage of this saying, as we must if we are to get down to its meaning, we will readily see that by the lack of common sense is meant some other defect of knowledge that is more noble and more peculiar to ourselves. And because there is nothing like the self-evidence of those first principles – which, being indemonstrable inasmuch as there is nothing more clear than they are, cannot be illuminated otherwise – we might think that it is in relation to the privation of this spiritual light that our common saying is to be understood. And certainly the mathematicians call their principles common notions, such as that the whole is greater than the part; that taking away equal parts of equal things, the remainders are equal; and that if two things are congruent to a third, they are mutually congruent. . . . But apart from the fact that it is never in this connection that we apply our saying, we must also admit that first principles reduce to a very few in each art or science, and yet we find our saying applied all the time to an infinity of subjects. Since we want to agree that our saying derives its origin from a certain thickness of mind, which renders its subject incapable of understanding these principles, and since our saying has an application much wider than to first principles, we must look elsewhere for its meaning.

There are people so thick, and so naturally stupid that, to be frank, one could well apply our proverb to them without doing them any injury. . . . But people of this sort, whose minds are as useful to their bodies as a grain of salt would be to keep something from rotting, and of whom we laughingly say that they could die without "giving up the ghost," since they have none, do not deserve to be thought of in this connection, nor should we consider them any further. For we do not accuse them of lacking common sense, but of lacking sense and judgment altogether.

The fact is that the most common use of our saying is in connection with those whose opinions we think are extravagant, when they do not agree with our own. Self-love being so powerful, we think of our opinions as belonging to our very being, without examining them further, like the doting mother who finds nothing so handsome as her child, whatever its defects, because it is hers. This is the source of the common animosity against those who disagree with us, and as soon as anyone parts company with our sense, taken for our judgment, we say that he has lost his common sense, that is, that he does not reason or speak as other reasonable men do. . . .

That said, I note first of all how mistaken one can be to take common sense for good sense, and to take the most widely held opinions for the best of all. For what is more common than error? And what is as idiotic as the mob? And is not the widely traveled road the way taken by animals? Could there be any greater spiritual blindness than to think that one cannot do better than to follow the procession, if one can use that

metaphor without being profane, or that there is no surer way of trav-
eling than in a throng? If we ever manage to free our mind to the point
where it can examine things without the customary impediments, it will
soon emerge that there are scarcely any opinions as certainly false as
those that are universally accepted. . . .

   And thus it is that so many great men have preferred solitude to
society, so as not to be infected by the breath of people. For whether
you are exposed to brutal ignorance or perverse theory, you cannot fail
to be affected: whether the plasterer whitewashes you or the coal man
blackens you, the mark remains all the same. . . .

   It is noteworthy that in the public combats between men and beasts
in ancient Rome, the crowd usually supported the beasts rather than the
men, as the multitude is always impertinent and naturally attracted to
the worst. But do we not see that, on the contrary, everything that is
excellent is found only in small numbers; that rubies and diamonds are
rare, and that pearls are called *singletons* by the Romans because beautiful
ones are found only one at a time. . . .

   We have a memorable story in this connection. The Council of the
Abderites sent, in great haste, for the divine old man Hippocrates (as
his followers called him) to cure Democritus, whom they took to be
mad and a perfect fool, for no other reason than that he had no common
sense and, as their letter put it, in view of the fact that he spoke of
infernal regions, idols, and images in the air, and the language of birds,
the infinity of worlds, and other similar things. . . . I have to say here on
behalf of Democritus that not only the great philosophers of antiquity
passed for fools in their time; in our own day I have seen quite a few
great minds and men of extraordinary merit of whom the public has
taken a similar view, regarding as mad those who depart from their
common sense. . . . It is perhaps the least of all offenses to be called a
fool, according to what we have just said, and given that, as the Spanish
proverb has it, we are practically all fools to one another.

   From this consideration I go on to another, which gives me the opportunity to express my wonder at the arrogance and temerity of the
human spirit, when it has condemned anything that seems to it new or
incongruous, as if it were the measure of all things; when it counts things
less common just because it has not heard of them, as if nature had no
greater extent than its knowledge. And this is why it sees the lack of
common sense as soon as anything departs from its manner of conception, as if all activity were within its intellectual sphere, and as if it took
account of all human opinions when in fact it knows only a fraction of

them. For, if it is only with great effort that one finds out how people reason in Europe, Asia, Africa, and America, how will it be when it emerges that there are more lands to be discovered than the geographers so far know? What if there are other worlds than this one? What if, as many philosophers think, there are infinitely many? Has the human spirit sifted through the thoughts of that many peoples and places, as we should expect it to, if it is to determine what is common sense? . . .

Without so perfect and so extensive a knowledge of all human imaginings, good sense is left to be determined by what the greatest number of people one knows will consent to; not only is this false in itself, but the reasoning leading to it is defective; it is also easy to show by induction and by a few examples appropriate to the subject just how erroneous the supposition is, and how many things that are universally regarded as good and virtuous in one place, are also reputed to be base and vicious in another. Let's start with a comparison of the new to the old world. . . .

We say commonly that dreams are lies, and that it is pointless to give them credence. The people of Canada think them very real and there are marvelous reports of their predictions by sleep. They always respond to those who wish to give them a new doctrine on this matter by saying that each nation has something of its own to offer and that theirs has prophetic dreams. This reminds me of what Pliny said of the Atlants people of Africa, that their dreams were altogether different from anyone else's. . . .

We wash here and carefully clean our faces to make them attractive. In New France the most painted, either by ink or some other rubbish, are the most pleasant, and it is not common sense there to judge otherwise.

We wear perfume and feel disgust at any stench. These savages find musk so bad-smelling that they cannot stand it, but they like the odor of something like old grease, so that they please their sense of smell with precisely the things we find unbearable.

Let's return to our old world and see if we find there a more uniform common sense. . . . Our battles take place by day, which is why they are called *journées*, it being only out of necessity or for surprise that anyone fights after dusk. The Massylians of Libya, we are told by our friend Augustus, never take up arms except at night, to such an extent that they always suspend hostilities by day, even during their bitterest wars.

Cicero remarks at the end of the second *Tusculan Disputations*, and Valerius Maximus also, that the Cimbres and Celtiberes sing while making war without fearing death, though they are sorrowful if confined to their beds, fearing that they will die there shamefully of some illness. The Greeks, on the other hand, according to the same authors, run away from danger in war and die quietly on their pallets, philosophizing there until the end; this also is called a lovely death, when we meet it between two sheets.

Our most serious actions seem ridiculous to the Tartars, who regard as criminal actions that we permit. . . .

Is there anything more widely believed, and felt, deferring to appearances, than the lightness of air? There are nevertheless philosophers who have maintained it is heavy, and the doctor of medicine Reyd has demonstrated that it is no less heavy than earth. The whiteness and coldness of snow – can they be put in doubt? Yet Anaxagoras, who said it was black, had followers, as did Thelesius, who held it was hot.

What is more evident, and more widely accepted in the schools, than that there are five senses in nature? I nevertheless see philosophers who recognize a sixth, for voluptuousness. And others, such as Campanella, only recognize one – the sense of touch – which they think is subtle in the case of the eye, and more gross elsewhere, with a certain proportion.

All of logic is based on the principle borrowed from metaphysics that two contradictory propositions cannot be true at the same time. Democritus and others have maintained the contrary.

The foundation of the physics of the most celebrated pagans is the principle that one can make nothing out of nothing. That is why they deny the creation of the world and believe for the most part in its eternity. . . .

Has medicine so much as a single rule or aphorism that is not disputed? I am reminded of the *Dictyaques* of a certain Denis Aegee whom Photius mentions, which was in two sections containing a hundred chapters on medical matters. The first section was always in favor of the positive proposition, the second the negative.

If we examine [in particular] moral matters by natural light [alone], we will soon discover that it is better, as Saint Augustine says, to take the divine laws – these being certain and immutable – as our guide in life in what concerns vice and virtue and good and evil, rather than a would-be science that seems to be almost conjectural, given how often it changes with time, place, and people. . . .

I might add that, though I find it strange that there is so little agreement about the different fields of philosophy on the part of those whose profession it is to examine them, I would be more astonished still if they were in agreement. For how can they know anything else if they do not

first know themselves? I don't know, said Socrates, whether I am a man
or some other kind of animal, perhaps more strange than any Typhon
painted. How can they see clearly what remains if the thing that is clearest in nature is unknown to them? How can they teach others the truth
if they cannot establish what it is, or whether it is in things or in the
understanding, or if it is real or only a relation and conformity of a thing
to the intellect? . . . In short, if we possessed the criterion of the dogmatic philosophers to discern it, or if our highest faculty of judging does
not extend further than the probability of the skeptics, to that extent it
may be that, though we have the means of looking for the truth, we do
not have what is necessary to recognize it. The most eminent among us
confess readily that the human mind is congenitally blind, lacking so
many resources. So much so that we are forced to recognize as a fact
about our humanity that truth lies well beyond nature and is God's
alone. . . .

Let us face it: this reason, which we call divine, which makes us so
glorious, and by means of which we pretend to tell the true from the
false, is a plaything, which the lie manages as it wishes, as well as and
often with more gracefulness than does truth. We like to think that our
understanding possesses this wonderful reason as its lawful wife; in fact,
it is a brazen prostitute who, under her mask, abandons herself shamefully to all kinds of people. With the little light that reason furnishes,
we claim that we can easily penetrate the celestial spheres, control the
works either of nature or of God, in a word, be all-seeing. Nevertheless,
not only ordinary minds, but even those with the greatest acuity, with
the arid splendor of Heraclitus, find themselves enclosed in shadows so
thick and unconquerable that we could well say here as on the day of
the Crucifixion, "and darkness covered the whole earth," and that the
darkness, which in this sense is in all things, prevents us from seeing
anything as it should be. . . .

Since we can know nothing without the aid of the senses, the so-
called gates to the soul, wherein nothing enters except by their means,
must we not hold our knowledge in great suspicion, given their natural
shortcomings and their errors, which are so often apparent? . . . But what
comes after sensation ought to give us greater pause, for it is at that
stage that that part of the spirit which ought to correct the other faculties often undermines them. And as the senses most of the time make
their demands on the understanding, it isn't in its turn more faithful,
making them represent something as beautiful and well formed in the

morning through a predisposition to love, that in the afternoon, by a contrary passion, it makes appear ugly and deformed. This is what philosophers base themselves on when they say that man is the worst of all animals. . . .

I have to develop another thought about reason. Is it not universally believed that if everyone possessed it to such a degree of perfection that each was very wise, the world would be very much improved and everything would go better? A bit of careful consideration would soon make us see that, on the contrary, it is madness that constitutes the world, and that it would be destroyed without it. . . . For is it not true that most of the arts that men enjoy are due to madness? Take games, dances, feasts, delicacies and so on until infinity; costumes and ornaments and other such fripperies: would these otherwise have seen the light of day? Is it not madness that makes nations go to war? And yet the people who make their living from war are uncountable. What would judicial offices do without the mania of the people who employ them? . . .

It is thus easy to conclude that madness, seen from this point of view, is also useful to the world, and that wisdom causes confusion which it is hard to clear up. If one says that wise men would easily occupy themselves more gainfully, I must reply that without wars, murders, and the pleasures of all the bad actions wise people decry, the Earth would not have half of what is required to feed the human race, so great would be their numbers, given the way they live; and notwithstanding the fact that they kill themselves in various ways, they would never stop fighting to take bread from one another or remove by violence and cunning the necessities of life. For these plagues, which often come from the dissoluteness of men, would cease, and those that are sent from heaven – floods and fires and periodic worsenings of things (since it is our sins that bring them down on us from on high) – if men were wise, they would be exempt from them. And then we would be in an even more calamitous state than can be imagined, reduced to death from hunger, if madness did not intervene in our affairs. But, thanks be to God, we have little to fear on that score. So long as there are human beings, we will not be short of madness. . . .

And if our reason is so negligible a thing, and if madness, which we think to be worse, is its inevitable counterpart, which the heavens wanted to give as a gift or inheritance to our humanity, whereas the greatest wisdom of men is pure nonsense in the sight of God, why should we wonder at the opinions of others, however strange they may seem? Why do we accuse them of lacking common sense, we who are perhaps even further from being good persons, if there are any. And why do we take this same reproach as an injury when, however it is taken, it is no more than an empty sound, and has no sense that should scandalize an honest man?

TWELVE

Charles Sorel, *Universal Science*

[*La science universelle*, 1634–41]

Introduction

Charles Sorel (1602?–1674) was a man of letters best known for satirical histories and novels. He appears to have written some criticism of Descartes' friend Balzac, to which Descartes replied. He also outlined a "universal science" which on the surface appears to anticipate the project for an inclusive science outlined in Descartes' *Discourse*. In fact, and as the excerpts here show, Sorel's universal science is not Descartes'. For one thing, although its cardinal distinction is between spiritual and corporeal things, corporeal things come first in Sorel's order of investigation. In Descartes it is the other way round. Next, although Sorel's science is supposed to supplant what is taught in the schools, and includes much that was not included in the traditional curriculum, it does not appear to include or to be specially attuned to a reformed mathematics or to other reformed sciences. And it makes room for findings from alchemy and divination, the Cabala, and so on, that Descartes, whatever his sympathies for believers in these things, excludes from his science. On the other hand, Sorel does make room in universal science for a new grammar and a new art of reasoning, both reminiscent of Cartesian innovations. He thinks a new science ought to help people to live better and longer (as Descartes also believed), and that it ought to culminate in self-control and the elimination of vice. Whether there is an agreement at a level deeper than these generalities is not so clear, and perhaps there were many different ways in the 1630s and 1640s of describing and making good the promise of a new kind of understanding.

The excerpts given here come from two sources in the multivolume exposition of Sorel's system. First, there are extracts from *La proposition de la science universelle* (*Proposal of a universal science*), a kind of preface to the statement of the whole system, in which systematic understanding is recommended as a cure for human moral shortcomings – in fact, a vast range of vices, headed by the varieties of pride and ambition. *La proposition d'une science universelle* appears in Sorel's text as the sequel to *Remonstrance sur les erreurs et les vices* (*Admonition concerning errors and vices*), a text that goes into human shortcomings in reasonable detail. It is the *Admonition* that Sorel refers to when he tells his reader in *Proposal* that he has been dwelling on human ills.

Sorel's universal science is geared to a distinction between spiritual and corporeal things, but the distinction as said is an un-Cartesian one. Intriguingly enough, the task of responding to the skeptics is assigned to the part of the system dealing with the enhancement and control of spiritual things, which, again superficially, recalls the approach of the *Meditations*. Selections from chapter 1 of the section of the universal science dealing with spiritual things make up the second extract from Sorel. The resemblance between them and the *Meditations* is not much more than skin deep. According to Sorel's theory the soul turns out to have internal resources against the deceptions of the senses, but this on account of an unexplained elevation of the common sense and reason over the external senses. Sorel thinks that the senses can sometimes be corrected by reflections on the difference such things as distance or minuteness made to visual perception. There are signs that he thought that acting on objects might reveal hidden powers. When it comes to spiritual and invisible things, Sorel thinks we can have inferential knowledge of some of them, and that the understanding has direct (but unexplained) access to others (it is not clear which). The general outlines of Sorel's project probably have more enduring significance than the details. They suggest that Descartes was not alone in thinking about large-scale reform of science in the 1630s and 1640s, and though Sorel's doctrine stays much closer to Scholasticism than Descartes' does, the project of the reform of science and of answering the Skeptics was evidently not Descartes' personal property or even that of his intellectual circle.

[TS]

UNIVERSAL SCIENCE

Science of Corporeal Things

First Part of Human Science

*In Which One Knows the Truth of All Things in the World
through the Forces of Reason and One Finds
the Refutation of the Errors of Vulgar Philosophy*

Proposal of a Universal Science in Accordance with True Reason to Act as a Remedy for Errors and Vices

This time, fellow men, you ought to listen to me freely. I have dwelt up to now on your ills; but now you are going to hear more agreeable things. I announce the end of your troubles and tell you that you can overcome them, provided you want to. There are many among you who, having considered them, supposed they were incurable. According to the people you have studied, your nature is below that of animals. They have said that mere beasts know how to control their appetites better than you, that they never want to eat when they are not hungry; and that they are never subject to the disquiet of ambition or want. But some unjust despair made that plausible to certain people, who did not realize that animals need no more than blind instinct, and that they do not enjoy the advantages attributed to them. Men have a faculty of judgment that can make up for all of their defects and can guide them through difficulties. That is why they can be assured that, so long as they make use of it as they should, they can achieve supreme happiness. Many presume to think that [men] cannot do this for themselves, but they know that the character of man is sufficient for his finding those things that are necessary for him, and that by governing ourselves according to the rules that right reason implants in us, we will not lack the knowledge necessary to escape the corruption of the world. There are all kinds of evidence of this. But even though the nature of man is that of a reasonable creature, it has to be admitted that men are not all rational to the highest degree, and that perfect reason is not present in all minds, as there are many that are spoiled by bad habits, and there are more than a few who are careless of their safety and are brought by their negligence to the same state as the wholly incapable, and need lots of instructions if they are to improve. All the same, so long as they are backed up by reasons, the admonitions of others can revive their nature.

However, in order to put the admonition in this form, it is important to recognize that just as there is only one reason, there is also only one truth and, consequently, that there is only one science, which one can call universal, because it includes all the others. By means of reason one comes to know the truth, and one acquires this infallible science, which if filled out with all that is necessary, enables us to remedy our defects. . . . It is necessary that there be just one book to deliver us from all these misfortunes. It is necessary that it contain the true science of all things that conform to right reason, and that, by an easy and certain route, it lead us to a perfect tranquillity of mind. It must show in what ways those people were lacking who thought they had the best opinions, and that of all the miseries that I have already gone through [in the *Remonstrance*] there will not be one that it will not help to banish from the Earth. But so that it may succeed in giving us such excellent guidance, it seems that its [practical teaching] should be left for last, and that beforehand it is necessary to know the truth of all things that subsist. As soon as we have become accustomed to having appropriate opinions about a whole range of different things, it will be possible to begin forming one's judgment and adapting it to things that are more esoteric. It is true that one can well have some peace of mind without any other science than that taught to us by blind nature; but let us leave that happiness for country fellows and savages who never hope to have anything above the life of brutes. If we want to be perfectly happy, we must not disregard any of what can be known.

The knowledge of all the marvels that one witnesses in the world raises the spirit higher and makes it better able to follow virtue. That is why if one attempts to understand everything, it is very much to the point to begin with the consideration of corporeal things, and, instead of this physics that philosophers broadcast, which is so full of absurdity and lies, give a doctrine that is supported by reason and experience. After this it is necessary to become acquainted with spiritual things in quite another way from how it is done in their metaphysics. By this method one will see which things exist, and what one should think of them; it has to be shown as well in what way one can bring the soul to perfection and strengthen its faculties, in such a way that this book will contain more than those courses of philosophy given to us by our doctors, who are pleased to tell us what logic, morals, physics, and metaphysics consist in. They vainly boast that in that way one can learn all things. One will never know spiritual and corporeal things adequately unless one is in-structed in many other particulars. Indeed, it is necessary that the doctrine that makes man perfect goes well beyond those things. All of the secrets of natural and supernatural science and those of the Cabala have to be revealed in this doctrine, as well as those of medicine, alchemy, aastrology, divination, and magic. One has to make room also for arithmetic, geometry, music, optics, and other parts of mathematics, grammar, rhetoric, the art of memory, the art of history, and poetry. One must not follow the example of some vulgar philosophers and have morals without economics and politics. Morals will govern individual as much as public life; and one has to teach methods of government so that those who are most discontent should have nothing to wish for.

In a word, the idea of the work is to mention nothing but what is necessary for a man to raise himself to perfection. So the universal science will never touch on things that can be changed as one fancies or where no certain rule applies. . . . It will be necessary to find as well new reasons for all of the effects that are observed in the world, and teach a method for making everything that is useful with an ease that is as yet unknown. I admit that there are truths so manifest that men have possessed them for all time, but they have not drawn the consequences from them that they should, or made the best use of them, so that in treating of them according to the required method, it cannot be said that we are doing nothing new. In addition, we will come upon other new sciences that have never before been conceived by any man, or at any rate no traces of them have been left. In particular, one needs to have a new grammar and many other teachings that must be universal, as the parts of our science are. It will similarly be necessary to provide a new art of reasoning and to discover sure ways of illuminating the mind of man on all occasions – so that it can never be deceived, and so it can govern itself and others with such moderation and prudence that we will no longer see injustice or poverty, or other ills. And we should not leave out the secrets of making the body healthier and life longer, so that everything reaches its best possible state. . . . My fellow men, be sure of this. Whoever has universal science will be capable of everything in the world. His judgment will be purified to such an extent that his opinions will be exactly appropriate to anything that presents itself. He will be able to judge and speak on any subject whatever, and do in a day what others are unable to do in a month. He will know himself and others and will be able to tell in an instant who is good or bad and who subscribes to false or true doctrine.

The Use and Perfection of All the Things in the World

Third Volume of Sorel's Universal Science

*Wherein One Finds the Most Striking Secrets of the Arts
and the Most Curious of Man's Inventions*

The Use and Perfection of Spiritual Things
The Use, Perfection, or Improvement of the Common Sense of Man; Means of Correcting Errors, and Sure Reasons against Those Who Doubt Everything, Called Skeptics or Pyrrhonists
CHAPTER ONE

To begin this treatise concerning the use of spiritual things, nothing is more urgent to address than the human soul. All other truly spiritual things are so far elevated above it that they do not need to be considered first. As nothing commends itself to man's attention so much as the use and improvement of his principal faculty, it would have seemed to some that they should start by hoping for the improvement of the body, but the improvement of the body is a necessary first step on the ascent to the improvement of the soul, and the infirmity of our nature permits us to spend all our time on it, even though the purpose is no more than to make the basest part of us capable of serving the highest. The whole course of our instruction taking for granted this gradation, we will assume it in our consideration of the use of the soul. To proceed, then, we note that as the soul has two controlling faculties, which are the understanding and the will, it is necessary in the first place that the understanding be illuminated by the real understanding of things, in order that the will be well guided and so that it flees the bad and seeks the good. The faculties that come under the understanding are the common sense, imagination, memory, judgment or reason, and foresight or prudence. It is necessary to see how they work, and how they admit of improvement, even perfection. It is important first to speak of the internal sense called the common sense, which alone takes in all that the external senses receive. It is certain that it can judge wisely when guided by reason, and the right way to perfect the common sense is by putting reason in control and making sure that it possesses the truth on all occasions. But many have said that this is impossible and that everything we can think about the things we consider is uncertain and that we should not affirm anything.

Those who speak in that way are known as Skeptics (that's to say, searchers, for they are always looking for the true opinion) or by the name of Pyrrhonists, after the leader of their sect. There are many who doubt everything. There are those who claim that the soul only knows things by means of the senses, by which it is deceived at all times in such a way that one cannot establish with any certainty what they report. Here in detail is what they suppose in order to maintain indifference [in judgment]. That which seems hard to some seems soft to others, and what seems dry or heavy or hot to these people seems damp, light, or cold to those, and there is no one who has any better access to the truth than anyone else. As for the sense of taste, men can scarcely take any pride in that either; moreover, as the beasts have the same bodily senses as men, and possess them more perfectly, it seems that one should somehow defer to them in this area. Again, there are vegetables, fruits, and other foods that men think have a bad taste, while other animals relish them. In addition, this diversity of taste is no less pronounced among men themselves. . . . As for sight, many animals see what men cannot; and among men there are those who notice things that their companions cannot perceive at all. . . . But, besides that, at any given time, [men] have always had a variety of opinions about the diversity that objects present according to location and distance, and especially in regard to colors, which vary for them according to whether they receive light or shade, candlelight or sunlight. One can infer from all of this that there is no telling whether to defer to the opinions of animals or men, or, if men, which men. One doesn't know whether to believe the old or the young; the healthy or the sick; those of one temperament or those of another; and it would be even more difficult to discern the truth in the variety one takes in oneself, at one time or another; so much so in fact that one is forced to conclude that common sense must never rely on the report of the external senses, though it cannot get away from them, and though it receives nothing but what they deliver. Thus, common sense is only confronted with lies and this keeps it at a great distance from the perfection one intends for it in crediting it with knowledge of things.

The reply to all of that is that the external senses are of too low a degree to have the power always to deceive the common sense, so elevated is it over them. We have already noted that as far as they [the external senses] are concerned, they are not even deceived, since they receive species from objects in just the way they are brought [to the senses], and in just the way they are capable of receiving them; and, above all, it is not in them that the power of knowing resides. But this is no help to us here, since we have also said that this does not prevent the common sense from being deceived when it gives credence to their reports. We would go so far as to say that if we consider it in isolation, the senses can deceive it all the time. But this consideration applies only to the common sense of beasts, which is at the same time the fantasy, the highest part of the soul [but] devoid of reason, and guided only by natural instinct. In the case of the common sense of men, it is a faculty of their souls, attached to their understanding, which has the ability to reason, that is, to distinguish things, to know them combined or divided, to compare them, to draw consequences. This is why the human senses are always accompanied by reason, provided that man is as he should be. And this reason, which corrects the deficiencies of the bodily senses, does not let the poor common sense go so terribly wrong, as those who deprecate their powers suppose. We freely admit that this internal sense can be deceived if what it believes is determined by what the external senses perceive. But it must be entirely disturbed for that to happen, because having once discovered their deceptions, it is forewarned of them in the future. Our opinions therefore need not be held in suspense continually. . . .

After all of that, we are starting to have an inkling of the reason the Skeptics have for being uncertain about everything. If they say in addition that the beasts surpass men in the power of their external senses, [the answer is that] this is not true in general, and that men equal them in this respect. Besides, even if they are equipped with good organs, they lack the means of making good use of them. Men are not similarly disadvantaged. Not only can they have organs proper to all sorts of operations and the physical reception of objects, but in addition they have a spiritual faculty to receive and judge them – to such an extent that they lower themselves unduly if they turn to lesser animals to determine what to believe about objects. Their common sense, which is a faculty of their soul, being wholly spiritual, must preside over what is corporeal. It can safeguard itself against deception by the senses. Things are perceived by all men just as they are, or as they appear in whatever way they are open to being known, and insofar as one knows this manner of reception, one cannot be taken in. After the universal and spiritual reception of the common sense, exact distinctions can be made among the different receptions of each corporeal sense. If the appearances of things vary with the organs of each man, the truth can be discovered by considering what is the subject of this variety. If things appear to each man differently from how they are when they are at a distance or in a mixture, that also will not prevent one knowing them, since the appearance, whatever it is, makes one judge how things truly are, whereas one knows how they must really be when they appear in a certain way. The tests that one makes produce a judgment in this connection, and though there are men who let themselves be taken in by trusting their external senses too much, they are not necessarily representative. In any case, they do not prevent others knowing according to the truth, and those who go astray can be led back by those who have proper knowledge. There are some who instruct themselves and use one of their senses to correct the errors of another, as when by touching we learn that there is nothing hollow or humped in an object that appears thus to sight. Others, listening to the protestations of the more judicious, correct their mistakes and register the truth of things, and by this means we can say that they clear up their errors by the sense of hearing.

In this way all men can make good use of the senses, and if one imagines a time when they were incapable of receiving instruction from anyone else, their common sense, guided by their understanding, has always made them know the truth about any objects that present themselves after some experience, and having noticed often that a distant thing appears small even though it is big, that something that seems small from a distance need not fail to be large. They have thought that way about differences between the whole range of objects, and at times their acuity has been such that they have conjectured that different things are the same – not in virtue of having seen entirely similar ones, but in virtue of having drawn conclusions about some from others, or having hit upon secret connections or other proofs, which several have attested to on different occasions. And on the other hand, they have also thought that several things were different, even though they resembled one another in some of their most evident qualities. . . . If they saw smoke from sufficiently far away, they did not say for certain that there was fire and flame there, because, when one extinguishes a fire one raises pretty heavy smoke, and there are mists and other damp vapors that from a distance resemble the driest exhalations; and because many can see these different things at different times, they have not jumped to conclusions about what they see if they have not judged by all the circumstances, which do not mislead them in the least. All men of good sense can do likewise, the older they are and the more experience of the world they have, the more expert they become, to the point where even old people make up for the weakness of their bodily organs by the subtlety of their common sense. It will not do, therefore, to complain that age, or illness, or the variety of locations, multiplies impressions of things, since one can conjecture what they are according to how they appear; and insofar as taking one for another is concerned, the majority of men do not let themselves be taken in this way if they are careful; for whether [things] appear similar or different, [men] can examine all of their qualities and the source from which they derive, and all these results contribute to knowing whether the bodies in which we see such and such an appearance are what they appear to be, and whether they can be found where they appear to be, and if there are not any others. . . .

If the internal sense proves useful in judging the various deliverances of the external senses without error, it comes into its own even more in conjunction with memory and imagination, which are two faculties of the understanding that are more elevated than it is. The imagination consists in forming a proper idea of present objects and in forming other [ideas], or the same or similar ones. The more it takes in of what the senses perceive, the more it can consider of other things which the senses have not perceived, but which they can make use of in objects. The utility of this faculty is that having already found out what certain things are, it can also represent others it has never encountered, with no more than another man's testimony to go by. The memory brings back to the mind images that were once depicted there, and gathers them together in such a way that the common sense, seeing them all, can come to some judgment, with the help of the higher faculties.

All the same, those who want to show that this doesn't help in the least to improve the common sense, claim that the imagination and memories of those who have some mania are altogether different from others. . . . But in any case it is a big mistake to think that it is necessary to relate the existence of things to people like that or that this should make us have some doubts. Madmen, sick people, and drunkards have their sense organs corrupted, so that they see things other than as they are; from their imaginations are formed bizarre and unreasonable things, and their memories forget the truth and make them remember only lies. . . . It is just as bad to assert that while asleep we do a number of difficult and strange actions and that we see in a short time many extraordinary places very far away from one another, but that nevertheless there is as much truth in that as in anything that happens while we are awake. What can the skeptics understand by that? Do they think that we go to another world when we sleep? If that were so, it would only be spiritually. We see asleep a man who does not stir from his bed, and nevertheless on waking he says that he has taken a walk in some gardens, and that he has seen some dancing and plays. If his body was always there, how could he have gone to all of the places he tells us about? It must be his soul that went. But the soul only leaves the body at death: he only represented the image of various things; and because in addition he thought that the action of his body was joined to it in many ways, which never happened at all, we have a manifest illusion. But since the body and the soul have to act in equal and corresponding ways in the real actions of life, we must not put in doubt, as some do, that the time spent asleep or dreaming is not all real life, or that it is more so than waking life. The body and soul really act in waking life: they are certainly real actions. The body can also act in sleep, according to the thought of the soul, as happens to those who sleepwalk and even appear to flee or pursue someone, or do something similar. But most people act by the soul alone and, staying immobile in bed, think they are doing what they are not. Those who really do what they think they do only do it at best imperfectly, and the imagination works more in that case than the body. . . .

It is not in this area at all that we should look for the truth of things. Most dreams are nothing but an outlandish mishmash. In sleep our external senses are dormant and even the internal sense that has the brain for its organ is so darkened by vapors that it hasn't got its ordinary freedom, and the imagination doesn't discharge its normal well-ordered functions either, so that what it does has no upshot. . . .

However, there is still the objection that one only sees the surfaces of things and that invisible things, especially spiritual ones, can't be known. . . . As for spiritual things whose power is invisible, their effects are apparent even so, and one can judge about their states on that basis. If one sees nothing more, there is nothing more that is visible, and it is necessary for the understanding to act alone to represent these things, and it is in its power to do so, contrary to what the Skeptics and doubters say, because it can go beyond the senses in many operations; and if it is not able to represent spiritual and invisible things in all their perfection, at least it is able to understand that they are more excellent than visible and corporeal things, and it can define their qualities and distinguish them – so much so, in fact, that the judgment of man and his soul do not have the narrow limits they are often thought to have.

THIRTEEN

Jean-Baptiste Morin, *That God Exists*
[Quod Deus sit, 1635]

Introduction

Jean-Baptiste Morin (1583–1656) was professor of mathematics at
the Collège de France from 1629 until his death, and his interests
included physics and astronomy as well as mathematics. A year after
the condemnation of Galileo by the Inquisition in 1633, he published *Pro telluris quiete*, defending the traditional doctrine of the
immobility of the Earth. Descartes read this, and also Morin's *Quod
Deus sit*, which appeared the following year. This short work, con-
structed on Euclidean principles, with Definitions, Axioms, and
Theorems, illustrates a way of doing metaphysics to which many
were attracted about this time; Descartes himself offered a brief
example of the genre (in his *Replies to the Second Set of Objections*), and
its most celebrated later exponent was Spinoza. The project of establishing God's existence using the kind of self-evident reasoning
characteristic of geometry clearly appealed to Descartes, but he re-
corded his disappointment with Morin's work in a letter to Mersenne written shortly before the publication of his own *Meditations*:

> M. Morin's main fault is that he always discusses the infinite as
> if he had completely mastered it and could comprehend its prop-
> erties. This is an almost universal fault which I have tried carefully
> to avoid. I have never written about the infinite except to submit
> myself to it, and not to determine what it is or is not. Then,
> before giving any explanation of controversial points, in his six-
> teenth theorem, where he sets about proving that God exists, he
> rests his argument on his alleged refutation of the Earth's move-
> ment, and on the revolution of the whole sky around it, which he
> has in no way proved. He supposes also that there cannot be an

infinite number, which he could never prove. Right up to the end, everything that he says is very far from the geometrical self-evidence and certainty which he seemed to promise at the beginning. This is between ourselves, please, since I have no desire to hurt his feelings.[1]

Despite Descartes' criticisms, Morin's work remains of considerable interest as an illustration of the kind of philosophical theology that was prevalent when Descartes was composing the *Meditations*. Moreover, though Descartes' arguments for God's existence are more sophisticated than Morin's, the two writers share many of the same background assumptions, particularly with regard to such central concepts as being, substance, causality, the indivisibility of the divine attributes, creation, and conservation. There are of course many differences: Morin is a conservative and a traditionalist, both in his support of the pre-Copernican cosmology, and in his orthodox providentialism. But to read Morin's work alongside the discussion of God in the Third Meditation is to see, nonetheless, that for all Descartes' innovations in science, much of his metaphysics was very much a creature of its time.

[JC]

THAT GOD EXISTS,
AND THE WORLD WAS CREATED BY HIM IN TIME,
AND IS GOVERNED BY HIS PROVIDENCE.
SOME SELECTED THEOREMS AGAINST THE ATHEISTS,
BY JEAN-BAPTISTE MORIN,
DOCTOR OF MEDICINE AND REGIUS PROFESSOR OF
MATHEMATICS AT PARIS.

To the Most Illustrious and Reverend Doctors, the Archbishops, Bishops and all the Clergy of the Holy Convocation of France.

1. Letter to Mersenne of 28 January 1641, AT III 293–294; CSMK 171–172. Descartes' desire not to offend Morin was no doubt partly due to his habitual caution, but may also owe something to the fact that Morin had earlier provided some criticisms of the *Discourse* that Descartes apparently valued (Letter of Mersenne of 29 June 1638, AT II 191; CSMK 105). For more on Descartes' relations with Morin, see D. Garber, "Morin and the Second Objections" in Ariew and Grene (eds.), *Descartes and His Contemporaries*, pp. 63–82.

It would be nothing, or at least a small thing, most illustrious and reverend doctors, to complete a mental and visual survey of this entire universe; to distinguish the element into its primary regions, the ether and the heavens, and to describe each accurately; to show whether the primary motion belongs to the Earth or the heavens, to uncover the principles of universal physics, astronomy, and astrology, and the true way in which the celestial bodies act on these lower regions; in short, to provide a fully adequate knowledge of the nature of physical bodies, by means of all the relevant principles and powers and actions – all this would be worth nothing unless, by such continuous progress of the mind, the creator of the world, God, were not finally discovered, allowing the human intellect, so long troubled up till now, to find rest and calm in him.

This was the goal to which so much effort was devoted not just by Plato, Aristotle, Plotinus, and the other ancient philosophers and theologians, but also by many more recent Christian writers, who have produced massive volumes to this end. But they did not meet with such success as to remove the first principle of all religion, that God exists, from obscurity; so much so that there arose a rampant sect of atheists, which since that time has steadily grown. But Nature herself cannot lie, and provides such people with certain inner sparks of awareness that God exists, disturbing them against their will. Yet either because in a matter of such moment they resist giving serious attention to their own natural light of reason, or because they are unwilling to submit to any laws of religion, they constrain their will to the point of madness, and with a willed blindness bent on self-deception they empty their minds. Alternatively, they may see that, while many call into question the existence of God, no one has proved it by arguments and methods that compel them to assent. And hence they are tossed around by these lethal storms, and suppose falsely that atheism will be that calm harbor of intelligence and freedom that they so long for. Thus, in the very midst of those lights which God himself has kindled in the heavens and the ether and the Earth, they perish in misery, incapable of being called back by any authority of philosophy or theology or Holy Scripture, since these are all things they fly from or despise.

For my part, I have never doubted that not just the nature but the existence of God can be proved most evidently by means of the natural light alone. And I have discerned his supreme goodness principally in this, that he has not taken away the natural light even from atheists, by means of which alone they remain capable of grasping the first principles of nature, which despite themselves they cannot but perceive, since such principles are in themselves the object of this very light. And hence at least this way is open to us to debate the existence of God with the atheists, to make them acknowledge their own supreme error. Accordingly, I have set about this task for the glory of God, and to strengthen the faithful, and enlighten the atheists, using a mathematical method; and I have established that, once we grant the principles I set out, which are perceivable by the natural light alone, it cannot be denied by the atheists that God exists, and this world was created in time by him, and is governed by his providence, unless they are prepared to deny their own existence.

Since I have been assured by the testimony of men renowned for their intelligence and learning that this little work of mine ... would be neither unwelcome nor lacking in value for the Christian state, I have been unwilling to let it see the light of day without some protection. And as I reflected on this, the safest, most fitting, and illustrious protection to occur to me was that which you, most illustrious and reverend doctors, might supply. . . . Hence, I have ventured to dedicate this poor product of my intellect, small though it be, yet infinite in its subject matter, to you. If I see you welcome it, the principles I put forward and the theorems I demonstrate will easily enable it to yield many other truths of importance concerning God and his creatures; indeed, the immortality of the rational soul and all the natural sciences may be demonstrated by the same method, as anyone will discover. Hence, I will endeavor all the more earnestly to deserve your grace and benevolence. Paris, the first of September in the year of our Lord 1635.

Your most humble and obedient servant
Jean-Baptiste Morin

APPROVAL[2]

We the undersigned, Doctors in the Sacred Faculty of Theology at Paris, certify that we have attentively read the book *That God Exists* . . . by Jean-Baptiste Morin, Regius Professor of Mathematics at Paris, and that we find nothing in the book which is out of tune with, or contra-

2. Descartes hoped to obtain a similar seal of approval from the Sorbonne for his own *Meditations*, and wrote a dedicatory letter to the Theology Faculty with this aim; he was, however, unsuccessful. See however J.-R. Armogathe, "L'approbation des *Meditationes* par la faculté de théologie de Paris (1641)."

dicts, the Roman Catholic and Apostolic Faith. Signed on the third of
August, in the year of our Lord 1635.

F. Jullien
P. D'Ardivillier

THAT GOD EXISTS,
AND THE WORLD WAS CREATED BY HIM IN TIME,
AND IS GOVERNED BY HIS PROVIDENCE.
SOME SELECTED THEOREMS AGAINST THE ATHEISTS

DEFINITIONS

1. *Being* is that whereby whatever is is.
2. *A being* is that which has being.
3. *Nothing* is that which has no being.
4. *A finite being* is whatever is circumscribed by some limits in its being.
5. *An infinite Being* is whatever is circumscribed by no limits in its being, or what transcends all limits of being.
6. *Eternity* is duration that is closed by no limits and is, hence, infinite.
7. *Creation* is the transition of a being from nothing to actual existence, or the production of a being from nothing.
8. *Providence* is that whereby things are rationally ordered to some end.
9. *Number* is a plurality composed from unities.
10. Pure *activity* is a perfection of a being that excludes all potentiality for anything.

AXIOMS

1. Nothing is outside itself (in the way it is in itself).
2. A thing does not exist prior to its own existence.
3. What does not exist has no power.
4. What exists is not in potentiality to be what it itself is.
5. Whatever is, either exists in virtue of itself or has its being from some other.
6. Nothing can bestow what it does not itself possess.
7. The virtue of a finite being is finite.
8. The effect of a finite virtue cannot be infinite.
9. With respect to anything finite, something greater or more ample can always exist or be conceived.

10. With respect to the infinite, nothing greater or more ample can exist or be conceived.
11. The whole is greater than its part.
12. Two items that are identical with a third are themselves identical.
13. What is the cause of a cause is also the cause of its effect.
14. What is not eternal has a beginning in time, or another inchoate duration proper to itself.
15. In the case of something that exists from eternity, there is no beginning of its duration.
16. Every composite can be divided into the elements from which it is composed.

Theorem 1

An Infinite Being Is, in Itself, Whatever Is or Can Be

Otherwise an infinite Being would be circumscribed by some limits in its being (contrary to definition 5). Hence, an infinite Being is in itself whatever is or can be. And it follows from this that an infinite Being is any finite being, yet beyond or above any limits of being, in accordance with the definition of the infinite . . . or, as some would put it, "eminently."

Theorem 2

An Infinite Being Is Pure Activity

Otherwise it would be in potentiality with respect to something (definition 10), and hence it would not be everything that it is or can be (contrary to theorem 1), or it would be circumscribed by limits in its being (contrary to definition 5). Hence, an infinite Being is pure activity.

Theorem 3

An Infinite Being Is Infinite Activity, or Every Activity That Is or Can Be

Otherwise an infinite Being would not be everything that is or can be (contrary to theorem 1). Nor will the activity itself be pure (contrary to theorem 2). Hence, an infinite Being is infinite activity. And in consequence it is good, true, powerful, wise, and whatever else can be or be conceived under the notion of activity and perfection.

Theorem 4

An Infinite Being Is Immutable

Otherwise it would be in potentiality with respect to that into which it is capable of changing and, hence, it would not be pure activity (contrary to theorem 2) or be infinite activity (contrary to theorem 3).

Theorem 5

There Are Not Two Infinite Beings

If there were, it would be possible for there to be two infinite beings A and B at a given moment of time. And since A is an infinite Being, it will be whatever is or can be at that moment of time. And similarly B will be whatever is or can be at that same moment of time. But whatever is or can be in this same moment of time admits of no difference from itself, whether generic, specific, or individual, or of any other kind. Hence, A and B do not admit of any difference whatsoever between each other and will be entirely one and the same (axiom 12). Hence, they will not be two infinite beings, as we began by assuming. Hence, there are not two infinite beings.

It could be said that the result established in this theorem is valid of two infinites of the same kind or order – for example, two things that are infinite in being or substance or quantity or quality, and so forth, but not of two infinites of different orders. For example, one might be infinite in being, the other in substance, and so on.

This is an empty objection as is clear from the following. Let there be two infinites, A infinite in being and B in substance. Now since A is infinite in being it will be whatever is or can be, by theorem 1, since that theorem is understood as applying to an infinity entity or a being that is infinite qua being. Yet we are supposing that there is infinite substance in B; hence, A will be infinite substance and, hence, infinite in substance. Yet B is supposed to be infinite in substance. Hence, there will be two things that are infinite in substance, contrary to the premise of the objection. Therefore there cannot be two infinites, of whatever kind, but one alone. For if we conceive there to be two other infinites, one in quantity and the other in quality, either of these will be liable to the comparison just made with something infinite in being (which it is impossible not to conceive of), and in the course of this comparison each of the two supposed other infinites will be eliminated, as in the preceding argument.

Theorem 6

An Infinite Being Is Indivisible

It cannot be divided into two infinite beings, since there cannot be two infinite beings (theorem 5). Nor can it be divided into two finite beings, since for any finite being something greater or more ample can exist or be conceived (axiom 9); hence, from any two finite beings the infinite could not arise – otherwise it would be possible to have something greater than the infinite (contrary to axiom 10). Finally, it cannot be divided into a finite and an infinite being. For if we take away the finite, the infinite itself would always be left. Hence, an infinite Being is indivisible. And from this it follows that in an infinite Being there is nothing prior or posterior; otherwise it would be capable of being divided into that which is prior and that which is posterior.

Theorem 7

An Infinite Being Is Supremely Simple

For if it were in any way composite, it would be divisible into the elements of which it is composed (contrary to theorem 6). Hence, an infinite Being is supremely simple. Therefore, although it is single, true, good, powerful, and so on (theorem 3), yet in the case of an infinite Being, all these singular features are to be identified with itself (by this theorem), and with each other (axiom 12), and are a single infinite and supremely simple Being. Indeed, since an infinite Being may seem from the meaning of the terms to be conceived as composed of being and infinity, it turns out to be purer and more simple if it is simply conceived as a being in itself; for a being in itself is everything that is or can be and, hence, is identical with an infinite Being (theorem 1 and axiom 12). Again, since "a being in itself" still seems a concept made up of two elements – a subject possessing being, on the one hand (definition 2), and the being possessed by that subject, on the other, the concept of an infinite Being turns out purer and simpler if it is conceived simply as Being in itself. For "Being" is everything that is or can be, since it is that whereby whatever is is (definition 1), and is the essence of a being. Similarly, an infinite Being will be conceived of in a purer and simpler fashion if it is conceived as being unity itself, truth itself, goodness itself, wisdom itself, and so on, rather than being conceived as being one, true good, wise, and so on. Moreover, unity itself is, in itself, all the unity that is or can be; for it is a unity that is infinite and transcends all the limits of finite unity. And again, unity itself is goodness itself, and truth itself, and so on, since each of these, considered as infinite, is to be identified both with the infinite Being and with each other (as stated earlier). And the same must be said of truth itself, goodness itself, and so on. Now since an infinite Being is something unique and supremely simple, unity itself and truth itself and goodness itself, and so on are included in the supremely simple concept of Being itself. The intellect – at least the human intellect – cannot conceive of an infinite Being in any simpler fashion than under the concept of Being or Essence itself.

Theorem 8

An Infinite Being Is Neither Part nor Whole

It is not a part, since in that case it would be a part either of a finite or of an infinite Being: if of a finite being, the part would be greater than its whole (contrary to axiom 11); if of an infinite Being, an infinite Being would be divisible (contrary to theorem 6). On the other hand, it is not a whole either. For a whole qua whole consists of parts into which it is divisible; but an infinite Being is indivisible (theorem 6). Therefore, an infinite Being is neither part nor whole.

Theorem 9

The Difference between a Finite Being and an Infinite Being Is Infinite

For an infinite Being would exceed a finite being in a way falling short of the infinite, if the excess or difference were finite. And hence the infinite would be composed either of two finites or of a finite and an infinite, contrary to theorem 7. Therefore, the difference between an infinite and a finite being is infinite.

Theorem 10

An Infinite Being Differs in Itself from a Finite Being

Otherwise either the difference between an infinite and a finite being would not be infinite, contrary to theorem 9, or failing that there would be two different infinites, contrary to theorem 5. Hence, an infinite Being differs in itself from a finite being.

Theorem 11

Nothing Can by Itself Cross from Nothing to Actual Being

Otherwise, it would be able to do so either while it is not, or while it is. The first is ruled out, since what does not exist has no power (axiom 3). The second is ruled out, since what exists is not in potentiality to be that which it itself is (axiom 4). Hence, nothing can by itself cross from nothing to actual being.

Theorem 12

No Finite Thing Exists in Virtue of Itself

Otherwise, since every finite being is circumscribed by limits in its being, as this thing and not another (definition 4), if some finite being existed in virtue of itself, the question would arise as to why it was this thing and not another. And there would be no valid reason to be supplied but the following, namely that the finite being had chosen this rather than that nature from all possible ones, and had imposed on itself limits of being, so as to be this thing and not another. Yet it would follow from this that the finite being in question had existed prior to its own existence, since such choice and limitation could not possibly arise from something that does not exist (axiom 3). Yet it is impossible for something to exist prior to its own existence (axiom 2). Hence, no finite thing exists in virtue of itself.

Theorem 13

In the Production of Beings There Is No Circle

If A bestowed being on another, B, and B on another, C, and C bestowed being on the original A, it would follow that A was with respect to C both efficient cause and effect, and hence that it existed prior to its own existence, contrary to axiom 2. Hence, in the production of beings there is no circle.

Theorem 14

Every Finite Being Derives Its Existence from an Infinite Being

It is wholly necessary that whatever exists either exists in virtue of itself, or derives existence from some other being (axiom 5). For nothingness, which has no being (definition 3) cannot give existence to anything (axiom 6). Now no finite being exists in virtue of itself (theorem 12). So if a finite being has its existence from some being, it must be from either a finite or an infinite Being. If the latter, the desired result follows; if the former, we may say once again that this finite being derives its existence either from another finite being or from an infinite Being, and thus either the desired result once more follows, or the regress will continue to an indefinite number of finite beings. This number cannot be infinite, since the infinite is indivisible (theorem 6), whereas the number in question is a plurality composed of unities of singular produced entities (definition 9), and hence will be divisible into these unities or entities (axiom 16). Hence the number in question cannot be infinite (theorem 6), but will be finite. Consequently, this collection of finite entities will have a first member from which the others were produced, but which was not produced by any of them, since in the production of things there is no circle (theorem 14). And of this first finite entity we may again say that it does not exist from itself but derives its existence from some other entity, whether finite or infinite. Yet it cannot be finite, or else this further finite being would be the first among finite entities, in place of the original one we were supposing to be the first, thus violating our hypothesis. Hence, it must be infinite. And once we have posited a first finite being derived from an infinite Being, the other finite beings that come from the first being will be, at least in this sense, derived from the infinite Being; for what is the cause of a cause is the cause of its effect (axiom 13). Hence, every finite being derives its existence from an infinite Being.

This reasoning shows incidentally that the number of finite beings produced by other finite beings cannot be infinite. For let it be supposed that the number of human beings so far produced is infinite: in this case it will contain all the human beings who have been, are, and can be (axiom 10), and thus it will not be possible to produce a single additional human being. Yet every day, and every moment, new human beings are produced, as is obvious from experience (and this happens, moreover, without any circle of production: theorem 13). Hence, it cannot be supposed that the number of human beings produced is infinite, but only that it is finite. Consequently, there will be a first human being, and the same reasoning applies as previously given. Thus, since the argument is the same with respect to all other finite beings, where one derives its existence from some finite being, it necessarily follows that every finite being derives its existence from an infinite Being.

Let us pause here for a moment. If a being that is circumscribed by limits to its being is correctly called finite, it will follow that a Being that is conceived to be circumscribed by no limits to its being will correctly be called infinite. Now we have so far mentioned various properties of each kind of being, comparing each of them, but without settling in any way whether these entities do in fact exist, especially an infinite Being. We have however shown most manifestly that no finite being can exist in virtue of itself, but that all of them come from an infinite Being. We now proceed as follows.

Theorem 15

This Universe Is Finite

The terrestrial globe is finite, as is clear. And around it the remaining machinery of the universe moves in a circle, as is established by my thorough refutation of the view of the Copernicans. And hence the remaining machinery is finite, for otherwise it would occupy infinite space, and thus would in a finite time (the diurnal revolution of the heavens) cross this infinite space, which is impossible. Hence, the entire universe is finite; otherwise, there would be an infinite composed of two finites, contrary to theorem 6.

This also shows that the terrestrial globe is not the entire universe, but a part of the universe; and the same may be said of the Sun, and Moon, and any given star, and even of the heavens. Hence, the universe is a whole made up of these parts and, hence, is divisible into them (axiom 16). Therefore, it is not infinite, since the infinite is neither divisible (theorem 6) nor a whole (theorem 8). Hence, this universe is finite, both in respect of its being and its quantity; the argument establishes the same result for both. And therefore, although there may be a world soul, as several maintain following Plato, this is not the whole universe, but a part of it, just as the soul of a man is not the whole man but a part of him; even more so will the world soul be finite.

An alternative proof: Everything that is a quantity in respect of its form is divisible; but the universe is a quantity in respect of its form; hence, it is divisible. Therefore, it is not infinite (theorem 6); hence, it is finite, which is the proposition to be established.

Theorem 16

An Infinite Being Exists

A finite being exists, namely the Earth, the Sun, the Moon, man, and so on. Hence, an infinite Being exists from which these things derive their existence (theorem 14). It cannot be said that there was once an infinite Being from which these finite things derived their existence, but that it no longer exists. For this would certainly entail that such an infinite Being was circumscribed by limits to its duration and, hence, would not have been infinite (definition 5), which is a contradiction. Hence, an infinite Being[3] exists.

Theorem 17

An Infinite Being Exists in Virtue of Itself

Otherwise it derived its existence from another (axiom 5), which was either finite or infinite. The former is ruled out since the virtue of a finite being is finite (axiom 7), and its effect cannot be infinite (axiom

---

3. Or "the infinite Being." It should be remembered that Latin has no definite or indefinite article. The phrase *infinitum Ens* has generally been translated as "an infinite Being," since Morin's strategy throughout most of the work is to explore in general terms the necessary features of any being that qualifies as infinite (he has in any case demonstrated that there can be at most one such being; theorem 5).

8). The latter is ruled out since there cannot be two infinite beings (theorem 5). Hence, an infinite Being exists in virtue of itself.

Theorem 18

An Infinite Being Is Independent

For it exists in virtue of itself (theorem 17). Hence, it is independent of any other.

Theorem 19

An Infinite Being Is Eternal

Otherwise it either derived existence from another than itself (contrary to theorem 17), or it crossed by itself from nothingness to actual existence (contrary to theorem 11). Hence, an infinite Being is eternal; indeed, it is its own eternity, or eternity itself (theorems 6 and 7).

Theorem 20

From an Infinite Being Nothing Real Emanates Outside of Itself by Means of Which It Might Produce a Finite Being

Since an infinite Being is indivisible (theorem 6), if anything real emanated outside of it, then it would itself emanate outside of itself. But since it is immutable (theorem 4), it would in this case be outside itself, just as it is in itself (contrary to axiom 1). Therefore, from an infinite Being nothing real emanates and so on.

Theorem 21

An Infinite Being Produces a Finite Being by a Simple Act of Will

Since from an infinite Being nothing real emanates outside of itself which might produce a finite being (theorem 20), it is necessary that it produces a finite being by means of some immanent act. Now I maintain this act is an act of will. For in the production of a series of finite beings, we must eventually reach some first being that was produced by an infinite Being alone (theorem 14). But there are countless beings capable of being produced, no one of which has any greater claim to be produced than any other. So either all possible beings are simultaneously produced by an infinite Being that produces them outside of itself, or none are produced – and both the two alternatives just mentioned are clearly false – or else we must agree that there will be a choice or act of will in the infinite Being, which leads to the production of one possible thing rather than another. For the infinite Being itself is supremely free, wise, and powerful in the production of beings outside of itself; indeed, it is supreme freedom, infinite wisdom, and omnipotence (theorem 7). The way in which the production of a finite being is attributed to the infinite Being is, however, a peculiar one: such production depends on a simple act of will. For although the infinite Being is infinite wisdom and omnipotence, yet it neither produced outside of itself whatever it can produce, nor whatever it knows it can produce, but merely that which it wills to produce from among possible beings. Now given this act of will, a finite being cannot but be produced at the moment when the infinite Being willed from eternity that this should be done; for the will of the infinite Being is identical with its omnipotence (theorem 7), and is therefore most efficacious in itself, and needs no other cause, either efficient or inherent, to cooperate in its productive activity (otherwise it would not be supremely free and omnipotent, contrary to what has been said). Hence, the infinite Being produces a finite being by a simple act of will.

Theorem 22

A Finite Being Produced by an Infinite Being Is Continually Produced by the Same Infinite Being

Since a finite being is produced by an act of will of the infinite Being (theorem 21), it exists only insofar as the infinite Being wills this to be so. But as long as an infinite Being wills a finite being to exist, so long does it continue to produce it, since the omnipotent will of an infinite Being is supremely efficacious (theorem 21). Hence, a finite being produced by an infinite Being is continually produced by the same infinite Being. This continuous production of a finite being is generally called its "conservation" by the infinite Being, and if it ceased, the finite being would forthwith cease to exist.

Theorem 23

*All the Real Effects of a Finite Being Are Brought about by the
Efficient and Immediate Concurrence of the Infinite Being*

Since the infinite Being continually produces a finite being by an act of
will, thereby bestowing existence and the power of action (theorem 22),
it follows that at any given moment of time when a finite being acts,
the infinite Being wills it so to act. For otherwise its gift of the power
of action would be empty, and hence the infinite Being would not be
infinite wisdom (contrary to theorems 7 and 21); or else the finite being
would be acting against the will of the infinite Being, making it neither
infinitely free nor infinitely powerful (contrary to theorem 21). But insofar as the infinite Being wills a finite being to act, or to produce a real
new effect, so far does it bring about such action, and will the relevant
effect; and insofar as it wills this, so far does it also produce it, since its
will is supremely efficacious (theorem 21). Hence, all the real effects of
a finite being are brought about by the efficient and immediate concurrence of the infinite Being. The kind of "immediacy" we are talking of
here must be understood of the subject, and of some emanating power;
for no power emanates from an infinite Being outside of itself whereby
it might produce a finite being (theorem 20).

Theorem 24

*Every Finite Being Immediately Depends for Its Existence on the
Infinite Being*

A finite being is either produced by the infinite Being alone, or by some
other finite being. If the first, the truth of the theorem is obvious. If the second, since the infinite Being provides its efficient and immediate concurrence in the production of all the real effects of the finite being (theorem
23), it follows that a finite being produced by a finite being depends immediately on the infinite Being for its existence. Hence, the theorem is established.

Theorem 25

No Finite Being Exists or Can Exist Actually from Eternity

Let us suppose that some finite being actually exists from eternity. Since
it was produced by a simple act of will of the infinite Being (theorem

21), and is continually produced or conserved by this same act (theorem 22), then if the infinite Being wills (or can will) that this finite being will be eternal, it follows that we are supposing its duration, circumscribed by no limits, to be infinite, and hence indivisible; and, hence, that it will contain nothing prior or posterior (by the same theorem), and therefore will be all at once and once for all, and thus pure eternity (definition 6). But the infinite Being is also eternal (theorem 19), and is indeed its own eternity, or eternity itself (theorem 7). So either the eternities of the infinite Being and the finite being are numerically distinct, or they are one and the same. If the first, since each is infinite, there will be two infinites, contrary to theorem 5. If the second, since the eternity of an infinite being is identical with its being (theorem 7), then if the infinite Being can give its eternity to a finite being, it will also give it its infinite being, and hence this finite being will be infinite, contrary to our supposition. Hence, no finite being exists or can exist from eternity. (There is no force in the objection that eternity is essential to an infinite Being, but merely accidental and participatory in the case of a merely finite being. For this does not remove the infinity from the eternity of the finite being, and hence we are always brought back to the previous argument, namely that these eternities are either numerically distinct, or one and the same, and so forth.)

An alternative proof. No finite being can actually exist that was not capable of being produced from eternity. Hence, no finite being existed or was capable of existing actually from eternity. Otherwise it would have been simultaneously both actual and potential, or actual and not actual, which is a contradiction. This last point is self-evident. As for the initial premise, it is proved from the fact that any finite being can only be produced by an act of will of the infinite Being, and the will of such a being is supremely free with respect to the production of a finite being (theorem 21). Hence, it is in itself indifferent with respect to bestowing or not bestowing actual existence on the finite being, and this therefore presupposes that the finite being exists merely in potentiality. Otherwise the indifference of the infinite Being would be concerned with giving or not giving existence to something that is already actual, or to something impossible, each of which is utterly absurd. Hence, no finite being can exist actually from eternity, even if it is possible from eternity.

Theorem 26

*This Universe Did Not Derive Its Existence from a Physical Process
of Generation*

All physical generation yields something that is a unity in itself. But this
universe is not a unity in itself but only accidentally – namely, as the
result of an aggregation of many bodies, the Earth, the Sun, the Moon,
and so on, which are mutually discontinuous and of different species.
Hence, this universe did not derive its existence from a physical process
of generation.

Theorem 27

This Universe Was Created in Time by an Infinite Being

Since the universe is finite (theorem 15), it is not eternal (theorem 25).
Moreover, those who suppose with Aristotle that this universe is eternal
thereby suppose that its motion or that of the heavens is eternal, since
they declare that the prime mover of the universe is eternal. But on this
supposition, the number of revolutions of the prime mover from eternity
up to now is either finite or infinite. If the first, there will be a first
revolution, and hence a beginning to the duration of the universe, contrary to axiom 15. If the second, the number will include all the revolutions that have been, are, and can be (axiom 10), and as a result no
further revolution will be possible; yet every day there is a new revolution of the first heaven. Hence, this universe is not eternal. Therefore,
it began to exist in time, with a duration proper to itself (axiom 14). And
it did not derive its existence by means of physical generation (theorem
26), nor finally did it cross by itself from nothingness to actual existence
(theorem 11). Hence, it was brought from nothing to actual existence
immediately by that from which every finite being derives its existence,
namely from an infinite Being (theorem 24). And what is produced in
this way is said to be created (definition 7). Hence, this universe was
created in time by an infinite Being – which was the proposition to be
demonstrated.

Theorem 28

This Universe and the Individual Beings in It Are Ruled by the Providence of an Infinite Being

The infinite Being is the efficient immediate cause of this universe and the individual beings produced in it (theorem 24). Now every efficient cause acts for an end, and this is especially true of the infinite Being, which is infinite wisdom (theorem 7). Hence, either it is groundless to say the infinite Being acts for an end, or else this Being ordains the universe itself, and its individual finite entities, by appropriate means, toward an end that it intended in creating them; this is providence, or the rule of providence (definition 8). Hence, this universe and the individual beings in it are ruled by the providence of an infinite Being.

An alternative proof. It is most clearly to be seen that providence resides in all animals. For the brutes provide for their young, parents for their children, the head of the household for his family, the king for his kingdom and subjects. Hence, this finite providence derives from the infinite Being (theorem 24), and therefore the infinite Being itself will be provident (axiom 6 and theorem 3) and, indeed, will be infinite providence itself (theorem 7) – that is, providence extended to any finite being whatsoever, for otherwise it would not be infinite. Hence, this universe and the individual beings in it are ruled by the providence of an infinite Being.

Another proof. Every finite being is continually produced by the infinite Being, and this continual production is called the conservation of the finite being (theorem 22). It is produced, however, by an act of will, which is identical with infinite wisdom (theorem 21) and hence is not exercised rashly or pointlessly, but with a view to some end. Hence, every being is continually directed to this end by the same infinite Being, which would surely not be infinite, but circumscribed by limits to its being if it were not provident, and indeed [if it were not] infinite providence, having complete knowledge of itself and not overlooking even the smallest thing anywhere.

There are three benefits in the universe arising from the providence of the infinite Being. First, the placing of individual finite beings in their proper places and orders; second, their conservation in these places and orders; third, their motion and direction toward a proper end in accordance with the nature of each. For the infinite Being providentially ensures that necessary causes should act necessarily, contingent causes contingently, and free causes freely. The infinite Being willed that some of its creatures should be free and endowed with intellect and will, so that among all the finite beings created by it, it should not itself remain unknown. Its purpose was that, in the case of these free creatures at least (which in this respect it ennobled above all others and made like itself), it should be recognized by their intellect as the first principle of all things, their middle or conserver, and their ultimate end, and also chosen by their will as an object to be worshiped, loved, and longed for above all created things. Thus, these creatures quite freely, in virtue of their likeness to the infinite Being itself, would continually strive toward it in purity, justice, love, holiness, and the like, and would at length attain to it, and find their fulfillment there. If indeed they are free creatures, they are created with the capacity for distinguishing truth from falsehood, good from evil, and justice from injustice and, hence, for recognizing their own excellence above other finite creatures, and their greater obligations. And thus, by a decree of infinite providence, they must either do what is just or suffer their just deserts; if they do not pursue the first voluntarily, they will incur the second necessarily.

Theorem 29

There Is an Ultimate End of All Individual Finite Beings

Each finite being is produced by the infinite Being (theorem 24) with a view to some end; and the finite being is directed to this end by the infinite (theorem 28). Hence, this end exists – else it would be pointless for the finite being to be directed to it by infinite wisdom, which cannot be said. So either this end is the ultimate end of the finite being and is that at which it aims, or else it is merely a means to the ultimate end. If this ultimate end exists, then once again it will be what is aimed at; if not, then the original action will not be the means to it, contrary to our hypothesis. Therefore, there is necessarily an ultimate end of individual finite beings; and in this way every finite being arrives at the fulfillment of its perfection, according to its own nature. And therefore, it is in this end that a finite being seeks to find rest from the motion whereby it proceeds from its cause, striving toward its longed for goal.

Theorem 30

The Infinite Being Is the Ultimate End af All Finite Beings

Otherwise there would be an infinite regress in ends, entailing that a finite being could never reach the end intended in its production by the infinite Being, but would be directed in vain toward it by infinite wisdom. Or alternatively there would be a finite end produced by the infinite Being with no other purpose than to be the ultimate end of some finite beings (theorem 29). This would mean that some finite beings were the ultimate end of this finite being, and thus they would be mutual causes to each other within the same kind, which all philosophers admit is impossible. Furthermore, the ultimate end is sought above all by those that strive toward it, since it is sufficient for them; and hence, once it is attained, they come wholly to rest. But each finite end is never sufficient for itself alone, but continuously requires to be produced and conserved, to prevent it ceasing to be (theorem 22). Hence, it is even less sufficient for other beings, especially for the infinite appetite of man. Therefore, no finite being can be the ultimate end for itself or for another. Finally, since a rational creature is constrained to strive with its entire intellect and entire will toward the ultimate end to which it is directed, if this end were other than the infinite Being, it would tend with its entire intellect and will to turn away from the infinite Being; yet we have already said that the infinite Being made rational creatures in order to be recognized by their intellect and loved by their will. Hence, the infinite Being is the ultimate end of all finite beings and, in conclusion, is attained by any creature that tends toward it, in accordance with the nature proper to each thing. Hence, it is attained immediately by means of the intellect and the will, or by knowledge and love, by the rational creatures that use their intellect and will to strive toward it, and indirectly, via the agency of such creatures, by other created things.

Now this infinite Being, unique, supremely simple, immutable, independent, eternal, the creator of the universe, the conserver, the most providential ruler, and the ultimate end, is by the agreement of all the nations called GOD. He is infinite goodness, infinite wisdom, infinite love, infinite liberality, infinite justice, infinite blessedness, and everything else that is most fittingly attributed to him, for otherwise he would not be the infinite Being itself. Every creature, on account of the existence and power of action received from him, and on account of its conservation both immediate and via secondary causes, is in debt to him for its very existence, its power of action, and all the actions that come from this, or their entire use. But most of all, rational creatures are in debt to him for the entire use of their intellect and their will, since such creatures cannot be ignorant of his existence (if they are willing to inquire into the matter by the natural light, as has been shown already), nor should they be. They can conduct such an inquiry, and are obliged to do so, since the highest pitch of blessedness for a rational creature consists in the knowledge and love of God. And to God, finally, let there be given thanks, praise, honor, virtue, and glory, world without end, Amen.

Appendix: Condemnations of Cartesianism

Descartes made converts to his new philosophy with the publication of the *Principles*, the systematic exposition of his thought, set out in Scholastic style, but, on the whole, he did not succeed in getting the work adopted in the curriculum of the schools. Here and there one can find Cartesian principles taught, as with the ill-fated Oratorians at Angers in the 1670s and Edmond Pourchot at Paris in the 1690s. One can also find Cartesian propositions included in some disputations, but the discussion is mostly negative. The official response to Descartes' philosophy was unfavorable for most of the seventeenth century. At various times, Descartes waged fierce battles with his opponents. In the 1640s, he thought himself "at war" with the Jesuits, a war precipitated by a Jesuit disputation at Clermont College and continuing through Pierre Bourdin's *Seventh Set of Objections*, published, together with Descartes' *Replies* and the *Letter to Dinet*, in the second edition of the *Meditations* (1642).[1] There were troubles and official condemnations by Protestants at Utrecht, circa 1642, and Leyden, 1647.[2] The battles continued and intensified after Descartes' death in 1650. There were condemnations by Catholics at Louvain in 1662, culminating with Descartes' works being put on the *Index of Prohibited Books* by the censors of Rome in 1663. The fighting raged in the second half of the seventeenth century: the Jesuits held more anti-Cartesian disputations at Clermont College

---

1. See R. Ariew, "Pierre Bourdin and the *Seventh Objections*," in R. Ariew and M. Grene, eds., *Descartes and His Contemporaries*, pp. 208–225.
2. See *La querelle d'Utrecht*, ed. and trans. Theo Verbeek, and also Verbeek's *Descartes and the Dutch*.

in 1665, some clearly intended to make Descartes look ridiculous.[3] It intensified with numerous attacks in print.[4] The Cartesians counterattacked with satires[5] and learned essays.[6] The anti-Cartesians also responded with their own satires.[7] Ultimately, the dispute spilled into the official political arena, the domains of the king, of the universities, and of the teaching orders. The king issued an edict in 1671; the faculty of arts at Paris tried to condemn Cartesianism in 1671 and succeeded in 1691; there were skirmishes at Angers and Caen during 1675–1678;[8] the Jesuits, in a congress with the Oratorians, ultimately prohibited the teaching of Cartesianism in 1678, and formally condemned it in 1706. Only the condemnations of Aristotelianism in the thirteenth century were as frequent and as wide-sweeping as the condemnations of Cartesianism in the late seventeenth century; however, the reasons for the prohibitions of Cartesianism were even more diverse than those given against Peripatetic philosophy. Cartesianism was censured not only for doctrinal reasons, but also on pragmatic and pedagogical grounds. Reflecting the pedagogical judgment of the authorities of Utrecht was the assertion that being taught Cartesian philosophy would leave one unprepared for the higher faculties of theology, law, and med-

3. For example, Ludovicus Prou, *De hypothesi cartesiana positiones physico mathematica* (1665).
4. See, for example, J. Vincent, *Discussio peripatetica in qua philosophiae cartesianae principia* (1677); Louis de la Ville [Louis le Valois], *Sentimens de Monsieur Descartes touchant l'essence et les proprietez du corps opposez à la Doctrine de l'Eglise, et conforme aux erreurs de Calvin sur le sujet de l'Eucharistie* (1680); Jean-Baptiste de la Grange, *Les principes de la philosophie contre les nouveaux philosophes, Descartes, Rohault, Regius, Gassendi, le P. Maignan, etc.* (1682); Pierre Daniel Huet, *Censura philosophiae cartesianae* (1689); Jean Duhamel, *Reflexions critiques sur le système cartesien de la philosophie de mr. Régis* (1692).
5. See the "arret burlesque," in *Oeuvres de Boileau*, ed. Saint-Marc (1747), vol. 3, pp. 150–153; *Corpus*, 20–21 (1992), pp. 231–240.
6. [Antoine Arnauld?], *Plusieurs raisons pour empecher la censure ou la condemnation de la philosophie de Descartes*, in *Oeuvres de Boileau*, ed. Saint-Marc, vol. 3, pp. 117–141. See also Pierre Bayle, *Recueil de quelques pièces curieuses concernant la philosophie de Monsieur Descartes* (1684).
7. Gabriel Daniel, *Voyage du monde de Descartes* (1690); M. G. de L'A. [Pierre Daniel Huet], *Nouveaux mémoires pour servir à l'histoire du cartésianisme* (1692); Gabriel Daniel, *Nouvelles difficultés proposées par un péripatéticien à l'auteur du "Voyage du monde de Descartes"* (1693).
8. For an account of the events at Angers, see François Babin, *Journal ou relation fidele* (1675–1679).

icine. And the Jesuits, echoing Bourdin's preoccupation with hy-
perbolic doubt, often gave pragmatic reasons for dispensing with
Cartesianism. As René Rapin said, "In truth, Descartes teaches one
to doubt too much, and that is not a good model for minds who
are naturally credulous; but, in the end, he is more original than the
others."[9] A general assessment of the doctrinal difficulties of Cartesianism can be found in a summary of a disputation by the Jesuits
of Clermont College during 1665:

> To say no more, the Cartesian hypothesis must be distasteful to
> mathematics, philosophy, and theology. To philosophy because it
> overthrows all its principles and ideas[,] which common sense has
> accepted for centuries; to mathematics, because it is applied to
> the explanation of natural things, which are of another kind, not
> without great disturbance of order; to theology, because it seems
> to follow from the hypothesis that (i) too much is attributed to
> the fortuitous concourse of corpuscles, which favors the atheist;
> (ii) there is no necessity to allow a substantial form in man, which
> favors the impious and dissolute; (iii) there can be no conversion
> of bread and wine in the Eucharist into the blood and body of
> Christ, nor can it be determined what is destroyed in that con-
> version, which favors heretics.[10]

Here are some of the official condemnations of Cartesianism from
1662 to 1705.

[RA]

Faculty of Theology at Louvain, 1662[11]

1. *Principles of Philosophy* I articles 51 and 52: "By substance we can understand nothing other than a thing that exists in such a way as to depend on no other thing for its existence. And there is only one substance
that can be understood to depend on no other thing whatsoever, namely
God. In the case of all other substances, we perceive that they can exist
only with the help of God's concurrence." And also: "But as for cor-

9. René Rapin, *Reflexions sur la philosophie*, in *Oeuvres* (1725), p. 366.
10. A report of the disputation can be found in a letter from Oldenburg to Boyle
    of 4 July 1665, *The Correspondence of Henry Oldenburg*, vol. 2, pp. 430–435; the
    summary is on p. 435.
11. Charles Duplessis d'Argentré, *Collectio judiciorum de novis erroribus tomus ter-
    tium* (1736), part 2, pp. 303–304.

CONDEMNATIONS OF CARTESIANISM

poreal substance and mind (or created thinking substance), these can be understood to fall under this common concept: things that need only the concurrence of God in order to exist."[12] These are censured by the Holy Faculty of Theology, since, as a consequence of these, there would not be any substantial forms, except for the rational soul; indeed there would not be any substantial forms in animals and plants, as signaled in various places.

2. *Replies to the Sixth Set of Objections to the Meditations*, section 7: "It is completely contradictory that there should be real accidents, since whatever is real can exist separately from any other subject; yet anything that can exist separately in this way is a substance, not an accident. The claim that real accidents cannot be separated from their subjects 'naturally,' but only by the power of God, is irrelevant. For to occur 'naturally' is nothing other than to occur through the ordinary power of God, which in no way differs from his extraordinary power – the effect on the real world is exactly the same. Hence if everything which can naturally exist without a subject is a substance, anything that can exist without a substance even through the power of God, however extraordinary, should also be termed a substance."[13] The Holy Faculty is of the opinion that, as a consequence, the accidents of bread and wine would not remain without subject in the Eucharist.

3. In *Meditations*, p. 172, and *Principles of Philosophy* I, article 53: "The extension of bodies constitutes its essential and natural attribute."[14]

4. *Principles* II, article 21: "What is more we recognize that this world, that is, the whole universe of corporeal substance, has no limits to its extension."[15]

5. *Principles* II, article 22: "It can also easily be gathered from this that . . . if there were an infinite number of worlds, the matter of which they were composed would have to be identical; hence, there cannot in

---

12. Descartes, AT VIII 24–25; CSM I 210.
13. Descartes, AT VII 434–35; CSM II 293.
14. What is attributed to Descartes is not an exact quote: Descartes, *Replies Six*, AT VII, 442 (CSMK 298): "I did not attribute to gravity the extension that constitutes the nature of a body"; *Principles* I, 53 (AT VIII 25; CSM I 210): "each substance has one principal property that constitutes its nature and essence, and to which all its other properties are referred. Thus extension in length, breadth, and depth constitutes the nature of corporeal substance."
15. Descartes, AT VIII 52; CSM I 232.

fact be a plurality of worlds, but only one."[16] Our academy has acted in this manner, and the doctrine of Descartes has been rejected.

Verbal Order of the King, Communicated by Monsignor François de Harlay, Archbishop of Paris, to the Gentlemen and Deputies of the University of Paris, on Tuesday, 4 August 1671[17]

The king, having learned that certain opinions that the faculty of theology had once censored, and that the parliament had prohibited from teaching and from publishing, are now being disseminated, not only in the university, but also in the rest of this city and in certain parts of the kingdom, either by strangers, or by people within the kingdom, and wishing to prevent the course of this opinion that could bring some confusion in the explanation of our mysteries, pushed by his zeal and his ordinary piety, has commanded me to tell you of his intentions. The king exhorts you, sirs, to bring it about that no other doctrine than the one decreed by the rules and statutes of the university is taught in the universities and put into theses, and leaves you to your prudence and to your wise conduct to take the necessary path for this.[18]

Congregation of the Priests of the Oratory: Excerpts from the Acts following the General Congregation of the Oratorians Residing in Paris, September 1678[19]

According to the resolutions of our assemblies. . . .

In physics, we must not stray from Aristotle's physics or his principles of physics commonly taught in the colleges, in order to attach ourselves to the new doctrine of Descartes, which the king, for good reasons, has forbidden to be taught.

We must teach.

1. That actual and external extension is not the essence of matter.
2. That in each natural body there is a substantial form really distinct from matter.

16. Descartes, AT VIII 52; CSM I 232.
17. Bouillier, *Histoire de la philosophie cartésienne*, vol. 1, p. 469.
18. Ibid.
19. *Concordat entre les Jesuites et les Peres de l'Oratoire, Actes de la Sixiéme Assemblée, September 1678*, in Pierre Bayle, *Recueil de quelques pièces curieuses concernant la philosophie de Monsieur Descartes*, pp. 11–12.

3. That there are real and absolute accidents inherent in their subjects, which can be supernaturally without any subject.
4. That the soul is really present and united to the whole body and to every part of the body.
5. That thought or knowledge is not the essence of the rational soul.
6. That there is no repugnance in God's creating several worlds at the same time.
7. That the void is not impossible.

The Rector and Professors of Philosophy of the Parisian Academy Have Met and Written What Follows, 1691[20]

With respect to certain articles given to the rector by the archbishop from the king, containing several propositions, allegedly extracted from the writings of some professors of the University of Paris, which His Majesty desires not to be upheld in the schools:

1. One must rid oneself of all kinds of prejudices and doubt everything before being certain of any knowledge.
2. One must doubt whether there is a God until one has a clear and distinct knowledge of it.
3. We do not know whether God did not create us such that we are always deceived in the very things that appear the clearest.
4. As a philosopher, one must not develop fully the unfortunate consequences that an opinion might have for faith, even when the opinion appears incompatible with faith; notwithstanding this, one must stop at that opinion, if it is evident.
5. The matter of bodies is nothing other than their extension and one cannot be without the other.
6. One must reject all the reasons the theologians and the philosophers have used until now (with Saint Thomas) to demonstrate the existence of God.
7. Faith, hope, and charity and generally all the supernatural habits are nothing spiritual distinct from the soul, as the natural habits are nothing spiritual distinct from mind and will.
8. All the actions of the infidels are sins.

20. Charles Duplessis d'Argentré, *Collectio judiciorum de novis erroribus tomus tertium*, part I, p. 149.

9. The state of pure nature is impossible.
10. The invincible ignorance of natural right does not excuse sin.
11. One is free, provided that one acts with judgment and with full knowledge, even when one acts necessarily.

Prohibited Propositions, from the Fifteenth General Congress, Michele Angelo Tamburini, General of the Jesuits, 1706[21]

1. The human mind can and must doubt everything except that it thinks and consequently that it exists.
2. Of the remainder, one can have certain and reasoned knowledge only after having known clearly and distinctly that God exists, that he is supremely good, infallible, and incapable of inducing our minds into error.
3. Before having knowledge of the existence of God, each person could and should always remain in doubt about whether the nature with which one has been created is not such that it is mistaken about the judgments that appear most certain and evident to it.
4. Our minds, to the extent that they are finite, cannot know anything certain about the infinite; consequently, we should never make it the object of our discussions.
5. Beyond divine faith, no one can be certain that bodies exist – not even one's own body.
6. The modes or accidents, once produced in a subject, do not have need of a cause to conserve them by a positive action; but they may last as long as they are not destroyed by the positive action of an external cause.
7. In order to admit that some quantity of motion that God originally impressed on matter is lost, one would have to assume that God is changeable and inconstant.
8. No substance, whether spiritual or corporeal, can be annihilated by God.
9. The essence of each being depends upon God's free will, so that, in another order of things he was free to create, the essence and prop-

---

21. Camille de Rochemonteix, *Un collège de Jésuites*, vol. 4, pp. 89–93. See also the discussion of these censures in the letters from Des Bosses to Leibniz, 20 August 1706, and Leibniz to Des Bosses, 1 September 1706, in Leibniz, *Philosophischen Schriften*, vol. 2, pp. 311–313 and 313–315.

erties, for example, of matter, mind, circle, and so on, would have been other than they are at present.

10. The essence of matter or of body consists in its actual and external extension.

11. No part of matter can lose anything of its extension without losing as much of its substance.

12. The compenetration of bodies properly speaking and place void of all bodies imply a contradiction.

13. We can represent local extension everywhere to ourselves; for example, beyond the heavens, there really exists a space filled by bodies or by matter.

14. In itself, the extension of the world is indefinite.

15. There can be only one world.

16. There is, in the world, a precise and limited quantity of motion, which has never been augmented or diminished.

17. No body can move without all those from which it gets farther or to which it gets nearer moving at the same time.

18. For a body to move is for it to be conserved by God successively in different places.

19. Only God can move bodies; angels, rational souls, and bodies themselves are not the efficient causes, but the occasional causes of motion.

20. Creatures do not produce anything as efficient causes, but God alone produces all effects, *ad illarum praesentiam.*

21. Animals are mere automata deprived of all knowledge and sensation.

22. The union of the rational soul and the body is nothing other than the act by which God willed some perceptions in the soul to be excited in relation to some changes in the body and, reciprocally, to produce in the body some determined motions following some thoughts or volitions of the soul.

23. This communication of motions and effects is not required by the very nature of body and soul; it is the result of God's free decree.

24. Color, light, cold, hot, sound, and all properties called sensible are affections or modifications of the mind itself, and not of the bodies called hot, cold, and so on.

25. Mixed bodies, even of animals, do not differ from each other except by variations of magnitudes, shape, situation, texture, rest, or motion of atoms or particles of matter that constitute them.

26. In perception, the mind does not act; it is a purely passive faculty.

27. Judgment and reasoning are acts of the will, not of the intellect.

28. There are no substantial forms of bodies in matter.
29. There are no absolute accidents.
30. Descartes' system can be defended as a hypothesis whose principles harmonize among themselves and with their deductions.

Bibliography

Argentré, C. Duplessis d'. *Collectio judiciorum de novis erroribus tomus tertium* (Paris, 1736).

Ariew, R., and M. Grene, eds. *Descartes and His Contemporaries* (Chicago: University of Chicago Press, 1995).

Armogathe, J.-R. "L'approbation des *Meditations* par la faculté de théologie de Paris (1641)." *Bulletin Cartésien XXI, Archives de Philosophie* 57 (1994), pp. 1–3.

Babin, F. *Journal ou relation fidele de tout ce qui s'est passé dans l'université d'Angers au sujet de la philosophie de Des Carthes en l'execution des ordres du Roy pendant les années 1675, 1676, 1677, et 1678* (Angers, 1679).

Baldini, U. *Legem impone subactis: studi su filosofia e scienza dei Gesuiti in Italia 1540–1632* (Rome: Bulzoni Editore, 1992).

Bayle, P. *Recueil de quelques pièces curieuses concernant la philosophie de Monsieur Descartes* (Amsterdam, 1684).

Blair, A. "The Teaching of Natural Philosophy in Early Seventeenth-Century Paris: The Case of Jean-Cecile Frey." *History of Universities* 12 (1993), pp. 95–158.

Blanchet, L. *Les antécédents historiques du je pense, donc je suis* (Paris: Vrin, 1920).

Bloch, O. R. *La philosophie de Gassendi* (The Hague: Martinus Nijhoff, 1971).

Boileau. *Oeuvres de Boileau*, ed. Saint-Marc (1747).

Bouillier, F. *Histoire de la philosophie cartésienne*, 2 vols. (Paris: Delagrave, 1868).

Brockliss, L. W. B. *French Higher Education in the Seventeenth and Eighteenth Centuries: A Cultural History* (Oxford: Oxford University Press, 1987).

Charron, P. *De la sagesse* (1601; 2nd ed. 1604; Paris: Fayard, 1986).

Clavius, C. *Modus quo disciplinae mathematicae in scholis Societatis possent promoveri.* In *Monumenta paedagogica Societatis Jesu quae primam rationem studiorum anno 1586 praecessere* (1586; Matriti: Typis Augustini Avrial, 1901).

Conimbricenses. *Commentarii in octo libros physicorum Aristotelis* (Coimbra, 1592).
Commentarii in tres libros de anima (Coimbra, 1598).
Commentarii in universam dialecticam Aristotelis (Coimbra, 1606).

Cottingham, J. "The Cartesian Legacy." *Proceedings of the Aristotelian Society*, suppl. vol. 66 (1992), pp. 1–21.

ed. *Cambridge Companion to Descartes* (Cambridge: Cambridge University Press, 1992).

ed. *Reason, Will and Sensation* (Oxford: Clarendon Press, 1994).

Daniel, G. *Voyage du monde de Descartes* (Paris, 1690).

Nouvelles difficultés proposées par un péripatéticien à l'auteur du "Voyage du monde de Descartes" (Paris, 1693).

Dear, P. *Mersenne and the Learning of the Schools* (Ithaca: Cornell University Press, 1987).

Descartes, R. *The Philosophical Writings of Descartes*, vols. 1 and 2, trans. J. Cottingham, R. Stoothoff, and D. Murdoch. Vol. 3, *The Correspondence*, trans. J. Cottingham, R. Stoothoff, D. Murdoch, and A. Kenny (1619–1650; Cambridge: Cambridge University Press, 1985–1991).

Des Chene, D. *Physiologia: Philosophy of Nature in Late Aristotelian and Cartesian Thought* (Ithaca: Cornell University Press, 1996).

Duhamel, J. *Reflexions critiques sur le système cartesien de la philosophie de mr. Régis* (Paris, 1692).

Philosophia universalis sive commentarius in universam aristotelis philosophiam ad usum scholarum comparatam, 5 vols. (Paris, 1705).

Duhamel, J.-B. *Philosophia vetus et nova* (Amsterdam, 1677).

Dupleix, S. *Corps de philosophie, contenant la logique, la physique, la metaphysique et l'ethique* (Geneva, 1627).

La logique ou art de discourir et raisonner (1603; Paris: Fayard, 1984).

La physique ou science des choses naturelles (1603; Paris: Fayard, 1990).

La metaphysique ou science surnaturelle (1610; Paris: Fayard, 1992).

L'ethique ou philosophie morale (1610; Paris: Fayard, 1994).

Eustachius a Sancto Paulo (Eustache Asseline). *Summa philosophiae quadripartita de rebus dialecticis, moralibus, physicis, et metaphysicis* (Paris, 1609).

Garber, D. *Descartes' Metaphysical Physics* (Chicago: University of Chcago Press, 1992).

Gassendi, P. *Dissertations en forme de paradoxes contre les Aristoléliciens (Exercitationes paradoxicae adversus Aristoteleos)*, ed. and trans. B. Rochot (1624; Paris: Vrin, 1959).

Gilson, E. *Index scolastico-cartésien* (Paris: Félix Alcan, 1913).

Etudes sur le rôle de la pensée médiévale dans la formation du système cartésien, 2nd ed. (Paris: Vrin, 1976).

Goudin, A. *Philosophie suivant les principes de Saint Thomas*, trans. T. Bourard (1st Latin ed., 1668; Paris, 1864).

Grange, J.-B. de la. *Les principes de la philosophie contre les nouveaux philosophes, Descartes, Rohault, Regius, Gassendi, le P. Maignan, etc.* (Toulouse, 1682).

Grene, M. *Descartes among the Scholastics* (Milwaukee: Marquette University Press, 1992).

Hatfield, G. "The Senses and the Fleshless Eye: The Meditations as Cognitive Exercises." Pp. 45–79 in A. E. Rorty, ed., *Essays on Descartes' Meditations* (Berkeley: University of California Press, 1986).

Huet, P. D. *Censura philosophiae cartesianae* (Paris, 1689).

[M. G. de L'A., pseud.]. *Nouveaux mémoires pour servir à l'histoire du cartésianisme* (n. p., 1692).

Joy, L. S. *Gassendi the Atomist: Advocate of History in an Age of Science* (Cambridge: Cambridge University Press, 1987).

Kretzman, N., A. Kenny, and J. Pinborg, eds. *The Cambridge History of Later Medieval Philosophy* (Cambridge: Cambridge University Press, 1982).

Lattis, J. M. *Between Copernicus and Galileo. Christoph Clavius and the Collapse of Ptolemaic Cosmology* (Chicago: University of Chicago Press, 1994).

Leibniz, G. W. *Philosophischen Schiften*, ed. C. I. Gerhardt (Berlin: Olms, 1875–1890).

Lennon, T. *The Battle of the Gods and Giants: The Legacies of Descartes and Gassendi, 1655–1715* (Princeton: Princeton University Press, 1993).

Lennon, T., J. Nicholas, and J. Davis. *Problems of Cartesianism* (Kingston: McGill-Queen's University Press, 1982).

Lenoble, R. *Mersenne ou la naissance du mécanisme* (Paris: Vrin, 1971).

Mersenne, M. *L'usage de la raison* (Paris, 1623).

   La verité des sciences contre les sceptiques ou pyrrhoniens (1625; Stuttgart-Bad Cannstatt: Friedrich Fromman Verlag, 1969).

   L'impieté des deistes, athées et libertins de ce temps (1624; Stuttgart-Bad Cannstatt: Friedrich Fromman Verlag, 1975).

Morin, J.-B. *Quod Deus Sit* (1635; Lecce: Conte Editore, 1996).

Murr, S., ed. *Corpus*, 20–21 (1992).

Oldenburg, H. *The Correspondence of Henry Oldenburg*, ed. R. H. Hall and M. B. Hall (c. 1660; Madison: University of Wisconsin Press, 1966).

Ong, Walter J. *Ramus: Method and the Decay of Dialogue* (Cambridge, Mass.: Harvard University Press, 1983).

Osler, M. J. *Divine Will and the Mechanical Philosophy: Gassendi and Descartes on Contingency and Necessity in the Created World* (Cambridge: Cambridge University Press, 1994).

Péguy, C. *Oeuvres en prose 1909–1914* (Paris: Gallimard, 1957).

Pintard R. *Le libertinage erudit dans la première moitié du XVIIe siècle*, 2nd ed. (1943; Geneva: Slatkine, 1983).

Popkin, R. H. *History of Scepticism from Erasmus to Descartes* (New York: Humanities Press, 1964).

   The History of Scepticism from Erasmus to Spinoza (Berkeley: University of California Press, 1979).

Pourchot, E. *Institutio philosophica* (Paris, 1695).

Raconis, C. F. d'Abra de. *Summa totius philosophiae* (1617; Paris, 1651).

Ramée, P. de La (Petrus Ramus). *La dialectique*, ed. M. Dassonville (1555; Geneva: Droz, 1964).

Rapin, R. *Oeuvres* (Paris, 1725).

Régis, P. S. *Cours entier de la philosophie ou système général selon les principes de M. Descartes contenant la logique, la métaphysique, la physique, et la morale*, 3 vols. (Paris, 1691).

Rochemonteix, C. de. *Un collège de Jésuites aux 17e et 18e siècles: Le collège d'Henry IV à la Flèche* (Le Mans, 1899).

Rodis-Lewis, G. *L'anthropologie cartésienne* (Paris: P.U.F., 1990).

Rorty, A., ed. *Essays on Descartes' Meditations* (Berkeley: University of California Press, 1986).

Rubidge, B. "Descartes's Meditations and Devotional Meditations." *Journal of the History of Ideas* 51 (1990), pp. 27–49.

Sanches, F. *Quod nihil scitur* (Lyons,1581). Translated as *That Nothing Is Known* by

D. Thomson, with introduction and notes by E. Limbrick (Cambridge: Cambridge University Press, 1988).

Schmitt C. B. *Aristotle and the Renaissance* (Cambridge, Mass.: Harvard University Press, 1983).

Schmitt, C. B., and Q. Skinner. *The Cambridge History of Renaissance Philosophy* (Cambridge: Cambridge University Press, 1988).

Shea, W. R. *The Magic of Numbers and Motion* (Canton, Mass.: Science History Publications, 1991).

Silhon, J. de. *De l'immortalité de l'âme* (Paris, 1634).

Les deux vérités (1626; Paris: Fayard, 1991).

Sorel, C. *La science des choses corporelles. Première partie de la science humaine* (Paris, 1634).

De l'usage et de la perfection de toutes les choses du monde. Troisième volume de la science universelle (Paris, 1641).

Sorell, T. *The Rise of Modern Philosophy* (Oxford: Clarendon, 1993).

Sortais, G. *La philosophie moderne depuis Bacon jusqu'à Leibniz: études historiques* (Paris: P. Lethielleux, 1920).

Suárez, F. *Disputationes Metaphysicae* (Salmantica, 1597).

Disputationes Metaphysicae, 2 vols. (1597; Hildesheim: Olms, 1965).

On Efficient Causality: Metaphysical Disputations 17–19, trans. F. Freddoso, Yale Library of Medieval Philosophy (New Haven: Yale University Press, 1994).

Opera Omnia, 26 vols. (Paris: Vives, 1861).

Toletus, F. *Commentaria una cum quaestionibus in universam Aristotelis logicam* (Venice, 1572).

Commentaria una cum quaestionibus in octo libros de physica auscultatione (Venice, 1573).

Commentaria una cum quaestionibus in tres libros Aristotelis de amina (Venice, 1574).

Vayer, F. de la Mothe le. *Opuscule ou petit traitté sceptique sur cette commune façon de parler, n'aviur oas le sens commun* (Paris, 1646).

Dialogues faits à l'imitation des anciens (1630–1631; Paris: Fayard, 1988)

Verbeek, T. *Descartes and the Dutch* (Carbondale: Southern Illinois University Press, 1992).

ed. and trans. *La querelle d'Utrecht* (Paris: Les Impressions Nouvelles, 1988).

Ville, L. de la [Louis le Valois]. *Sentimens de Monsieur Descartes touchant l'essence et les proprietez du corps opposez à la Doctrine de l'Eglise, et conforme aux erreurs de Calvin sur le sujet de l'Eucharistie* (Caen, 1680).

Vincent, J. *Discussio peripatetica in qua philosophiae cartesianae principia* (Toulouse, 1677).

Index

act, 120
activity, 235
alchemists, alchemy, 137, 151–3, 163
Alexander Aphrodisias, 206
Alexander the Great, 207
analysis, 99
angel, 75, 91, 194, 196, 259
animal spirits, 88
animals/beasts, 21, 80, 83, 85, 221, 259
Anselm, 39, 137, 149
antiquity, 210
Apollonius, 163
Aquinas, Thomas, 31, 34, 47, 79, 80,
    119, 137, 164, 209, 257
Aristotle, xv, 2, 3, 5, 6, 9, 10, 13, 16,
    26–7, 30, 31, 32, 42, 72, 76, 81,
    83, 84, 85, 94, 97, 99, 102, 104,
    108, 109, 113, 114, 119, 120,
    122–4, 126, 134, 151, 153, 155–
    7, 163–5, 167–70, 174, 194,
    196, 207, 208, 210, 211, 232,
    247
atheists, 131, 142, 143, 146, 148, 151,
    182, 209, 232–3, 245
Archimedes, 163
Augustine, 38, 39, 41, 113, 126–8,
    137, 184, 215
authority, 12, 77
Averroes, 33
axioms, 94

Balzac, Guez de, 176
beasts. *See* animals

being
    infinite, 234–5
    as object of metaphysics, 92
    objective versus subjective, 93–4,
        95
    from oneself or from another, 40,
        45, 240–1
    virtual, 95
"bent stick" example, 21
Bible, 43
body/bodies
    animate, 83, 86
    interpenetration of, 48
    as object of physics, 80–1
    and quantity, 48
    See also corporeal things
Brahe, Tycho, 146
brain, as seat of imagination, 89

Cabala, 223
categories, 72
Catholic, 62
cause, 36–7, 101, 104, 122, 123, 125,
    154, 155, 181, 186–9
    efficient, 81–2, 101, 122–4, 259
    final, 101, 122–4
    formal, 101, 122–4
    material, 101, 122–4
    proximate, 101, 124
choice, free, 79–80
Charron, Pierre, xvi, 167
Christianity, 62
    and skepticism, 205, 206

physical versus metaphysical, 44
freedom. *See* liberty

Galen, 2, 3
Galileo Galilei, 136, 230
Gassendi, Pierre, xvi, 166, 167
"general and universal," 2, 3
generation and corruption, 10, 123,
    124
genus and *differentia*, 2, 3, 74
God, 18, 32–3, 45, 61, 63, 64, 127,
    128, 131, 138, 139, 141, 156,
    157, 160, 163, 164, 170–2, 174,
    179, 185, 188, 189, 191, 192,
    196–9, 205, 206, 208, 209, 216,
    217, 255, 258
a posteriori proof of, 46
a priori proofs of, 46–7, 149, 208–
    9
attributes of, 37–8, 150, 250
cause of his own being, 41, 181,
    242–3
conception of, 37, 144
concurrence of, 142, 184–6, 189,
    245, 254, 255
and creation, 34, 243–4, 115, 116,
    118, 131, 133, 137, 139, 141,
    142, 144, 150, 181, 184–6, 189,
    190, 191
and essences, 95
eternity of, 145, 148, 174, 243
existence of, 38–9, 142–4, 176–83,
    199, 242, 257, 258
existence pertains to essence of, 45–
    6, 47, 95–6
first motive force, 147
immutability of, 236
incomprehensibility of, 96
independence, 143
indivisibility of, 236
ineffability of, 42
infinite being, 144, 189
infiniteness of, 207
innate knowledge of, 38, 157, 199
knowledge of, 38, 96, 145, 150
perfection(s) of, 34–5, 40, 73, 236

providence of, 248–9, 123, 177,
    192, 210
simplicity of, 237–8
as supreme being, 38, 143, 146
truths revealed by, 57
as ultimate end, 145, 249–50, 182
uniqueness of, 236
will of, 186, 190, 243–5
gods, 210, 211
goodness, 140
grammar, approached methodically, 3

happiness, 78, 221
Harlay, François de, 256
heat, 17, 33
Heraclitus, 216
heresy, 62
Hieronymus, 41
Hippocrates, 2, 213
Homer, 3, 208

ideas, 127, 155, 156
images, 74, 93
imagination, 87–8, 88–9, 170, 198
imperfection, human (as proof of
    God), 39
indifference. *See* judgment
infinite, 20–1, 82–3, 234ff., 258
intelligence/intellect, 20, 32
    being in the intellect, 93
    independent of body, 85
    its knowledge of substances, 90–1
    relation to senses, 90
    and will, 78–9, 80
intuition, 15, 71

Jesuits, xv, 24, 25–8, 97, 136, 137,
    146, 252–4
judgment, 23, 36, 86
    can overcome human defects, 221
    corrigible by tests, 227
    bad judgment, 59
    of everything, 58
    and human nature, 58
    indifference in, 56, 60–2, 204

Pell, John, 17
perfection(s), 34–5, 36, 42, 43
Petronius, 209
philosophy/philosophers, 213
  aim of, 77–8
  parts of, 168
physics, object of, 80, 215, 222
Plato, 2, 4, 26–7, 232, 242, 100, 113,
    126, 131–5, 155–7, 163, 206,
    207
Pliny, 184, 214
Plotinus, 232
Plutarch, 123
privation, 43, 72, 109–11, 121, 122
Popkin, R., 8
potency, 120
postulate, 108
Pourchot, Edmond, 252
prayers, 210
principles, 94, 99, 102, 103, 107, 109,
    110, 113–15, 119, 121, 122,
    139, 144, 161, 162, 170, 182,
    84, 188, 192, 195, 197, 198,
    212
propositions, truth of, 75
Publicola, 204
Pyrrhonism, 204–7, 225
Pythagoras, 156

quantity, 47–8, 81, 167, 172–4
  distinct from corporeal substance,
    48
  versus form, 73–4
  infinite, 73
Quintilian, 2, 5

Raconis, Charles François d'Abra de,
    97
Ramus, Petrus, xvi, 167
remembrance, 131–8
reason
  divine, 216
  imperfection of in human beings,
    217
  as universal nature, 60
religion, 205
  diversity of, 207–11

and indifference of mind, 62
  true religion, 207
resolution, 55
Richelieu, 97, 166
Rodis-Lewis, G., xiv
Rubius, Antonius, 97

Sale, François de, 136, 158
Sanches, Francisco, xvi, 8–11
Scaliger, Julius, 128
science
  demonstrative, 76–7
  Euclid's geometry as an example
    of, 4
  unity of, 222
sciences, 31, 160
  defensibility of doubting, 205
  new, 223
  See also universal science
scientia, science, 15, 19, 22, 99–102,
    106, 108, 109, 127–9, 131, 133,
    134, 151, 157, 159, 169, 178
Scotus, John Duns, 119
self-knowledge, 52
self-love, 55, 212
senses, 17–18, 19, 20, 21, 22, 32, 90,
    98, 105, 129–2, 138, 151, 154,
    159, 160, 167, 168, 194–6, 215,
    216, 225, 227, 259
  and error, 86–7, 154, 225
  and illusions, 22, 87, 154
  internal/external, 211, 228
  not really deceived, 225
Sextus, 209
Silhon, Jean de, xvii, 176
skeptics, 138, 154, 159, 160, 167, 168,
    176, 199, 226
  See also Pyrrhonism
Socrates, 4, 5, 63, 98, 215
solitude, 53, 213
Sorel, Charles, xvii
soul, 23, 33, 138, 193, 198, 224
  apt to be united to body, 92, 257
  bodily seat of, 84
  as form of body, 83, 112
  immortal and spiritual nature (of